The Clerical Library.

ANECDOTES

ILLUSTRATIVE OF

OLD TESTAMENT TEXTS.

The Clerical Library.

COMPLETE IN TWELVE VOLUMES.

I. Three Hundred Outlines of Sermons on the New Testament.
II. Outlines of Sermons on the Old Testament.
III. Pulpit Prayers.
IV. Outline Sermons to Children.
V. Anecdotes Illustrative of New Testament Texts.
VI. Expository Sermons and Outlines on the Old Testament.
VII. Expository Sermons on the New Testament.
VIII. Platform Aids.
IX. New Outlines of Sermons on the New Testament.
X. Anecdotes Illustrative of Old Testament Texts.
XI. New Outlines of Sermons on the Old Testament.
XII. Outlines of Sermons for Special Occasions.

ANECDOTES

ILLUSTRATIVE OF

OLD TESTAMENT TEXTS.

REV. NICHOLAS J. KREMER

HODDER AND STOUGHTON
LONDON NEW YORK TORONTO

$\frac{34}{29{,}623}$

PREFATORY NOTE.

GREAT pains have been taken in the compilation of this volume to go to original sources, and very many volumes have been examined with the view of making as fresh a collection as possible. But it should be distinctly understood that no originality is claimed for the form of the anecdotes. In most cases this has been taken as it was found.

I. The Power and Comfort of God. GEN. i. 1.
"In the beginning God created the heaven and the earth."

WHEN Mr. Simeon, of Cambridge, was on his dying bed, his biographer relates that, "after a short pause, he looked round with one of his bright smiles, and asked, 'What do you think especially gives me comfort at this time? The creation! Did Jehovah create the world or did I? I think He did; now if He made the world, He can sufficiently take care of ME.'"

II. Sin Ready to Enter. GEN. iv. 7. *"Sin lieth at the door."*

A YOUNG friend was one day calling upon an old Christian woman, nearly eighty years of age, just waiting for the summons. Said this friend, "Oh, granny, I wish I was as sure of heaven, and as near it, as you are!" With a look of unspeakable emotion, the old woman answered, "And do you really think the devil cannot find his way up an old woman's garret-stair? Oh, if He hadn't said 'None shall pluck them out of My hand,' I would have been away wandering long ago!"

III. Sin Crouching at the Door. GEN. iv. 7. *"Sin lieth at the door."*

A TRAVELLER who had fallen into the hands of some robbers, was murdered by them. In his last moments, seeing some ravens flying over his head, he exclaimed to them, "I call upon you to avenge my death." Three days after, the robbers, going into the neighbouring town, saw some ravens on the roof of the inn where they were carousing. One of them said, sneeringly: "I suppose those are the ravens come to avenge the death of the traveller we despatched the other day." The servant of the inn, overhearing these words, ran and repeated them to the magistrate, who had the robbers taken up, and, on inquiry being made, they were convicted of the murder and hanged.

IV. Undone. GEN. iv. 10. *"And He said, What hast thou done?"*

THE Rev. Rowland Hill preaching on one occasion from this text, at Cowes, began his sermon as follows:—" In my way to your island, I visited the county jail at Winchester, and there I saw many who were accused of heavy crimes, but who seemed careless and indifferent, and to have but little sense of their awful situation. But one young man attracted my attention: he kept separate from the rest, and seemed very much troubled. I went up to him and said, 'And what have you done, young man?' 'Sir,' said he, deeply affected, 'I have done that which I cannot undo, and which has undone me.' This, my dear friends," said the minister, "is the situation of every one of you. You have each of you done that which has undone you, and which you cannot undo."

V. My Ministry. GEN. v. 24. *"And Enoch walked with God: and he was not; for God took him."*

ON the 22nd of February, 1880, Dr. Raleigh preached for the last time. His text was, "And Enoch walked with God: and he was not; for God took him." Had he known that he would never preach again, he could not have chosen a more appropriate text, or have spoken with more impressiveness and pathos. One of the members of the congregation said, on returning home, "I have heard to-day what I never expect to hear again in this world." Dr. Raleigh was compelled to rest; weeks passed away, but there was no amendment in his health, and at length he had to be told that there was no hope of his recovery. When he received the intelligence he said, "Then my ministry is ended." There was a pause, and then he added, "My ministry!—it is dearer than my life." On the Tuesday before his death, he was visited by the Rev.

Joshua Harrison, to whom he freely expressed his confidence in the glorious work of the Saviour, and said: "In any case I may well be content and thankful. I am not an old man, yet I have lived long and worked hard. I have had, on the whole, a most happy, and I think I may say successful, ministry. God has blessed my work, and has always given me true friends. If I have finished my work, I am ready to go. Indeed, I should have no regrets, but for these dear ones" (his wife and children). When reminded of the prayers which were being offered on his behalf, he replied, "Yes, my people's prayers make me sometimes think I may have a little more work to do, but if not, I shall calmly march up to the Gates." Still trusting in Christ, he went "through the gates," April, 1880. In the presence of a sorrowing multitude, his coffin was lowered into a grave in Abney Park Cemetery.

VI. An Ideal Christian Pastor. GEN. v. 24. *"And Enoch walked with God."*

OBERLIN'S motto may be summed up in three words, "Walk before God." We have in him the ideal of a Christian and of a pastor. He had holy, vigilant, tender love for souls. When, of an evening, some of his flock were passing in front of his house at Waldersbach, and saw a light burning at a certain window which they well knew, "Hush!" one said to the others, "our pastor is watching for us"; and so, indeed, this valiant soldier of the cross did watch and wrestle for his people. He prayed by name for each of these souls whom he presented before God, as of old they brought the sick to the Saviour for healing. In common with all generous spirits, Oberlin had hailed with transport the clear, fair morning of revolution; but when its aspect changed—when the day darkened in crimes and bloodshed—when the Gospel was proscribed in France turned pagan, and the Age of Reason substituted in its place—do you suppose Oberlin was dumb, and spoke no more to his flock of the Gospel and of Christ? Assuredly no. This good shepherd, under the needful disguise of president of a club, contrived to retain the right of still feeding his sheep with the Divine word. For example, when the Convention despatched to all the "club presidents" the common motto or text on which they were to speak on each decade, the subject on one occasion was this :—"Against tyrants." Oberlin was in no wise embarrassed thereby—not he! "Tyrants," said he to his parishioners, "all good republicans ought to hate ; yes, and to make war on them without truce or intermission. But who are these tyrants? The King of Prussia or the Emperor? No, the real tyrants are the vices, the passions, the evil lusts which war against the soul. Behold in them our worst enemies, with whom peace there must never be." And so, by a happy turn like this, the good Oberlin would soon find his way back to the Gospel he loved, and keep his people alive with the bread of life, of which there was a sore famine in other places.

VII. Gathering Flowers to Compose Him in the Hour of Death. GEN. v. 24. *"And Enoch walked with God: and he was not; for God took him."*

WE know it to be a Scripture fact, that men have "walked with God," in closest intimacy, and that God hath held converse with them, "even as a man converseth with his friend." Such was the case with Enoch, Abraham, Moses, and all that luminous cloud of witnesses so brightly and clearly revealed in the Bible.

The Church of God, even down to our own time, furnishes innumerable witnesses to this truth, which we will establish by the mouth of two of them.

John Holland was an old Puritan minister, who died two hundred and fifty years ago. Little is known of him, except what relates to his deathbed. Perceiving that he was near his end, he said : "Come, oh come ; death approaches. Let us gather some flowers to comfort this hour." He requested that the eighth chapter of Romans might be read to him. But at every verse he stopped the reading, while he expounded it to the comfort of his soul, and to the joy and wonder of his friends. Having thus continued his meditations above two hours, he suddenly cried out, "Oh, stay your reading. What brightness is this I see? Have you lighted any candles?" They told him, "No ; it is the sunshine." "Sunshine?" said he ; nay, my "Saviour's shine! Now, farewell world—welcome, heaven. The Day-star from on high hath visited my heart. Oh, speak when I am gone, and preach it at my funeral, *God dealeth familiarly with man.*" In such transports his soul soared toward heaven. His last words, after repeating the declaration that "God doth and will deal familiarly with man," were these: "And now, thou fiery chariot, that camest down to fetch up Elijah, carry me to my happy home. And all ye blessed angels, who attended the soul of Lazarus to bring it to heaven, bear me, oh bear me to the bosom of my best beloved, Amen; even so come, Lord Jesus, come quickly!"

Our other present witness is Gilbert Tennent, who was a main instrument, with Whitefield and Edwards, of the great revival in New England, one hundred years ago. In one of his letters to his brother, the holy William Tennent, he says, "Brother, shall I tell you an astonishing instance of the glorious grace of the Lord Jesus Christ? It is this, that one of the meanest of His servants has had His presence every day, in some degree, for above eleven weeks. Nor is the great, good Master yet gone. Oh, brother, it is heaven upon earth to live near to God! Verily our comfort does not depend so much upon our outward situation as is generally supposed. No, a Saviour's love is all in all. Oh, this will make any situation sweet, and turn the thickest darkness into day."

VIII. Quenching the Spirit. GEN. vi. 3. "*My Spirit shall not always strive with man.*"

A PREACHER says "It is long since I was a collegian, either as a senior here, or previously as a member of the lower classes elsewhere. I still remember vividly three young men who went about *swearing by the Holy Ghost*, which they considered the unpardonable sin. They were already hardened and reckless. One of them, who became a brilliant physician, died in middle age, a suicide; another of them, still earlier, a drunkard; the other yet lives, a physician, but with not a sign of religious thought or feeling. This reminiscence has led me to the subject of quenching not the Spirit, as one adapted to young men just laying the foundations of life.

"In the class of 1840, of which I was a member, were

two ministers' sons, of fine minds, but neither of them Christians. During revival services near by this edifice, at about this season of the year, one of them was converted; but the other held aloof. Under an urgent appeal from his friend he had, however, been touched. He did not quench the Spirit. He became, finally, a minister, and settled at New Rochelle. In the same class was a third member, an avowed infidel. After graduation he banded with others even worse than himself to go by sea to New Orleans, and thence overland into Texas, there to form a predatory band for the commission of all kinds of iniquity. They did not all reach New Orleans. A part went on, but were attacked by disease. This student buried the last one, and was left alone. From Galveston he worked his way home, sick, diseased, and ragged, to his mother's door. He got a little school at New Rochelle, but was a gambler and misanthrope, resisting long all his classmate's advances and appeals. Touched at length by them, he did not quench the Spirit. He began a higher, a Christian life; and these three students of this college within these walls nearly fifty years ago, are now all ministers of Christ, living at the West.

IX. GEN. vi. 5. *"Every imagination of the thoughts of his heart was only evil continually."*

EMMANUEL refuses even to allow a letter from Diabolus to enter the town of Mansoul. A preacher has well said: "There must be no correspondence whatever. The devil's letters are evil hints and suggestions, and if you entertain them, then you are opening up a correspondence with him. Whenever you get a letter addressed in his hand-writing, with the post-mark of hell on it, destroy it at once." Luther said, "I cannot help unclean birds flying over my head, but I can keep them from building and breeding in my hair." So we cannot help evil thoughts crossing our minds, but we can keep them from dwelling there.

X. The Shut Door. GEN. vii. 16. *"And the Lord shut him in."*

IN the life of the late Hugh Millar, we find the following passage from Mr. Stewart, of Cromarty, whom Millar considered one of the very best and ablest of Scotland's ministers: "Noah did not close the door. There are words that God keeps for Himself. The burden is too heavy for the back of man. To shut that door on a world about to perish would have been too great a responsibility for a son of Adam. Another moment, and another, and another might have been granted by Noah, and the door might never have been shut, and the ship that carried the life of the world might have been swamped. And so it is in the ark of salvation. It is not the Church nor the minister that shuts or opens the door. These do God's bidding; they preach righteousness; they offer salvation, and it is God that shuts and opens the door. Oh, what a sigh and shudder will pass through the listening universe when God will shut the door of the heavenly ark upon the lost!"

XI. A Quaint Epitaph. GEN. viii. 9. *"But the dove found no rest for the sole of her foot, and she returned unto him into the ark."*

THE following quaint epitaph has reference to a little girl buried at the age of five months: "But the dove found no rest for the sole of her foot, and she returned unto him into the ark."

XII. Noah's Prayer. GEN. viii. 20. *"And Noah built an altar unto the Lord."*

TRADITION has preserved the prayer of Noah, and the learned John Gregory gives it to us as he gathered it from the Arabic and Syriac. And assuredly the prayer is a beautiful one, a prayer which might not only have been well offered up in that floating church, but which may be even a pattern for many prayers. The following is John Gregory's translation from the floating words of the traditional original: "O Lord, excellent art Thou in Thy truth, and there is nothing great in comparison of Thee. Look upon us with the eye of mercy and compassion; deliver us from this deluge of waters and set our feet in a large room. By the sorrows of Adam Thy first-made man, by the blood of Abel Thy holy one, by the righteousness of Seth, in whom Thou art well pleased, number us not among those who have transgressed Thy statutes, but take us unto Thy merciful care, for Thou art our deliverer, and Thine is the praise from all the works of Thy hands for evermore. And the sons of Noah said, Amen, Lord."

XIII. The Covenant Sign. GEN. ix. 13. *"I do set My bow in the cloud, and it shall be for a token of a covenant between Me and the earth."*

THE native account of the last martyrdom in Madagascar concludes in these touching words:—"Then they prayed, 'O Lord, receive our spirits, for *Thy love to us hath caused this to come to us;* and lay not this sin to their charge.' Thus prayed they as long as they had any life, and then they died—softly, gently; *and there was at the time a rainbow in the heavens which seemed to touch the place of the burning.*"

XIV. One Language. GEN. xi. 1. *"The whole earth was of one language and of one speech."*

A HINDU and a New Zealander met upon the deck of a missionary ship. They had been converted from their heathenism, and were brothers in Christ; but they could not speak to each other. They pointed to their Bibles, shook hands, and smiled in each other's faces; but that was all. At last a happy thought occurred to the Hindu. With sudden joy, he exclaimed: "Halleluia!" The New Zealander, in delight, cried out "Amen!" These two words, not found in their own heathen tongues, were to them the beginning of "one language and one speech."

XV. The Confusion of Tongues. GEN. xi. 9. *"Therefore is the name of it called Babel, because the Lord did there confound the language of all the earth."*

THE late Bishop Selwyn devoted a great part of his time to visiting the Melanesian Isles, and he thus writes home about the difficulty of languages: "Nothing but a special interposition of the Divine Power could have produced such a confusion of tongues as we find here. In islands not larger than the Isle of Wight, we find dialects so distinct that the inhabitants of the various districts hold no communication one with another."

XVI. True Service must have Soul in it. GEN. xii. 5. *"And Abram took Sarai his wife, and Lot his brother's son, and all their substance that they had gathered, and the souls that they had gotten in Haran."*

A MINISTER makes the following remarks in his sermon:
—The want of this age—of all ages is—*soul*. Quaint old Matthew Henry points out that Abraham's slaves which he had gotten in Haran are called *souls*. In these times servants are called *hands*. A world of difference. *Hands* —four fingers and a thumb to get as much out of as one can, and to put as little into, from the master's standpoint. And from the servants—to pick up as much as they can and to give as little back again. When master and man can find in each other's relationship a soul—a living, earnest, brotherly soul, then only are the work and wages alike right. In least and commonest works we want not *hands* only but souls. If I hire a man to do my garden and I find him scarcely playing at the work, for men put their souls into their play, but 'dawdling' only, tickling the earth with a rake as if he expected it to laugh into flowers, I would sooner fling him his half-crown, and do the work right earnestly myself. So do we value soul, we who see but the outside of men. Think then of Him Whose eyes do look us through—*the Father of spirits*, Whose contact is even with the inner man, the soul. If that sleeps, how poor in His sight, how vain and mocking, is any service that we pretend to render Him. Here all is worse than nothing if there be not reality, heart, earnestness."

XVII. Magnanimity. GEN. xiii. 9. *"If thou wilt take the left hand, then I will go to the right; or if thou depart to the right hand, then I will go to the left."*

AN instance of the practical effectiveness of Mr. Sherman's preaching is narrated thus. In one of his Monday evening lectures to teachers, the subject was the parting of Abraham and Lot: in the course of which he spoke of the magnanimity of Abraham, and, as a contrast to it, said that he had just visited a family belonging to the congregation that was rent by discord about the ownership of an old bedstead. It happened that amongst his hearers was a man who had not been in Surrey Chapel for years. He was greatly amused by the illustration. As he left the chapel, he called on an old friend, and told him that he was at the very time arranging the distribution of some property left by a relative, amongst which there was an old bedstead, which had been matter of dispute : but the effect of the address upon him was such that the bedstead difficulty was soon amicably settled.

XVIII. Unconscious Surveillance. GEN. xvi. 13.
"And she called the name of the Lord that spake unto her, Thou God seest me."

SOME years since a trio of gentlemen, members of a large mercantile firm, came into the office of the writer, and, under injunctions of profound secrecy, desired the favour of using the window for a few days. The privilege was readily granted, and one of their number was at once installed behind a curtain, where, with a powerful glass, he could rigidly scrutinize every movement of a certain clerk in a large building across the way. The young man, all unconscious of the vigilant eye constantly upon him, was absorbed in his duties, making entries and receiving money ; and, whatever consciousness of innocence or guilt was carried about with him, the suspicion of a rigid watch upon his actions—every movement closely scanned and weighed by his employers—doubtless had never entered his mind. The surveillance was continued nearly a week when it was abruptly terminated, and the result, whether in discovery of wrong or establishing innocence, I never learned.

The incident made a profound impression upon me, suggesting, with thrilling distinctness, the solemn truth which men are so prone to forget, "Thou God seest me," and enabling me as never before to realize how open before Him are the hearts and ways of men, their desires, volitions, actions ; and that at last He shall bring every work into judgment, whether it be good or whether it be evil.

XIX. God Makes no Mistakes. GEN. xviii. 25.
"Shall not the Judge of all the earth do right?"

THERE is here a young man of about thirty, of fine talents and capabilities for active life, but for years a cripple, paralytic, and helpless. He would starve, if left alone. A friend was commiserating his condition, when, with deep earnestness, he exclaimed, as he slowly raised his withered hand, "*God makes no mistakes.*" How noble the sentiment! "Shall not the Judge of all the earth do right?" This is piety. Only a heart divinely taught could thus speak.

XX. Protection from evil. GEN. xix. 26. "*But his wife looked back from behind him, and she became a pillar of salt.*"

AN evil is never a thing to play with. When God promises His protection against evil, it is understood that we, on our part, shall keep aloof from it as much as possible; that we shall not, at any rate, go recklessly or carelessly into it.

I can remember an event in my early life. I had come home from school for a holiday. My father had just bought a fine large dog. Of course I was rather afraid of the powerful animal, and as we were going out to walk, I was rather uneasy when I saw that my father was to take the dog along with us. But he bade me relinquish all fear, as he would keep the animal under his own command, and he assured me that the dog would do me no harm if I let him alone. I found that my father spoke the truth, and as I walked on cheerfully by his side I soon lost all dread. But seeing that the animal was peaceful, I became bold and forward, and began to tease him when my father's back was turned. The consequence was, that soon the blood streamed down my hand and my cries filled the air. "You promised me that the dog should not hurt me," I said sobbing. "Yes," was the answer, "but you did not tell me that you were going to torment him. It was understood that *you* were to let *him* alone."

I always look at this scar of mine when I think of God's promises to His children with reference to their protection against evil. It is understood that *we* shall keep aloof. You know the sad story of Lot's wife. God had promised her a safe escape from the evils of Sodom. But in her recklessness she chose to turn her face towards the burning furnace and the fiery shower. Of course, no protection was promised against such a foolhardiness. When God promises that He will carry our cares for us, it is understood that we shall not unnecessarily and neglectfully try to increase the burden. If so, we may expect our Father to allow the dog to bite us, that we may learn to behave wisely.

XXI. A Motto. GEN. xxii. 14. *"The Lord will provide."*

THE celebrated Richard Boyle, Earl of Cork, who rose from a humble station in life to the highest rank, and passed through strange and trying vicissitudes, used these words as his motto, and ordered them to be engraved on his tomb: "God's providence is my inheritance."

XXII. Three Bad Bargains. GEN. xxv. 34. *"Thus Esau despised his birthright."*

A Sunday school teacher remarked that he who buys the truth makes a good bargain, I inquired if any scholar recollected an instance in Scripture of a bad bargain. "I do," replied a boy, "Esau sold his birthright for a mess of pottage." A second said, "Judas made a bad bargain when he sold his Lord for thirty pieces of silver." A third boy observed, "Our Lord tells us that he makes a bad bargain who to gain the whole world loses his own soul."

XXIII. Beautiful Doors. GEN. xxviii. 17. *"The gate of heaven."*

MICHAEL ANGELO BUONARROTTI said of the doors of the Baptistery at Florence, executed by Lorenzo Ghiberti, when asked what he thought of them, "They are so beautiful that they might stand at the gates of Paradise."

XXIV. Give all you Can. GEN. xxviii. 22. *"And of all that Thou shalt give me, I will surely give the tenth unto Thee."*

THE late Bishop Selwyn used often to quote that motto of John Wesley's, "Save all you can and give all you save," and he did not think that charity began until after a tithe had been paid to God. "Whatever your income," he wrote once to his son, "remember that only nine-tenths of it are at your disposal."

XXV. A Tenth of All. Gen. xxviii. 22. *And of all that Thou shalt give me I will surely give the tenth unto Thee."*

"Take it quick, quick," said a merchant, who had promised, like Jacob, to return to the Lord a tenth of all that he should give him, and found that it amounted to so large a sum, that he said, " I cannot give so much," and set aside a smaller amount. Then his conscience smote him, and, coming to himself, he said, "What! can I be so mean? Because God has thus blessed me that I have this large profit, shall I now *rob Him* of his portion?" And fearing his own selfish nature, he made haste to place it beyond his reach in the treasury of the Lord, coming almost breathless to the pastor's house, and holding the money in his outstretched hand.

XXVI. Helping on the Work of God. Gen. xxviii. 22. *"Of all that thou shalt give me I will surely give the tenth unto Thee."*

A widow found pardon and peace in her Saviour in her sixty-ninth year. Her gratitude and love overflowed and often refreshed the hearts of Christians of long experience. The house of God became very dear to her, and she was often seen to drop a gift in the church door box though her income was only 2s. 6d. per week. A fall in her seventy-second year prevented her ever coming out again.

A little boy being seen to drop something into the box, was asked what it was. He said, "It is Mrs. W——'s penny." He was told to take it back to her, and to say that her good intention was prized, but that her friends could not let her thus reduce her small means, especially as she could not come out to worship. She replied, "Boy, why did you let them see you give it? Take it again and put it in when no one sees you." Then weeping she said, " What! and am I not to be allowed to help in the work of God any more because I can't get out?"

XXVII. A Christian Boyhood. Gen. xxxix. 2. *"And the Lord was with Joseph."*

Dr. Harold Schofield, the talented missionary to China, lived a life of singular beauty, purity, and devotion. He had that best of all earthly blessings—a good and godly mother. The gracious training of his childish days bore fruit early. "When nine years old he was truly converted to God." The circumstances of his conversion are singularly beautiful, and should encourage Christian parents not only to pray for, but to expect from, their children an early decision for Christ. An elder brother, who was away at school, had just found the Saviour, and had written to tell his brother of his new-found joy. After reading the letter, Harold was deeply affected, and a servant noticing his agitation went to his mother to tell her that "Harold was walking up and down the dining-room in great distress of mind." "I sent for him," his mother says, "and he handed me a letter from his brother, and stood by me in tears to think that he was not saved like him. I spoke simply of the sacrifice of Christ, and I shall never forget the ray of joy that beamed through his tearful eyes and lighted up his whole face as he owned that Christ had saved him too." Who can wonder that the spiritual life which had so gracious a beginning, had so fair a continuance and so glorious a close! Happy the child who at nine years of age is led to Jesus by a brother's letter and a mother's voice!

The gladness of that day, the settled conviction that he was Christ's and Christ his, seems never to have been lost, hardly dimmed in after years.

At school he soon won the highest place, and began his brilliant series of prize winnings. Here, too, he took his stand as a thorough-going Christian. "His piety was as well-known to all the boys as his diligence;" and in after years old schoolfellows testified to the blessing received through his earnest religious talk in the play-ground. He was, however, always ready for out-door exercises and holiday excursions, cycling and boating expeditions in which a touch of danger only added to the interest of the enterprise.

At the University, and at St. Bartholomew's Hospital, he never hesitated to declare himself Christ's servant; and it was soon recognised by the other students that Schofield's presence must put an end to everything wrong in word or act.

XXVIII. Praying First. GEN. xli. 9. *"I remember my faults this day."*

Two Christian men "fell out." One heard that the other was talking against him, and he went to him and said, "Will you be kind enough to tell me my faults to my face, that I may profit by your Christian candour and try to get rid of them?" "Yes, sir," replied the other; "I will do it." They went aside, and the former said: "Before you commence telling what you think wrong in me, will you please bow down with me and let us pray over it, that my eyes may be opened to see my faults as you will tell them? You lead in the prayer." It was done, and when the prayer was over the man who had sought the interview said, "Now proceed with what you have to complain of in me." But the other replied, "After praying over it, it looks so little that it is not worth talking about. The truth is, I feel now that in going around talking against you I have been serving the devil myself, and have need that you pray for me and forgive me the wrong I have done you."

Here and there in almost every community is a man or woman who might profit by this incident.

XXIX. Troubles. GEN. xli. 52. *"The land of my affliction."*

"When in Amsterdam, Holland, last summer," says a traveller, "I was much interested in a visit we made to a place then famous for polishing diamonds. We saw the men engaged in the work. When a diamond is found it is rough and dark like a common pebble. It takes a long time to polish it, and it is very hard work. It is held by means of a piece of metal close to the surface of a large wheel which is kept going round. Fine diamond dust is put on this wheel, nothing else being hard enough to polish the diamond. And this work is kept on for months and sometimes for several years before it is finished. And if a diamond is intended for a king then the greater trouble and time are spent upon it."

Jesus calls His people His jewels. To fit them for beautifying His crown, they must be polished like diamonds, and He makes use of the troubles He sends to polish His jewels.

XXX. A Son's Affection. Gen. xlv. 3. *"And Joseph said unto his brethren, I am Joseph; doth my father yet live?"*

THE Huguenots were persecuted beyond measure in southern France, and were not allowed to meet together for worship.

On New Year's Day, 1756, the Church at Nîmes held a service in the gorge in the desert. The people had scarcely assembled when they were surprised by the soldiers. They flew up the rocks like a scattered flock of goats. Among the more agile was a young man named Jules Fabre. Suddenly he remembered his father, a feeble old man of seventy. He was sure that he could not have escaped. Returning, he found his fears realized; his father and another man had been captured. He ran up to the soldiers and insisted on their accepting him in place of his father. The old man besought him to go. The altercation had gone on some time, when the young man seized his aged parent round the waist and carried him to a stone, where he gently laid him down, more dead than alive. Jules Fabre then gave himself up as a prisoner, was convicted of being present at an illegal assembly, and sent to the galleys, where he might have remained for life, had not the peculiarity of the case touched the hearts of some powerful people, and he was released at the end of six years.

XXXI. The Homesick Mount. Gen. xlvii. 9. *"The days of the years of my pilgrimage."*

WE are told that in the neighbourhood of Interlaken there is a prominent point, though not of great height, called the *"Heimweh Fluh,"* which means the *Homesick Mount*. It is so called because it is generally the last spot which the traveller visits before leaving that part of Switzerland, and at a time when his thoughts are turned homeward. It commands a view of the whole valley of Interlaken, with its cultivated fields and pastures and picturesque villages and lakes in the cup of mountain walls, and beyond the Jungfrau and other mountains, which never doff their caps of eternal snow. It is beautiful to look upon, but the heart of the tourist is not there. He is thinking of friends and loved ones, and his own country. It is the Homesick Mount. And so they to whom faith makes the invisible most real may have their moments of uplifting, standing on some "Heimweh Fluh," some Mount of Homesickness, and, while they acknowledge all the beauty, all the glory, all the gladness of the world, their hearts are not here; this sight does not enthral them, for their faces are turned toward home. They dwell in the Land of Promise as in a strange country.

XXXII. Eternity, and Where it is to be Spent. GEN. xlvii. 29. *"And the time drew nigh that Israel must die: and he called his son Joseph."*

A MINISTER was dying, and he called his son, who was a thoughtless lad, to his bedside. "Tom," he said, "will you promise me one thing before I die? I only ask that, when I am gone, you will go every evening alone for fifteen minutes and say, 'What is eternity? and where shall I spend it?'" The promise was given, and faithfully kept. At first the lad thought little of the words; but he went on doing as he had promised, until at last he was not able to face the awful question any longer, and gave himself up to Jesus.

XXXIII. The Great Pilot is on Board. GEN. xlviii. 21. *"And Israel said unto Joseph, Behold, I die: but God shall be with you."*

JOHN OWEN, two days before he died, thus wrote in a letter to a friend: "I am leaving the ship of the Church in a storm; but whilst the great Pilot is in it, the loss of a poor under-rower will be inconsiderable."

XXXIV. The Persecution of the Huguenots. EXOD. ii. 23. *"The children of Israel sighed by reason of the bondage, and they cried, and their cry came up unto God by reason of the bondage."*

MANY otherwise estimable people approved the Huguenot persecution at the time. Thus Madame de Sévigné, one of the most amiable women of the seventeenth century, a most tender mother, an example of virtue, and noted for extraordinary good sense, absolutely approved Louis XIV.'s attempt to exterminate Protestantism. In a letter to the Comte de Bussy she writes : " You have doubtless seen the edict by which the king revokes that of Nantes. Nothing can be more admirable than its contents, and no king has done, or ever will do, a more honourable act." To which the count replies : " I admire the conduct of the king in destroying the Huguenots ; the wars which have been waged against them before, and the St. Bartholomews, have multiplied and given vigour to this sect. His majesty has gradually undermined it, and the edict which he has just published, supported by dragoons and Bourdaloue, has been its *coup de grâce*" (1685).

To the elegent, refined gentlefolk of the court of Louis XIV., these Huguenots, who dared to claim the right to worship God according to their consciences, were human vermin, to be exterminated by fire and sword. Madame de Sévigné commiserates her nephew, the Marquis de Trousse, who was engaged in the "dreadfully fatiguing" work of shooting down "miserable Huguenots." He beat the country with armed bands, just as modern sportsmen beat the woods for game ; wherever a group of Protestants were found praying or singing hymns, the soldiers fired on them or cut them down.

XXXV. Egyptian Animal Worship. Exod. viii. 26.

"And Moses said, It is not meet so to do ; for we shall sacrifice the abomination of the Egyptians to the Lord our God : lo, shall we sacrifice the abomination of the Egyptians before their eyes, and will they not stone us ?"

THE veneration with which the Egyptians regarded such animals as were the objects of their religious worship might be illustrated by a variety of historical facts. On one occasion a Persian commander saved his army by placing craftily, in the foremost lines of his troops, some dogs, cats, and other sacred animals, at which the foiled Egyptians did not dare to aim an offensive weapon. A Roman in Egypt once killed a cat inadvertently, upon which the people met together, beset his house, and killed the man, in spite of the king and princes, who endeavoured to prevent it.

XXXVI. The Passover. EXOD. xii. 13. *"And the blood shall be to you for a token upon the houses where ye are."*

EPIPHANIUS tells us that the Egyptians used, at this time of the year, to mark their cattle, trees, and one another with red ochre, which they fancied to be a preservative from death; it probably took its rise from hence.

XXXVII. A Remedy against Despondence. EXOD. xiv. 15. *"Speak unto the children of Israel, that they go forward."*

"LET me mention," says Sir W. R. Hamilton in one of his letters, "what I think an important secret of experience; namely, that blessed a thing as meditation is, it is *action*, rather than meditation, which is the appointed remedy, the Divine specific, against despondence; and that present duties which may at first seem irksome, are part of the medicine wherewith God healeth the sickness of those that are broken in heart."

XXXVIII. Not slavishly Afraid of his Sins. EXOD. xx. 2. *"I am the Lord thy God."*

WHEN Ebenezer Erskine lay on his death-bed, one of his elders said to him, "Sir, you have given us many good advices, may I ask what you are now doing with your own soul?" "I am just doing with it," he replied, "what I did forty years ago; I am resting on that word, 'I am the Lord thy God.'" Another friend put the question, "Sir, are you not afraid of your sins?" "Indeed, no," was his answer; "ever since I knew Christ I have never thought highly of my frames and duties, nor am I *slavishly* afraid of my sins." At another time he said, "I know that when my soul forsakes this tabernacle of clay it will fly as naturally to my Saviour's bosom as the bird to its beloved nest."

XXXIX. The Heathen's Reply to the Jesuit. EXOD. xx. 4. *"Thou shalt not make unto thee any graven image."*

WHEN the Jesuit missionaries first arrived in the Sandwich Islands, they used many arguments with the natives to show that their instructions and those of the Protestant missionaries were alike. It was on one of these occasions that an old man, who made no pretensions to religion, replied that the missionaries had taught him about God. "Oh, yes," replied the priests, "Mr. Thurston taught about God, and that was right; you heard him, and now I wish you to hear me." The old man gravely answered, "But the Bible says I cannot serve two masters." He further objected to their images, when the priests said: "Oh! we do not call this God, and we do not pray to it. It is only a representation, shadow, of God." The old man replied: "Let me see it. That cannot be any representation of God. It is made of brass. *If there be any shadow or representation of God, it must be in the heart, not in an image.*"

XL. Look to Your Pockets. EXOD. xx. 7. *"Thou shalt not take the name of the Lord thy God in vain."*

HOWARD the philanthropist was standing in a crowd by the door of a post office, when a man uttered a volley of oaths. "Look to your pockets!" cried Howard, buttoning up his own tightly. "Always take care of your pockets when you find yourself amongst swearers. He who will take God's name in vain will think little of taking your purse, or doing anything else that is evil."

XLI. Swearing. EXOD. xx. 7. *"Thou shalt not take the name of the Lord thy God in vain; for the Lord will not hold him guiltless that taketh His name in vain."*

IT is interesting to know that when St. Paul's Cathedral was in building, Sir Christopher Wren, the architect, caused a printed notice to be affixed to the scaffolding, threatening with instant dismissal any workman guilty of swearing within those sacred precincts.

XLII. Who Taught you to Swear? EXOD. xx. 7. *"Thou shalt not take the name of the Lord thy God in vain."*

AN aged minister was once riding on the box-seat of a coach; the driver, a fine-looking young man, frequently swore at his horses. For some time the minister was silent; at length he asked in a kind voice : " Will you tell me, my friend, who taught you to swear? Was it your mother?"

A tender point was touched. "My mother? No, sir. Why, my mother is a praying woman! It would break her heart if she heard me swearing," he replied.

In loving words the aged Christian pleaded with the driver to honour, not only his mother's teachings, but also the commands of his mother's God.

"I thank you, sir," said the young lad, and during the remainder of the journey not another oath was heard.

XLIII. The Profanation of the Sabbath. Exod. xx. 8. *"Remember the Sabbath day, to keep it holy."*

BLACKSTONE declares somewhere that "a corruption of morals usually follows a profanation of the Sabbath"; and La Place said just before his death, "I have lived long enough to know what at one time I did not believe, that no society can be upheld without the sentiment of religion." The testimonies of other such men might be quoted in great numbers that, alike on moral, social, economical, and physical grounds, the disregard of the Lord's day is a dangerous evil both to the individual and the community.

XLIV. The Noblest Work of God. Exod. xx. 12. *"Honour thy father and thy mother."*

A LITTLE boy hearing a party of gentlemen applauding the sentiment "an honest man is the noblest work of God," boldly said, "No"; and being asked, "What do you think is the noblest work of God?" said, "My mother." That boy made a good man. Who can doubt it?

XLV. An Emaciated Body. Exod. xx. 13. *"Thou shalt not kill."*

IT is told of St. Francis of Assisi that, an hour or two before his death, gazing down on his poor, emaciated body, he exclaimed regretfully, "I fear I have ill-treated my brother, the ass!"

XLVI. Cursing. Exod. xxi. 17. "*He that curseth his father, or his mother, shall surely be put to death.*"

"Curses, like chickens, always come home to roost." Such is the proverb, and it is a very true saying. The evil wishes and threats which are spoken against another return on the swearer's own head. When an Arab is kicked by his camel, or when the beast refuses to go on, he solemnly curses the camel, at the same time throwing a handful of sand into the air, and most of that sand comes back into the Arab's eyes. So it is with curses.

XLVII. A Gift which Blindeth the Wise. Exod. xxiii. 8. "*And thou shalt take no gift: for the gift blindeth the wise, and perverteth the words of the righteous.*"

It is recorded of Sir Matthew Hale that upon his circuit as a judge he refused to try the cause of a gentleman who had sent him the customary present of venison, until he had paid for it ; for he well understood the spirit of the excellent law in Exodus xxiii. 8.

XLVIII. The Plan of Strasburg Cathedral. Exod. xxv. 9. "*According to all that I show thee, after the pattern of the tabernacle, and the pattern of all the instruments thereof, even so shall ye make it.*"

There is a beautiful story told of the plan by which Strasburg Cathedral was made. The architect, Erwin von Steinbach, who was given the commission to build it, was greatly troubled lest he should not get his plan sufficiently noble. He had a daughter named Sabine, who was skilful in drawing, and one night after they had wept together over the plans, she said to her father, "Don't despair, God will help us." After she fell asleep she dreamed that a beautiful angel came, and, when she had told her story, said, "You shall make the plan for the minster." The angel and Sabine then set to work, and soon the plan was done. When she awoke she uttered a loud scream, for there was a paper before her covered with wonderful drawing. Her father exclaimed : "Child, it was no dream. The angel really visited you, bringing the inspiration from heaven to help us." He built the cathedral after the plan, and it was so beautiful that the people really believed the story.

XLIX. Burning with Pure Oil. EXOD. xxvii. 20.
"And thou shalt command the children of Israel, that they bring thee pure oil olive beaten for the light, to cause the lamp to burn always."

IT is related in the biography of one who lived to become a devoted Christian man, that while he was yet a little boy, the passage read from the Bible in the family on a certain occasion was Exodus xxvii. 20, describing the oil used in the vessels of the tabernacle. The meaning and application of the verse was explained by other passages from the New Testament. This boy was then but five years old, and it was not supposed that he could understand or feel the slightest interest in a subject considered far beyond his age. The older children left the room after family worship, but the little boy was detained, as usual, to be taught some simple verses of the Bible by his mother, and to pray with her. He kneeled down at length to pray, and in the midst of his prayer, he paused, and exclaimed earnestly, "O my God, make *me* to burn this day with *pure oil!*"

The morning lesson had not been lost upon him; he had understood its import. "Most evidently," says his biographer, "was this prayer heard and answered throughout the day of his life."

How appropriate is this petition for the morning offering of every Christian, "Make me to burn this day with pure oil"! If He who hath all hearts in His keeping vouchsafe a gracious answer to that prayer, the example of the disciple must be one that will glorify the name of Jesus. Such a man will walk with God. No unhallowed fires will be lighted in his bosom. Neither revenge nor hate can burn there. The peace and joy of the believer will fill his soul.

L. Talent without Sanctity. EXOD. xxix. 44. *"I will sanctify also both Aaron and his sons, to minister to Me in the priest's office."*

WILLIAM GRIMSHAW, of Haworth, administered a severe reproof to a lady with whom one day he was conversing. She had expressed her admiration of a certain minister who was more gifted in talent than in grace. "Madam,"

said Grimshaw, "I am glad you never saw the devil."
When asked why he made this remark, he said : "Because
he has greater talents than all the ministers in the world.
I am fearful if you were to see him you would fall in love
with him, as you seem to have so high a regard for talent
without sanctity. Pray do not be led away with the sound
of talents. Let the ministry under which Providence has
called you never be deserted under the influence of novelty.
There dwell, and pray that it may prove to you increasingly
edifying, consolatory, and instructive."

LI. Sabbath Desecration. EXOD. xxxi. 13. *"Verily My sabbaths ye shall keep."*

MR. GRIMSHAW'S ministry at Haworth was one of ceaseless
energy, labour, and prayer.

On entering upon the charge there, he found little
attention paid to the observance of the Lord's day. The
church was situated at the extremity of the parish, and it
was thought the people from the remoter districts would
not come so great a distance to worship, unless they had
the further inducement of being able to purchase such
stores for their families as were not to be procured nearer
their own dwellings. Sabbath had become a busy market-
ing day. To check this desecration, he adopted the most
vigorous means. It was the custom in that locality for the
churchwardens to leave their pew in the course of the
morning service, and visit the public-houses, and the usual
places of resort for the village idlers, to ascertain whether
idlers might be there lurking. Not content with requiring
these officers to do their duty, the incumbent was accustomed to leave the church himself when the psalm before
the sermon was sung, and if any was found wandering
in the streets, or lounging in the churchyard, he was
driven before him into the house of God. It has been
said that in this service the horse-whip was used, and that
on some occasions he told the clerk to give out the 119th
psalm, that he might have the longer time in which to
prosecute his search. But this is probably a myth or
exaggeration. John Newton relates, that as a friend of
his was passing a public-house in Haworth on the Lord's
day, his attention was attracted towards a number of

persons who were making their escape from it, some by jumping out of the lower windows, and others by climbing over a wall. At first he supposed from the hurry of their flight that the house must be on fire; but on inquiring the reason of the sudden rush, he found that it all arose from their having discovered the near approach of the parson. At another time, a man was passing the village on his way to call the doctor, when his horse lost a shoe. On applying to the blacksmith to have his loss repaired, the reply was, that unless the minister granted leave it could not be done. Grimshaw, learning that the case required haste, consented that the horse should be shod.

LII. Moses' Argument. EXOD. xxxii. 12. "*Wherefore should the Egyptians speak and say, For mischief did He bring them out, to slay them in the mountains, and to consume them from the face of the earth? Turn from Thy fierce wrath, and repent of this evil against Thy people.*"

THE pious Mr. Flavel, on the occasion of his escape to London from the persecution which was raging against the Nonconformists during his settlement at Dartmouth, is said to have made use of a similar argument to this of Moses. Being overtaken on his voyage by a violent storm, in which he and his companions all expected to be drowned, Mr. Flavel called the ship's company together in the cabin to invoke God's mercy and deliverance. Among other arguments he made use of this, that if he and his company perished in that storm the name of God would be blasphemed; the enemies of religion would say, that, though he escaped their hands on shore, yet Divine vengeance had overtaken him at sea. No sooner was his prayer ended than a person came from the deck crying: "Deliverance! God is the hearer of prayer! In a moment the wind is come fair west." And so sailing before it, they were brought safely to London.

LIII. Truthfulness. EXOD. xxxii. 24. "*So they gave it me: then I cast it into the fire, and there came out this calf.*"

HENRY VENN ELLIOT, the pious Brighton minister, writes thus in late life: "If there is one point more than another in morality concerning which I have been especially watchful in my own words, and earnest in teaching my children, it has been *strict truth*, even to the banishment of ordinary exaggerations." If a child had made some trifling mistake, and said, "I am so very sorry," "Keep your sorrow, my child," he would say, "for a greater occasion." He used to refer to Adam's self-justification, "The woman gave unto me"; to Aaron's, "There came out this calf"; to Saul's, "The people took of the spoil"; as compared with David's earnest, ingenuous "I have sinned against the Lord."

LIV. Christ our Rest-Stone. Exod. xxxiii. 14.
"And He said, My presence shall go with thee, and I will give thee rest."

IN India, where burdens are carried on men's heads and backs, it is customary to provide resting-places for them along the road. Stones are set up along the hot, dusty roads, just the right height for a man to rest his burden upon until he is refreshed and able to go on his way.

"Ah, sahib," said a native Christian to an English gentleman, "Christ is my rest-stone, Christ is all my hope."

LV. Leprosy. Lev. xiv. 1, 2. *"And the Lord spake unto Moses, saying, This shall be the law of the leper."*

THE crusaders were the means of introducing the leprosy of the East into all the countries bordering the Mediterranean Sea, and a feeling of pity, and even of reverence, for these sufferers was widely diffused through Europe at that time. The churchmen of the times encouraged this feeling, and taught that Christ Himself had regarded the lepers with special tenderness, and quoted from the fifty-third of Isaiah a prophecy, in which, as they maintained, the Messiah was foretold under the image of a leper. Francis of Assisi had faith to see and charity to love even in the leprous the imperishable traces of the Divine image. He became an inmate of the lepers' hospital at Assisi, and with his own hands washed and dressed the poor sufferers, and once kissed a leper, who, we are told, instantly became whole. Even they who reject the miracle will revere the lovingkindness.

LVI. Transferring of Sins. LEV. xvi. 21. *"And Aaron shall lay both his hands upon the head of the live goat, and confess over him all the iniquities of the children of Israel, and all their transgressions in all their sins, putting them upon the head of the goat."*

CHARLES SIMEON, of Cambridge, thus speaks of his attaining peace in believing:

"In passion week," he tells, "as I was reading 'Bishop Wilson on the Lord's Supper,' I met with an expression to this effect, *That the Jews knew what they did when they transferred their sin to the head of their offering.* The thought rushed into my mind, What! may I transfer all my guilt to another? Has God provided an Offering for me, that I may lay my sins on his Head? Then, God willing, I will not bear them on my own soul one moment longer. Accordingly I sought to lay my sins upon the sacred head of Jesus, and on the Wednesday began to have a hope of mercy; on the Thursday that hope increased; on the Friday and Saturday it became more strong; and on Easter Sunday (April 4) I awoke early with these words upon my heart and lips, 'Jesus Christ is risen to-day! Alleluia! Alleluia!' From that hour peace flowed in rich abundance into my soul."

LVII. Some Rules for the Christian Life. LEV. xviii. 4, 5. *"Ye shall do My judgments, and keep My ordinances, to walk therein: I am the Lord your God. Ye shall therefore keep My statutes, and My judgments; which if a man do, he shall live in them: I am the Lord."*

JOSEPH ALLEINE tells in a letter to a clergyman what were the rules he imposed upon himself in the Christian life and ministry.

"Never to lie down, but in the name of God: not barely for natural refreshment, but that a wearied servant of Christ may be recruited and fitted to serve Him better next day.

"Never to rise up but with this resolution, Well, I will go forth this day in the name of God, and will make religion my business, and spend the day for eternity.

"Never to enter upon my calling but first thinking, I will do these things as unto God.

"Never to sit down to the table, but resolving, I will not eat merely to please my appetite, but to strengthen myself for my Master's work.

"Never to make a visit but upon some holy design, resolving to leave something of God where I go, and in every company to leave some good savour behind.

"This is what I have been for some time learning, and am pressing hard after: and if I strive not to walk by these rules, let this paper witness against me."

LVIII. Honesty of the Huguenots. LEV. xix. 36.

"Just balances, just weights, a just ephah, and a just hin, shall ye have: I am the Lord your God, which brought you out of the land of Egypt."

THE name "Huguenot" has received several explanations, but the most plausible one is suggested by Dr. Baird, that it was derived from a popular hobgoblin, known as "Huguet" or "Le Roy Huguon," to which the superstitious folk likened the Protestants whom they saw flitting under cover of the darkness to their secret conventicles.

The testimony to the character of these people, as distinguished from some of their military and political leaders, is very explicit and honourable. "The Huguenot never swears," was a common saying. Their honesty was also a proverb. The manufacturers called them "a silly sort of people," because the silk which they brought did not have to be re-weighed. They were people of great industry and thrift. Hon. John Jay, who has made a life-long study of the history of the Huguenots in America, says that he "never heard of one of them who asked or received alms"; nor has he reason to think that, notwithstanding their privations, "any of them came to this country in a destitute condition." Gov. Lovelace wrote to the king of England: "I find some of these people have the breeding of courts, and I cannot conceive how such is acquired." The devout and practical quality of their religion is exemplified by such instances as that which attended the arrival of the party which settled at New Paltz, on the Hudson River. They had no sooner hitched their horses than they gathered in a group, when Psalm xlvi. was read, and they kneeled together in a prayer of thankfulness and dedication to the Lord, who had led them in the wilderness.

A single case may be cited as an illustration of the whole. Amadée was a youth of eighteen, living in the province of Perigord. His mother, a widow, had twenty-two soldiers quartered upon her during the dragonnades. For the sake of her children she signed a recantation. But because she added "compelled by fear," they were carried off to convents, except Amadée, who escaped, but was arrested on the frontier with a young comrade. Every effort was made to intimidate or seduce this young Christian and Faithful into abjuring their belief. A rich and beautiful wife was promised to Amadée if he would become a Papist. An attractive and attracted young Catholic girl even visited him in his cell, and offered herself to him with tears of pity and tenderness. Standing firm even against this allurement, he was condemned to the galleys.

The labour of the galley-slave is thus described in the memoir which was published of him: "Six men are chained to each bench wholly naked, sitting with one foot on a block of timber, the other resting on the bench before them, holding in their hands an enormous oar fifty feet long. Imagine them lengthening their bodies, their arms stretched out to push the oar over the backs of those before them; they then plunged the oar into the sea, and fall back into the hollow below, to repeat again and again the same muscular exertion. The fatigue and misery of their labour seems to be without a parallel. They often faint, and are brought to life by the lash; sometimes they are thrown into the sea, and another takes the place."

By reason of his intelligence and integrity this young man was offered the position of keeper of the supplies, which exempted him from labour at the oar. But he relinquished it in favour of another Huguenot, an old and feeble man, and returned to his torture and his vile companions. In an engagement with an English frigate he was the only survivor of eighteen who occupied three benches, and was himself severely mutilated.

The story of the woes of this noble young confessor as he and his companions were transferred from the galleys of Dunkirk to those of Marseilles; marched across the country on foot for three hundred miles with shackles about their necks; confined in a horrible prison in Paris, so chained in ranks that they could neither stand nor lie down; in winter chained upon the wharves with neither fire nor blankets; obliged to exhibit themselves in all sorts of ridiculous attitudes and degrading antics for the amusement of visitors—all this is too painful to be recapitulated. More fortunate than most of his brethren, Amadée, with a few others, was released by the intercession of Queen Anne of England, on condition of quitting France. They repaired to Geneva, where they were received with joy and tenderness.

LIX. The Duty of Charity. Lev. xxv. 35. *"And if thy brother be waxen poor, and fallen in decay, with thee; then thou shalt relieve him: yea, though he be a stranger, or a sojourner; that he may live with thee."*

THERE are eight degrees or steps, says Maimonides, in the duty of charity:

The first and lowest degree is to give, but with reluctance or regret—the gift of the hand, but not of the heart.

The second is to give cheerfully, but not proportionably to the distress of the sufferer.

The third is to give cheerfully and proportionably, but not until we are solicited.

The fourth is to give cheerfully, proportionably, and even unsolicited; but to put it in the poor man's hand, thereby exciting in him the painful emotion of shame.

The fifth is to give charity in such a way that the distressed may receive the bounty and know the benefactor, without their being known to him. Such was the conduct of some of our ancestors, who used to tie up money in the hind-corners of their cloaks, so that the poor might take it unperceived.

The sixth, which rises still higher, is to know the objects of our bounty, but remain unknown to them. Such was the conduct of those who used to convey their charitable gifts into poor people's homes, taking care that their own names should remain unknown.

The seventh is still more meritorious; namely, to bestow charity in such a way that the benefactor may not know the relieved objects, nor they the name of their benefactor: as was done by our charitable forefathers during the existence of the temple; for there was in the holy building a place, called the Chamber of Silence or Unostentation, wherein the good deposited secretly whatever their generous hearts suggested, and from which the most respectable poor families were maintained with equal secrecy.

Lastly, the eighth, and most meritorious of all, is to anticipate charity by preventing poverty, to assist the reduced brother before he be forced to hold out his hand for charity. This is the highest step, and the summit of charity's golden ladder.

LX. Reverencing the Sanctuary. LEV. xxvi. 2.
"*Ye shall keep My sabbaths, and reverence My sanctuary: I am the Lord.*"

WHEN Colonel Turner, a gallant cavalier, was hanged for burglary, he told the crowd gathered round the gallows that his mind received great consolation from the thought that he had always taken his hat off when he went into a church.

LXI. Trivial Hindrances keeping back from Public Worship. LEV. xxvi. 2.
"*Ye shall keep My sabbaths, and reverence My sanctuary: I am the Lord.*"

OF good Archbishop Leighton it is said, that the Sabbath was his delight; no slight hindrance could detain him from the house of prayer. Upon one occasion, when he was indisposed, the day being stormy, his friends urged him, on account of his health, not to venture to church.

"Were the weather fair," was the reply, "I would stay at home; but since it is otherwise I must go, lest I be thought to countenance by my example the irreligious practice of allowing trivial hindrances to keep me back from public worship."

LXII. A Boy Martyr. NUM. vi. 25, 26.
"*The Lord make His face shine upon thee, . . . and give thee peace.*"

WILLIAM BROWN was a poor boy martyr in the reign of Queen Mary. He was burnt at Brentwood. "Pray for me," he said to the bystanders. One of them replied, "I will pray no more for thee than I will pray for a dog." "Then," said William, "Son of God, shine Thou upon me!" And lo! at once on a dark, cloudy day, the sunshine burst forth upon him, and kindled a glory upon his youthful face; "whereat the people mused, because it was so dark a little time before." Happy are they on whom the Son of God shall thus smile.

LXIII. How John Williams was Converted.
NUM. x. 29. "*Come thou with us, and we will do thee good.*"

JOHN WILLIAMS, the well-known missionary to the South Sea Islands, when loitering about on a Sabbath evening in early life, was persuaded to go and hear a sermon; by the grace of God, by that sermon he was converted, and became one of the greatest missionaries of modern times.

LXIV. Building up in their most holy Faith.
NUM xii. 3. "*Now the man Moses was very meek.*"

MR. MOSTYN, one of Wales' early ministers, was remarkably humble. When he was assistant to another minister, some good people in his hearing ascribing their conversion, under God, to that minister's preaching, he seemed dejected, as if he were of no use. A sensible countryman present, who had a particular value for his ministry, made this observation for his encouragement: "An ordinary workman may hew down timber, but it must be an accomplished artist that shall frame it for the building." Mr. Mostyn cheerfully replied, "If I am of any use, I am satisfied." His preaching was eminently useful to Christians.

LXV. Aaron's Rod.
NUM. xvii. 8. "*Behold the rod of Aaron for the house of Levi was budded.*"

MR. RUSKIN takes up the legend of St. Christopher, and writes thus:

"I do not know," he says, "how far the tale of St. Christopher is proposed by the Catholic Church for belief as history, or with interpretation as myth. I could myself much more easily explain it as the gradually enriched and sunset-gilded tradition of a dream and vision seen by a hermit-ferryman, than I can interpret its incidents as symbolizing any course of facts of spiritual life. Reading it as a myth, I am myself utterly uncertain of the meaning of the king, the hermit, the river, or the oppression felt by the saint in bearing Him whose yoke is easy and whose burden is light. But I will hope for the reader's pleasure in being reminded of Tintoret's figure of St. Christopher in paradise (in the Ducal Palace at Venice), bearing the globe of the world, which is surmounted by a cross, and by whose surface a beam of light descending from the enthroned Christ is reflected in a dazzling star. By which I have always understood Tintoret to mean what Holman Hunt means by his "Light of the World," but with the further lesson that the visitation which was to sanctify our world for us with eternal day would come first through the deepest night, and in the heaviest toil of the occupation which was our earthly duty. I think also that Tintoret may have intended to make us feel how greatly the story of St. Christopher had been itself a light to all the Christian, and might be to all the future, world. But none of these lessons by great imaginative interpreters, however probable, guides us to any clear reading of the legend for all men, in the continuous action of it; nor, if any such could be given, would the application be other than forced and untrustworthy. At first thought most of us would suppose the river meant human life; but that river we do not cross, but descend: we are troubled when it is troubled, calm when it is calm. We do not resist its current nor refuse its peace. Again, in memory of more recent fables, we might think of it as the river of death; but the travellers whom the saint carried over resumed their journey, and he himself, finally fording it, begins his true ministry of the gospel. Take it for some chief time of trouble, and we might perhaps, without much strain, suppose the meaning to be that the man who had sustained others in their chief earthly trials afterwards had Christ for companion in his own; but this idea would never occur easily and naturally to very simple persons who heard the story; it is rare that, among the many confused evils of existence, any of us can fix on that which, once traversed, was to be feared no more; and I should

D

be extremely reluctant to offer to my Protestant readers, as the true sense of the loveliest of Catholic legends, the thought that common people were only to have a saint to comfort them in their troubles, while the saint himself had Christ. More and more, as I think over it, I am led to take it for the memory of what really once happened to some kindly warden of a river ford, bearing by the grace of natural human feeling comfort afterwards to all who hear of it for ever."

The legend goes on to relate how the dry fir tree that St. Christopher carried in his hand became green, after his ministry, and was covered with fresh leaves. Mr. Ruskin compares with this the blossoming of the spears of Charlemagne's knights in the windows of Chartres cathedral, and adds, "It is, I suppose, only by the coincidence of thought which runs through all great literature and legend, that the putting forth of blossom by the rod of Aaron, and of leaf by the staff of St. Christopher, teach the life and beneficence of the sceptres of the just, as the for ever leafless sceptre of Achilles, and the spear whose image was the pine, hewn for ships of battle from the Norwegian hills, show in their own death the power of the kings of death."

LXVI. Results are in God's Hands. NUM. xxi. 4. *"The soul of the people was much discouraged because of the way."*

A DISCOURAGED minister had the following strange dream. He thought he was standing on the top of a great granite rock, trying to break it with a pickaxe. Hour after hour he worked on with no result. At last he said, "It is useless; I will stop." Suddenly a man stood by him and asked: "Were you not allotted this task? and if so, why are you going to abandon it?" "My work is vain; I can make no impression on the granite." Then the stranger solemnly replied: "That is nothing to you; your duty is to pick, whether the rock yield or no. The work is yours, the results are in other hands; work on." In his dream he saw himself setting himself anew to his labour, and at his first blow the rock flew into hundreds of pieces. This was only a dream, but it proved a valuable and never forgotten lesson to the minister, and a means of comfort and cheer to his soul.

LXVII. Solid Happiness. NUM. xxiii. 10. *"Let me die the death of the righteous, and let my last end be like his!"*

"MY first convictions on the subject of religion," says the late Rev. R. Cecil, "were confirmed by observing that really religious persons had some solid happiness among them, which I felt the vanities of the world could not give. I shall never forget standing by the bedside of my sick mother. 'Are not you afraid to die?' I asked. 'No.' 'Why does the uncertainty of another state give you no concern?' 'Because God has said: "Fear not. . . When thou passest through the waters, I will be with thee; and through the rivers, they shall not overflow thee." 'Let me die the death of the righteous.'"

LXVIII. The Bliss of Dying. NUM. xxiii. 10. *"The death of the righteous."*

THE Rev. Henry Venn, of Huddersfield, and latterly of Yelling, in Huntingdonshire, was so elated at the prospect of death, that it actually proved a stimulus to life. Upon one occasion, as he lay on his death-bed, he himself remarked some bad symptoms, and said to Mr. Pearson, "Surely these are good symptoms for me"; to which his medical attendant replied, "Sir, in this state of joyous excitement you cannot die." The joy of dying kept him alive.

LXIX. Ready to Go. NUM. xxiii. 10. *"Let me die the death of the righteous, and let my last end be like his."*

JOHN ELIAS, the great Welsh preacher, had a happy death. It may be said of him in the exquisite lines of Dr. Watts—

> "He stood, but with his starry pinions on,
> Dressed for the flight, and ready to be gone."

As he lay on his death-bed he said: "I am as happy as it is possible for a redeemed man to be, though in pain, in pain. There is not a cloud between me and the face of my God. The blessings and mercies I used to enjoy in my ministry are still flowing freely into my soul. They are more powerful, more lively in their effects on my soul than ever I felt them when I preached them to others." Thus he passed away on June 8th, 1841, to his Saviour and his reward. His body was carried at the head of a funeral procession a mile and a half long, to the grave at Llanfaes, near Beaumaris.

The Lord God of Elijah is still present in Israel, but the sons of the prophets need a double portion of the Spirit. Let the Churches lift up their cry, "Oh that Thou wouldest rend the heavens, that Thou wouldest come down!" So shall greater deeds be wrought, and ministries given to the Church as powerful and as fruitful as was that of John Elias.

LXX. The First Telegram in America. NUM. xxiii. 23. *"According to this time it shall be said of Jacob and of Israel, What hath God wrought!"*

THE first words ever flashed along an electric wire in America were, "What hath God wrought!" sent by a young girl from Washington to Baltimore. And when man's science subdued the forces of the lightning and the ocean, and the electric cable first flashed its words from hemisphere to hemisphere, almost the first message was, "Glory to God in the highest, and on earth peace, goodwill toward men."

LXXI. The Detection of Sin is Certain. NUM. xxxii. 23. *"Be sure your sin will find you out."*

IN the most mysterious manner does the providence of God sometimes expose crime. The singular movements of some domestic animals; the words written upon the wadding of some discharged gun; the caving in of banks, in the sand of which dead bodies have been buried; and other things as trivial, lead to the detection of criminals who suppose they have concealed all tokens of guilt in the graves of their victims. It is related of an eminent clergyman, that on one occasion, while walking in a graveyard, he saw the sexton throwing up the bones of a human being. He took the skull in his hands, and on examination saw a nail sticking into the temple. He drew it out, placed it in his pocket, and asked the sexton whose skull it was. On receiving the necessary information, he went to the widow, now an aged woman, and entered into conversation with her. He asked her of what disease her husband died, and while she was giving an answer drew the nail from his vest, and asked her if she had ever seen it before. Struck with horror, the wretched woman confessed that she had murdered her husband, and that her own hand had driven into his temple that nail.

LXXII. Good turned to Evil. DEUT. xxiv. 24.
"For the Lord thy God is a consuming fire."

A GLASS inkstand was placed on the table so that the sun's rays fell upon it. Brightly and cheerily, no doubt, they played upon its facets and angles; but that inkstand affected these beautiful sunbeams in such a way as to extract from them heat in sufficient force to set the table upon which it stood on fire, reducing it, and all it came in contact with, into ashes. What is there more beautiful than the sunbeams? How they cheer and cherish and inspire nature all around! yet there are some objects which can convert this thing of beauty and health and life into a consuming fire. So there are moral characters which extract death out of life; transform the loving, life-giving gospel into an instrument of destruction; in short, cause the God of love to become to them a consuming fire.

LXXIII. The Stranger within thy Gates.
DEUT. v. 14. *"Thy stranger that is within thy gates."*

A HIGHLY cultivated lawyer relates this incident of his early days. When a thoughtless youth, he wandered away to a distant city. The Sabbath came, and he was alone, with nothing but his own fancy or inclination to guide him in his selection of a place of worship. As he was going along the street, he passed by the door of a Bethel chapel. Hearing the voice of prayer, he turned back and entered. Scarcely was he seated, before the preacher, among the subjects of petition prayed for "the stranger within our gates." He remained till the service was concluded, and went to his room in tears. The words of supplication gathered around the word "stranger" rang in his memory. After relating the circumstance the lawyer adds: "In public ministrations never forget the 'stranger within thy gates.' You will touch some heart, which will vibrate to the appeal."

LXXIV. The Arithmetic of Heaven. DEUT. vi. 4.
"The Lord our God is one Lord."

DANIEL WEBSTER had been attending Divine service in the Park-street Church, Boston. It is a staunch, orthodox church, and at that time was not in high favour with the Unitarians. Coming away from church, he was met by a Unitarian gentleman, who said to him, "So you have been to church, where they teach that three times one are one!" Mr. Webster replied with that solemn voice of his, now more intensely solemn than usual, "My friend, you and I do not understand the arithmetic of heaven."

If any man less than Mr. Webster had made this reply, it might be considered an evasion of the difficulty suggested. Mr. Webster had been attending a church where the doctrine of the Trinity is taught, Three Persons in one Godhead, Father, Son, and Holy Spirit, Three in One. No human intellect can comprehend the mode of such existence; and some there are who reject the truth, because it does not seem to them reasonable that One should be Three, and Three should be One.

LXXV. Loving God. DEUT. vi. 5. *"And thou shalt love the Lord thy God with all thine heart, and with all thy soul, and with all thy might."*

SIR DAVID BREWSTER was an earnest searcher after light. A memorable incident we give in the words of his loving biographer. She is recording a conversation which her father had with her sister-in-law, Mrs. Macpherson, who says: "I had a long talk with dear papa upon the suffering of Christ, from which we passed on to speaking of the gratitude due to God. . . . We spoke of the possibility of feeling any love towards God, and agreed that such a sentiment of love as is possible between man and man was impossible between man and God. 'How can we love Him,' he said, 'One whom we have not seen? We admire Him in His works, and trust from the wisdom seen in these that He is wise in all His dealings; but how can we LOVE Him?'" After this conversation, his daughter-in-law, being herself led to understand how alone the love of the unseen Christ can be shed abroad in the heart by the working of the Holy Spirit, felt that she must confess this change in her views and feelings. "He listened most attentively, and when I had finished, took me in his arms, kissed me, and said, in such a child-like manner, 'Go now then, and pray that I may know it too.'"

LXXVI. A Question for Parents. DEUT. vi. 7.
"And thou shalt teach them diligently unto thy children."

IT is related of Ben Ezra, that when yet a child he asked his teacher to be instructed in the law of God; but he was told that he was yet too young to be taught these sacred mysteries. "But, master," said the boy, "I have been in the burial-ground, and I have measured the graves, and I find some shorter than myself. Now if I should be taken away by death before I know the word of God, what will become of me after?"

LXXVII. The Haus-Segen. DEUT. vi. 9. *"And thou shalt write them upon the posts of thy house, and on thy gates."*

THE mountainous region in the south-east of Bavaria is the home of a race of people, simple, pious, and primitive in their habits, even to the present day. It is the common custom of the Bavarian peasants to affix the "Haus-Segen" to their house doors. This is a paper, with the outline of a heart printed in the centre, and surrounded by a circlet of smaller hearts. Each heart contains a prayer or some sacred verse, and the paper is sometimes decorated with tints of red, blue, and yellow.

LXXVIII. Scripture Texts. DEUT. xi. 18. *"Therefore shall ye lay up these my words in your heart and in your soul, and bind them for a sign upon your hand, that they may be as frontlets between your eyes."*

TEXTS of Scripture used to be painted on the doors of the Puritans, and over their fireplaces. Texts used to be stamped on kettles and skillets, wrought into garments, and even carved on the wooden cradles. The language of the Bible was with them the language of every-day life.

LXXIX. Duty of Liberality. DEUT. xv. 7. "*Thou shalt not harden thine heart, nor shut thine hand from thy poor brother.*"

MR. SHERMAN had the cause of the poor and needy very much at heart. On a Friday morning's service, when his congregation was, as it often was, a scanty one, the subject was Elisha multiplying the poor widow's oil to pay the demands of her creditors. He depicted the need of poor widows, especially of ministers' widows, often left utterly destitute, and mentioned a case just then known to him, where £25 pounds were needed to apprentice a minister's son ; and with such effect, that the dozen or two people present subscribed £18 before leaving the hall, more than enough to complete the sum required being sent in afterwards. Mr. Sherman was himself a man of great benevolence. He gave liberally himself. We are told that his house was like the house of the relieving officer, besieged by needy applicants, and a deserving case was never sent unhelped away. The old people in the almshouses were often gladdened by parcels of tea and sugar or by small presents of money, and he never failed to remember them in his Christmas gifts.

LXXX. Succour Men in Distress. DEUT. xv. 11. "*For the poor shall never cease out of the land: therefore I command thee, saying, Thou shalt open thine hand wide unto thy brother, to thy poor, and to thy needy, in thy land.*"

I WAS very much struck with an old Englishman that I knew, who used to do a great deal of amateur preaching and amateur teaching, visiting jails and poorhouses, who said to me one day, "I make them understand, wherever I go, that I am never going to give them anything." I said to myself, "That being the general rule of your ministration, I would not give the turn of my hand for all the good that you will do." A man who determines that he will not succour men that are in physical distress, through all the range of his ministration, will not do any good.

I did not then believe that he did any good ; I do not believe it now ; and since he is dead, I do not think he believes it.

LXXXI. Moral Training of the Young. DEUT. xxxii. 46. *"And he said unto them, Set your hearts unto all the words which I testify among you this day, which ye shall command your children to observe to do, all the words of this law."*

THE strong feeling which Erasmus always had in regard to the careful moral training of the young appears in his "Manual." "Let parents," he says, "who are Christians, not utter words before their children which give the lie to their faith. Let not the Christian mother indulge in unreasonable grief after bereavement, and let the father beware of praising before his children the man who has made a fortune by doubtful means."

LXXXII. Venture on Him. DEUT. xxxiii. 27. *"Underneath are the everlasting arms."*

I ONCE saw a lad on the roof of a very high building where several men were at work. He was gazing about with apparent unconcern, when his foot slipped, and he fell. In falling he caught by a rope, and hung suspended in mid air, where he could sustain himself but a short time. He perfectly knew his situation, and expected in a few minutes to be dashed on the stones below. At this moment a kind and powerful man rushed out of the house, and standing beneath him with extended arms called out, "Let go of the rope ; I will catch you." "I can't do it," said the boy, "Let go, and I promise you shall escape unhurt." The boy hesitated for a moment, and then quitting his hold, dropped easily and safely into the arms of his deliverer. Here is a simple act of faith. The poor boy knew his danger ; he saw his deliverer, and heard his voice. He believed him, and letting go every other dependence and hope, he dropped into his arms.

> "Venture on Him, venture freely,
> Let no other trust intrude ;
> None but Jesus
> Can do helpless sinners good."

LXXXIII. A Farewell Scene. DEUT. xxxiv. 8.

"And the children of Israel wept for Moses in the plain of Moab thirty days."

ROBERT MOFFAT laboured for more than fifty years in South Africa, and chiefly at Kuruman, amongst the Bechwanas. On Sunday, March 20th, 1870, he preached for the last time in the Kuruman church. In all that great congregation there were few of his own contemporaries left. The older people were for the most part children when he first came among them. With a pathetic grace, he pleaded with those who still remained unbelieving amid the gospel privileges they had now enjoyed for so many years, and he commended to the grace of God those converts who had been his joy and crown. It was an impressive close to an impressive career. On the Friday following the aged missionary and his wife took their departure. As they came out of their house and walked to their wagon, they were beset by crowds of the Bechwanas, each longing for a hand-shake and another word of farewell; and as the wagon drove away it was followed by all who could walk, and a long and pitiful wail arose, enough to melt the hardest heart.

LXXXIV. Ruskin's Bible. JOSH. i. 8.

"This book of the law shall not depart out of thy mouth; but thou shalt meditate therein day and night."

JOHN RUSKIN writes thus in his "Outlines of Scenes and Thoughts in my Past Life": "I have just opened my oldest (in use) Bible; a small, closely, and very neatly printed volume it is, printed in Edinburgh by Sir D. Hunter, Blain & J. Bruce, in 1816. Yellow now with age, and flexible, but not unclean, with much use, except that the lowest corners of the pages at 1 Kings viii., and Deuteronomy xxxii. are worn somewhat thin and dark, the learning of these two chapters having cost me much pains. My mother's list of the chapters with which, thus learned, she established my soul in life, has just fallen out of it. I will take what indulgence the incurious reader can give me for printing the list thus accidentally occurrent.

Exodus xv., xx.
2 Samuel i. from seventeenth verse to the end.
1 Kings viii.
Psalms xxiii., xxxii., xc., xci., ciii., cxii., cxix., cxxxix.
Proverbs ii., iii., viii., xii.
Isaiah lviii.
Matthew v., vi., vii.
Acts xxvi.
1 Corinthians xiii., xv.
James iv.
Revelation v., vi.

"And truly, though I have picked up the elements of a little further knowledge—in mathematics, meteorology, and the like—in after life, and owe not a little to the teaching of many people, this maternal installation of my mind in that property of chapters I count very confidently the most precious, and, on the whole, the one *essential* part of all my education."

LXXXV. Rahab. JOSH. ii. 1. *"And they went, and came into a harlot's house, named Rahab, and lodged there."*

"RAHAB had wrecked her life; mast was broken, sail was gone, rudder was lost! She was a helpless, ruined woman. But as sailors have found a mere timber of what was a ship with the compass clinging to it, and pointing away to its northern star, so from amidst the fragments of what was once a woman's life, as they drifted along the streets of Jericho, Rahab's heart was trembling away towards the Star that should come out of Jacob, and the Sceptre that would rise out of Israel."

LXXXVI. A Moravian Missionary. JOSH. xiii. 33. *"But unto the tribe of Levi Moses gave not any inheritance: the Lord God of Israel was their inheritance, as he said unto them."*

THE Moravian missionary, Zeisberger, who laboured for sixty-three years among the Red Indians, never took a penny from the Church for his support. "I am no hireling," he said quietly; "God set me this work."

Zeisberger died in extreme old age in an Indian village.

Bishop de Schweinitz, in his history of the Moravian missionary, tells us that, when the hour of his death drew nigh, the passing bell tolled, and his white friends, the Brethren, withdrew and gave way to the Lenape Indians, who gathered around his bed. They sang the hymns in their own tongue, which he had written for them, and on these strains of lofty hope his soul passed. "Then," says the chronicler, "the red men fell upon their knees, and wept aloud, for they knew that their best friend was gone for ever."

LXXXVII. A Soldier of Jesus Christ. JOSH. xxiv. 24. *"The Lord our God will we serve, and His voice will we obey."*

THE following anecdotes are told of David Sandeman, the devoted missionary :

"Delighting as he did in vigorous exercise and gymnastic feats, he one day, in a walk with two companions, joined for a few minutes in the amusement of leaping over the stile at one corner of the old Queen's Park. While his companions failed, he cleared the stile so easily and gracefully as to draw forth the admiration of a dragoon who stood by. When about to walk on Mr. Sandeman turned to the soldier, got him into conversation, and spoke of the perils and honours of a life like his. Then suddenly drawing himself up to his full height, he exclaimed with deep feeling : 'There is something far better yet! It is to be a soldier of Jesus Christ. Are *you* that ? ' The dragoon looked with wonder on the man of muscle and sinew who could thus speak to his soul, and shook hands at parting, evidently deeply interested. Scenes like these were continually recurring ; but this power of gracefully turning every little event into a means of usefulness could exist only in one whose natural atmosphere was the love of God, and in whose soul there was an uninterrupted gravitation towards his Divine Saviour.

"One day, in harvest, finding by the roadside a woman cutting grass, he plucked a head of wheat, and told her how a corn of wheat must die before that beautiful head could spring up, and that so Christ must needs die ere we could be saved. The woman was astonished, and the young missionary went on his way, praying that the Lord might send his word to her heart. So continually did he act upon his favourite text, 'Whose I am, and whom I serve,' that in a brief summer excursion in the west of Scotland, a companion of his journey informs us, that he believes that he must have spoken to not less than *five hundred persons* in the course of their pedestrian excursion, and that when opportunity occurred he was as direct and ready in addressing the rich as the poor."

LXXXVIII. Devoutness of Spirit. Jud. v. 16.
" Great searchings of heart."

THE great secret of all Sherman's success as a preacher lay in the devoutness of his spirit, and the closeness of his communion with God, and his earnest, humble searching of heart. Here are some of his "resolves," dated Feb. 20th, 1841 :

" 1. To rise at seven o'clock every morning, and to spend half an hour with God before breakfast in reading the Scriptures and prayer.

" 2. To select some portion out of one of the chapters for meditation through the day.

" 3. To retire some time during the day for prayer, and to give as much time as possible in the evening to this exercise.

" 4. To pray with my dear wife.

" 5. To seek specially the salvation of my family by prayer and correspondence.

" 6. Not to go where temptations to any of my besetting sins are sure to abound.

" 7. To plead with God for more conversions amongst the people, and to visit them, and to labour at my sermons more and more. Oh, how wonderful that the people will come and hear me! O Lord, strengthen me, help me to put these resolves into practice, and never to depart from them. Now help me to plead for grace to perform my vows. Oh, kiss the prodigal, and welcome him to his Father's heart!"

LXXXIX. An African Convert. RUTH ii. 12.
" Under whose wings thou art come to trust."

IN an article by Robert Moffat, the famed missionary to the Africans, he tells of a young man who accompanied him in a missionary tour. Marelolé was clever and intelligent and an inquirer, who would soon have been received into Church fellowship. The camp was visited by the well-known African fever, and Marelolé was seized, and had a relapse. He became insensible, and lay for two days motionless in a comatose condition, from which no effort could rouse him. On the evening of the second day Moffat was at work repairing a wagon, when he heard some one singing in a clear voice, and on inquiring who was singing to the sick man, was told, " It is himself." He hastened to the spot, and found it even so. The sick man was singing one of the hymns which embodied some of the thrilling parts of Psalm lxxxiv. Moffat knelt down beside him, and listened with inexpressible feelings of gratitude. As he sang the last verse he spoke to him ; he was deaf, and his pulse was performing its last beats ; and while the missionary looked at the now motionless lips, the spirit departed to that heavenly Zion about which he had just been singing.

XC. The Most Unfashionable of all Books.
1 SAM. iii. 4. *" The Lord called Samuel: and he answered, Here am I."*

SIR JOSHUA REYNOLDS tells us that he was exceedingly mortified when he showed his picture of the prophet Samuel's call to some of the great, because they asked him who Samuel was. One of his friends told him " that he must get somebody to make an oratorio of Samuel, and then it would not be vulgar to confess they knew something of him. I tell him that I hope the poets and painters will at last bring the Bible into fashion, and that people will get to like it from taste, though they are insensible to its spirit, and afraid of its doctrines. I love this great genius for not being ashamed to take his subjects from the most unfashionable of all books."

XCI. Called of God. 1 SAM. iii. 4. *" The Lord called Samuel: and he answered, Here am I."*

DAVID ZEISBERGER was a most devoted worker amongst the Red Indians of America, and did a noble work in

Christianizing and civilizing these wild tribes. His early history is interesting.

David Zeisberger's forefathers were peasants, the followers of John Huss. When he was five years old his family fled, to escape persecution, to Herrnhut, where Count Zinzendorf then had gathered the remaining Hussites. David's father and mother were among the Herrnhutters sent by Zinzendorf to Georgia, but the boy was left in Moravia, to be educated by the Church of the Unitas Fratrum. He was a small, delicate lad, with something in his face which attracted the notice of Zinzendorf. He sent the boy to a prosperous community of the Church near Utrecht, where education, as in godly private families of the time, was given through the lash. David went through a steady discipline of work, beatings, and fastings.

One day a stranger whom he helped, when he was lost in the morasses near the town, gave him two pieces of gold, bidding him keep them and not give them to the community. David's conscience however forced him to give one piece to the Brethren, who immediately charged him with having stolen it, and publicly punished him as a liar and a thief.

This was the stroke too much. That night David, with another boy named Shober, escaped from the community and set off to America, with no means but the solitary piece of gold which he had kept. It paid their way to London; there General Oglethorpe met the lads, and, struck by David's sensitive face and singular gravity, procured them a free passage to Savannah.

In the backwoods of Georgia, Zeisberger at last found his father and mother.

He was much impressed by the sight of the poor savages around him, and often pondered the question whether or not he should devote his life to the work of bringing those lost heathen to God.

Just at this juncture arrived Count Zinzendorf. He saw the lad, and detected again the same singular hint of promise on his face—a prophecy which he could not interpret.

He told the Brethren that the boy must have a chance, and appointed him one of his staff to return with him to Moravia. David came with him to Philadelphia, and embarked, with the understanding that a clear road to fortune lay before him in Europe, and that he never was to return to America.

The ship weighed anchor. Bishop Nitschmann, passing down the deck, saw the lad, pale and haggard, gazing at the receding shore.

"Zeisberger," he said, "is it possible that you wish to return?"

"Yes."

"But for what reason?"

"That I may learn to know Christ, and teach Him to the Indians," said David, finding speech at last in his extremity.

"Then if that be your mind, in God's name even now go back!"

The ship was brought to, and the boy sent back. After this the Moravians regarded him as Eli did Samuel: he was called of God. His name was entered on the list of the Brethren and their trades, as David Zeisberger, *destinirter Heidenbote*.

The lad at once left the community and went to the lodge of the great sachem of the Mohawks, and there lived and worked to learn thoroughly the habits and language of the Indians. He was adopted into the tribe of the Onondagas.

Thus began the remarkable history of a work which extended over sixty-two years.

XCII. A Noble Resignation to God's Will.

1 SAM. iii. 18. "*It is the Lord: let Him do what seemeth Him good.*"

"Do you know *this*, Master Cameron?" said an executioner, startling the old Christian in his cell, and showing something in a basket. It was a fair-haired, youthful head, just stricken off. "I know it, I know it; my son's, my own dear son's. It is the Lord; good is the will of the Lord, who cannot wrong me nor mine, but has made goodness and mercy follow us all our days."

XCIII. A Man of Prayer. 1 Sam. xv. 11. "*He cried unto the Lord all night.*"

JOHN WELCH, of Ayr, was pre-eminently a man of prayer. Whilst minister at Ettrick he was boarded in the house of one named Mitchelhill. A son of his landlord, who slept with Welch, used to tell, in after years, how he would lay a Scot's plaid above his bedclothes, and would rise and cover himself with it when he went to prayer; for, from the beginning of his ministry, "he reckoned the day ill-spent if he stayed not seven or eight hours in prayer."

He would, we are told, retire many nights to the church, and spend the whole night in prayer—praying with an audible and sometimes with a loud voice. Once his wife, going at night to his closet, where he had been long at prayer, and fearing he should catch cold, heard him say, "Lord, wilt Thou not grant me Scotland?" and, after a pause, "Enough, Lord, enough." Once he got such nearness to the Lord in prayer that he exclaimed, "Hold Thy hand, Lord; remember Thy servant is a clay vessel, and can hold no more."

XCIV. Impure Motives in Religious Work. 1 Sam. xv. 22. "*Hath the Lord as great delight in burnt offerings and sacrifices as in obeying the voice of the Lord?*"

THE traveller from Rome to Gaeta crosses the Maremma. He watches the sun setting over its dim, dismal, and yet majestic fanes; he sees a white mist rising soft, beautiful, tinged now with the fair glow of sunlight, now with the paler shades of moonlight—a beautiful mist indeed; but plunge into it, and the mist is poison. Just as fatal are the effects of religious work when engaged in from impure motives.

XCV. The Intellect and the Heart. 1 Sam. xvi. 7. "*For the Lord seeth not as man seeth: . . . the Lord looketh on the heart.*"

ON some Church festival, when the morning services were over, Massillon, the great preacher, entertained a party at dinner. A remark made by one of the guests, that it was time that something should be done to turn the holy day to edification, induced Massillon to fetch one of his sermons and read it to the company. A lady, by way of expressing admiration, exclaimed that if she had written such a sermon, she would certainly be reckoned among the saints. "Ah, madame!" was the old bishop's reply, "it is a long bridge which leads from the intellect to the heart." "Yes, indeed," muttered an Oratorian of Jansenist proclivities, who happened to be present; "and there are quite four arches of the bridge already broken down."

XCVI. The Soothing Power of Music. 1 SAM. xvi. 23. *"So Saul was refreshed, and was well, and the evil spirit departed from him."*

THIS remarkable instance of the power of music over the mind, especially in soothing its perturbations and allaying its disorders, is in conformity with the experience of physicians, and with various intimations which may be found in ancient authors. More or less so are those other scriptural instances, which evince the power of music over the moods of even the sanest minds, as in the case of Elisha, who called for the aid of a minstrel to bring his mind into the frame best suited to receive the impulses of the prophetic spirit. One would almost think, that there was some power in ancient music, which has since been lost, or that there existed, amid the simple manners of ancient times, a susceptibility to the influence of sweet and solemn sounds, which has been lost in the multitudinous business and varied pursuits of modern existence. But in truth, the wonderful effects so often described resulted from the concurrence of masterly skill in the minstrel with a peculiar sensibility to the influence of sweet sounds in the patient. And that where this concurrence is found it will still produce the same effect as of old, one or two "modern instances" may be cited to show.

In the *Mémoires* of the French Royal Academy of Sciences for 1707 are recorded many accounts of diseases, which, having obstinately resisted the remedies prescribed by the most able of the faculty, at length yielded to the powerful impression of harmony. One of these is the case of a person who was seized with fever, which soon threw him into a very violent delirium, almost without any interval, accompanied by bitter cries, by tears, by terrors, and by an almost constant wakefulness. On the third day, a hint that fell from himself suggested the idea of trying the effect of music. Gradually as the strain proceeded his troubled visage relaxed into a most serene expression, his restless eyes became tranquil, his convulsions ceased, and the fever absolutely left him. It is true, that when the music was discontinued his symptoms returned ; but, by frequent repetitions of the experiment, during which the delirium always ceased, the power of the disease was broken, and the habits of a sound mind re-established. Six days sufficed to accomplish the cure.

XCVII. The Habit of Prayer. 1 SAM. xxii. 4. "*I will call on the Lord.*"

FELIX NEFF, in speaking on the subject of prayer, has strikingly remarked : "When a pump is frequently used, but little pains are necessary to obtain water ; it flows out at the first stroke, because the water is high. But if the pump has not been used for a long time, the water gets low, and when it is wanted, you must pump a great while, and the stream comes only after great efforts. And so it is with prayer; if we are instant in it and faithful to it, every little circumstance awakens the disposition to pray, and desires and words are always ready. But if we neglect prayer, it is difficult for us to pray, for the water in the well gets low."

The thought is full of suggestions, of counsel, admonition, instruction. *The human heart is a leaky vessel;* and in a world like this, the tendency of spirituality, like that of water, is *downward*. If we neglect prayer, little by little we soon lose its *spirit;* and its spirit declining, its *habit* is soon laid aside, or retained only in the form ; and as the next step the *form* itself will soon be given up, the soul becoming prayerless, and the heart and life alike forsaken of God.

XCVIII. An Emperor's Shame. 1 SAM. xxiv. 19.
"*For if a man find his enemy, will he let him go well away ?*"

JOHN HUSS, in spite of the pledged safe-conduct of the Emperor Sigismund, was thrust into a miserable prison cell,

CIII. The Sweetest Name. 2 Sam. xxii. 3. "*In Him will I trust: He is my shield, and the horn of my salvation, my high tower, and my refuge, my Saviour.*"

The son of Sir James Mackintosh gives some account of the dying words of his father. "I observed that at every mention of the name of Jesus his eyes were unclosed. I said to him at one time, 'Jesus Christ loves you.' He answered slowly, and pausing between each word, 'Jesus Christ—love—the same thing.' He uttered these last words with a sweet smile. After a long silence, he said, 'I believe.' We said, in a voice of inquiry, 'In God?' He answered, 'In Jesus.' He spoke but once after this. Upon our inquiry how he felt, he said he was *happy*."

CIV. Tried before Trusted. 2 Sam. xxii. 31. "*The word of the Lord is tried.*"

A new steamboat has to be tried before passengers and freight can be trusted on board. A new railroad has its trial trips before it is thrown open to the public. A few years ago, at the opening of a railroad in Missouri, a train of cars filled with people, many of them gentlemen invited by the directors, set out from St. Louis on a trial trip. On swept the train. The party were in high spirits, when in an instant crash, crash! Timbers split, joists snapped, one terrible plunge, and down went the cars through a breaking bridge into the river below, a heap of ruins. *That* bridge was trusted *before* it had been tried.

CV. Fulfilling his Mission. 1 Kings xiii. 8, 9. "*If thou wilt give me half thine house, I will not go in with thee, neither will I eat bread nor drink water in this place: for so was it charged me by the word of the Lord.*"

The parish of R——, within the bounds of the presbytery of Edinburgh, had become vacant, and a presentation had been issued by the noble earl in whom the patronage was vested in favour of an individual who was obnoxious to the people, or, at least, who had not their consent to his becoming their pastor and spiritual instructor. In default of this Dr. Erskine strongly opposed his induction in the Church courts. His opposition was however fruitless; the necessary forms were ordered to be gone through, and the admission to take place, and, with a refinement of cruelty not unknown in those woeful days, Dr. Erskine himself was appointed to preside at the moderating of the call. This he did, in obedience to his ecclesiastical superiors. With his staff in his hand he walked from Edinburgh to R——, a distance of eight miles, on the morning of the appointed day; not being well acquainted with the place or the road, and immersed in deep thought, he went a considerable way beyond the church, and stopped only when he thought that he must have made a mistake, and had gone farther than was necessary. Meeting a man coming towards him, and dressed apparently in his Sunday suit, he conjectured that he might be going to the church, and inquired the road thither. The man told the doctor that he had gone a good bit too far, but that he would conduct him back to the church, as he was himself going there. In the door of the porch, and at the entrance to the churchyard, stood the patron peer and some others, who, observing Dr. Erskine to be fatigued, invited him to take some refreshment before entering on the duties of the day. This offer he gently declined, and passed directly into the church and to the pulpit. He went through the services with dignity and calmness, and fulfilled his mission. On returning from the church he was again accosted by the patron, who entreated him to rest a while and accept of some refreshment. His calm yet firm and solemn answer was to this effect: "I feel obliged by your politeness, my lord; but 'if thou wilt give me half thine house, I will not go in with thee, neither will I eat bread nor drink water in this place: for so was it charged me by the word of the Lord.'" And the good doctor walked his way back to Edinburgh, without a rest or even a halt.

CVI. Death of Children. 1 KINGS xiv. 17. *"The child died."*

MANY a little child Jesus has called to Him. Little Maggie was very ill of a fever, and the van had been sent to take her away to the infirmary. Maggie was dressed and ready. "Maggie, it's time for you to go," said her he could work no longer he was carried on a frame of wood with some grass and a blanket upon it. And when he could endure to be carried no farther, his faithful servants built him a little hut, and in that rude structure he died. He was a great traveller. He contributed much to our knowledge of Central Africa. The coloured races owe him a mighty debt of gratitude. He was one of the bravest of Christian men. But the journey of African exploration was too great for him.

CXI. A Martyr at the Stake. 1 KINGS xix. 14.
"Slain Thy prophets."

ON Huss firmly refusing to retract his opinions unless they were proved from the word of God to be erroneous, he was at length, with horrible solemnity, doomed to perish by fire as an obstinate heretic. On July 6th, 1415, sentence was formally pronounced upon him; and, after being stripped of his priestly garments, and subjected to various dreadful indignities, he was handed over to the secular arm for execution. A paper crown, painted over with figures of devils, and bearing the inscription "heresiarch," was put upon his head. "We thus devote thee to the infernal devils!" the prelates piously exclaimed; whereupon the martyr replied, "I am glad to wear this crown of ignominy, for the love of Him who wore a crown of thorns." He marched to the stake with wonderful composure, as if his heart were glad. A Roman historian who witnessed the scene says that he looked like a man going to a grand banquet. Arriving at the place of execution, Huss fell down on his knees and prayed aloud. Many of the people who heard him said to one another, "What this man has done before we know not; but now he has offered up most excellent prayers to God." When he had been tied to the stake, the faggots, piled up all round him, were kindled; and in less than a quarter of an hour John Huss expired amidst smoke and flame, with his last breath committing his soul to the Lord Jesus Christ, who had redeemed him. The ashes of his body were hastily gathered up by the executioners, and cast into the Rhine; but a good portion of the earth on which he was consumed, containing at least some of his remains, was conveyed to his native Bohemia, where to this day he is held in the highest veneration. The name of John Huss is as dear to the Bohemians as the name of William Tell is to the Swiss, or the names of William Wallace and John Knox are to the people of Scotland.

CXII. Soul Murder. 1 KINGS xxi. 25. "*Ahab, which did sell himself to work wickedness in the sight of the Lord.*"

AN American writer says: "When Charles IX. of France was importuned to kill Coligny, he for a long time refused to do so publicly or secretly; but at last he gave way, and consented in these memorable words, 'Assassinate Admiral Coligny, but leave not a Huguenot alive in France to reproach me.' So came the massacre of St. Bartholomew. When the soul resolves to assassinate some holy motive, when the spirit determines to kill, in the inner realm, Admiral Coligny, it too delays for a while; and, when it gives way, usually says, 'Assassinate this accuser of mine; but leave not an accusing accomplice of his in all my kingdom alive to reproach me.' So comes the massacre of the desire to be holy.

"Emerson quotes the Welsh Triad as saying, 'God Himself cannot procure good for the wicked.' Julius Müller, Dorner, Rothe, Schleiermacher, no less than Plato, Aristotle, and Socrates, assert that, in the nature of things, there *can* be no blessedness without holiness. Confucius said, 'Heaven means principle.' But what if a soul permanently loses principle? *Si vis fugere a Deo, fuge ad Deum*, is the Latin proverb. If you wish to flee from God, flee to Him. The soul cannot escape from God; and can two walk together unless they are agreed? Surely there are a few certainties in religion, or several points clear to exact ethical science in relation to the natural conditions of the peace of the soul."

CXIII. "Seed Corn." 2 KINGS ii. 3. "*The sons of the prophets that were at Bethel.*"

THE great importance of the work done in our educational institutions for young ministers was never more strikingly emphasized than by the missionary Judson, who said, as he to complete the trip himself, he committed his charge to natives, the result justifying his confidence in them.

These supplies had been made up into bundles for carrying on men's shoulders. It afterwards proved that these men faithfully discharged their trust. As privileged persons, carrying the packages of a missionary, they crossed the border country in safety and descended into the valley of the Zambesi, where there were none but their sworn enemies the Makololo, and at last presented themselves on the south bank of the river at a spot where they could shout across to an island in the river, and announce their errand. Small as their party was, they could get no one to approach them, for treachery was still suspected. They laid their packages on the bank, delivered their message across the stream, and departed hungry and tired and footsore. The Makololo, finding them really gone, took the bundles they had brought, placed them on an island, and built a roof over them; and there they were when Livingstone returned, some months afterward, from his journey to St. Paul de Loanda on the west coast, thankful indeed for the letters and supplies which reached him by this strange kind of parcel delivery.

CXIX. Praying and Working. 2 KINGS xx. 5. "*I have heard thy prayer, I have seen thy tears.*"

THERE are many instances on record of special answers to prayer. What shall we make of the instances of prayer in such lives as that of David Nasmith, or of the good men sketched in Mr. Stevenson's "Praying and Working," followed again and again and again by that which they had asked? The Rauhe Haus at Hamburg, a great Christian reformatory, has such a story as seems miraculous—as indeed is nothing less. Money came from unknown sources, as it was wanted. Step by step this work of God was built, extended, and sustained, with no exchequer but the never-failing goodness of the Lord. "I believe," says Wichern, its founder and head, "that whatever Christian household or person trusts the Lord utterly, and allows Him to be the only God and Saviour, although it be out of great faltering and weakness, that person or household shall never want, but shall have all it wants,

even if it should obtain it through daily need and peril."
This is the experience of a life in which such prayer has
been habitually put to the test. A case given by Major
Miller, governor of the military prison, Aldershot—than
whom we could surely have no safer authority—is quoted
in *Good Words.*

"One of our prisoners, on being checked at drill by one
of the warders, wished that God Almighty would strike the
warder dumb. The prisoner on the spot was struck dumb,
and did not recover his speech for seven days. During
the period he was deprived of speech he was strictly
watched. There was no feigning whatever; the man was
most wretched and alarmed."

CXX. Sun-dials. 2 KINGS xx. 11. *"And Isaiah the prophet cried unto the Lord: and He brought the shadow ten degrees backward, by which it had gone down in the dial of Ahaz."*

WHOEVER is fond of travelling through the villages of old
England will notice what innumerable fancies in various
places have been associated with the course and flight of
the hours. Very frequently the inscriptions on the sun-
dials are scriptural, such as, "Watch, for ye know not the
hour," or, "Yet a little while is the light with you: walk
while ye have the light." There is something very suggestive in the motto upon a sun-dial over an old cottage
at Bishopthorpe, near York, "Tempus labile," slipping
time. Over the porch of East Leake church, in Notting-
hamshire, are the words, "Now is yesterday's to-morrow."
It must have been in a spirit of hopeful expectancy that
such a motto as that famous one of Geneva was chosen,
"Post tenebras lux," After darkness light, or that other
form of it, "Post tenebras spero lucem," After darkness I
hope for light.

CXXI. True Nobility. 1 CHRON. vi. 49. *"Moses the servant of God."*

WHEN the female martyr Agatha was upbraided because,
being descended of an illustrious parentage, she stooped
to mean and humble offices for the relief of her fellow

believers. "Our nobility," she replied, "lies in this, that we are the servants of Christ." "Inasmuch as ye did it unto one of the least of these My brethren, ye did it unto Me."

CXXII. Sacred Silence. 1 CHRON. xvii. 16. *"And David the king came and sat before the Lord."*

TIME spent in quiet prostration of soul before the Lord is most invigorating. David "sat before the Lord"; it is a great thing to hold these sacred sittings, the mind being receptive, like an open flower drinking in the sunbeams, or the sensitive photographic plate accepting the image before it. Quietude, which some men cannot abide, because it reveals their inward poverty, is as a palace of cedar to the wise, for along its hallowed courts the King in His beauty deigns to walk.

> "Sacred silence! thou that art
> Floodgate of the deeper heart,
> Offspring of a heavenly kind,
> Frost o' the mouth, and thaw o' the mind."

CXXIII. The Best Way to get Riches. 2 CHRON. i. 10. *"Give me now wisdom and knowledge, that I may go out and come in before this people: for who can judge this Thy people, that is so great?"*

AN old Puritan divine says "that the best and surest way to have any outward mercy is to be content to want it. When men's desires are over-eager after the world, they must have thus much a year, and a house well furnished, and wife and children thus and thus qualified, or else they will not be content. God doth usually, if not constantly, break their wills by denying them, as one would cross a froward child of his stubborn humour; or else puts a sting into them, that a man had been as good he had been without them, as a man would give a thing to a froppish child, but it may be with a knock on his fingers and a frown to boot. The best way to get riches is, out of doubt, to set them lowest in one's desire. Solomon found it so. He did not ask riches, but wisdom and ability to discharge his great trust; but God was so pleased with his prayer, that He threw in riches into the bargain. If we seek the kingdom of God and His righteousness in the first place, and leave other things to Him, God will never be behindhand with us. Let our care be to build His house, and let Him alone to build ours."

CXXIV. The Patience of Unanswered Prayer.
2 CHRON. vi. 40. *"Now, my God, let, I beseech Thee, Thine eyes be open, and let Thine ears be attent unto the prayer that is made in this place."*

IN a biographical sketch of Miss Fletcher, an earnest Christian worker, the following incident is told. One Sabbath, at forenoon service, Miss Fletcher's eyes and heart were irresistibly drawn towards an old woman, who was evidently pinched with care, and bowed under some load of anxiety. She felt that she ought to give that old woman some money, and mentally resolved to do so if the opportunity presented itself at the evening service. Arrived at home, she found that her pocket-money consisted of one napoleon, and though loath to part with the whole of it, she felt she could neither break it nor leave it behind, but must take it with her to church. This she did, half hoping the old woman would not be among the worshippers. But there she was, with the mute and unconscious, but irresistible appeal as plainly written on her face as ever. On coming out of church Miss Fletcher somehow found herself beside her, and slipped the gold piece into the astonished old woman's hand, and ran off without waiting for thanks. It afterwards transpired that the poor woman at that very time was in the greatest destitution, and had been rolling her case on the Lord, and had left it with Him in confidence, and this was His answer.

CXXV. Seeking the Lord earnestly.
2 CHRON. xv. 15. *"They . . . sought Him with their whole desire; and He was found of them: and the Lord gave them rest."*

DURING a revival many years ago in Glasgow it was customary to hold meetings every night for prayer and conversation with inquirers after peace. One evening a Sunday-school teacher came to make known her case. She had been in distress for weeks. In her trouble she had tried to find relief by change of air and scenery, but soon found that this was no medicine for a soul diseased; and coming back she shut herself up in a room to plead for mercy. Her besetting temptation was a fear lest any one should discover her in the act of prayer; but after shutting herself up to pray in silence, her feelings became so excited that she literally screamed, and her prayer was heard in the house. At length she poured out her soul in this pathetic strain: "O Jesus, I am told Thou art the burden-bearer. Here is my burden; here I lay it. I will not lift it; I will have nothing more to do with it: do with it what Thou wilt." From that hour she rejoiced in Christ her Saviour. At another meeting one little girl, who had found peace to her own soul, was heard counselling another who was still in darkness, "I say, lassie, do as I did: grip a promise, and hold on to it."

CXXVI. The Widow's Son. 2 CHRON. xx. 21. *"He appointed singers unto the Lord, and that should praise the beauty of holiness."*

ONE of Queen Victoria's chaplains records the following story: "When I was in the island of Malta I heard a beautiful old legend, of about one thousand years ago, of a monastery on the banks of the Rhone, where it enters the Lake of Geneva. Into that monastery there entered a boy who was 'the only son of his mother, and she was a widow.' It was not with her desire, but not without her consent; and it became her consolation, morning and evening, to go outside the monastery walls, and, standing under the windows of the chapel, hear her boy's voice singing in the choir; and day by day this filled her heart with gladness. But one day she went, and could not hear it; and at last she demanded of the porter at the gate the reason, and was told that her boy was dead. So she thought, 'My last hope in life is gone.' At length, taking heart, she prayed that if it were possible she might hear her boy's voice singing in paradise; and the legend says that her prayer was granted."

CXXVII. Humility. 2 CHRON. xxxiv. 27. *"Because thine heart was tender, and thou didst humble thyself before God."*

MOLINOS, the Quietist, in his book, "The Spiritual Guide,"

thus writes : " Encourage thyself to be humble, embracing tribulations as instruments of thy good ; rejoice in contempt, and desire that God may be thy holy refuge, comfort, and protection. None, let him be never so great in this world, can be greater than he that is in the eye and favour of God ; and therefore the truly humble man despises whatever there is in the world, even to himself, and puts his trust and repose in God.

"The truly humble man finds God in all things, so that whatever contempt, injury, or affront comes to him by means of creatures, he receives it with great peace and quiet internal, as sent from the Divine hand, and greatly loves the instrument with which the Lord tries him."

CXXVIII. Social Intercourse. EZRA vi. 22. *"The Lord had made them joyful."*

DR. ROBERT HALL, the distinguished preacher, during the last years of his life at Bristol was in the habit of spending some evenings each week in social intercourse with his people. On these occasions some of the members of his own family occasionally accompanied him ; and if it did not happen that the conversation was particularly lively, these last were apt to complain that the evening had been dull. To this Dr. Hall would reply: "I don't think so. It was very pleasant. I enjoyed it. I enjoy everything."

CXXIX. Growing Love for the Word of God. EZRA vii. 6. *"And he was a ready scribe in the law of Moses; which the Lord God of Israel had given."*

THE following little anecdote of Dr. Kennicott, who lived at the end of the last century, strikingly proves how much the love of the sacred volume grows with its perusal. During the time that he was employed on his Polyglot Bible it was his wife's constant office, in their daily airings, to read to Dr. Kennicott those different portions of Scripture to which his immediate attention was called. When preparing for their ride, the day after this great work was completed, upon her asking what book she should *now* take, "Oh!" exclaimed he, "let us begin the Bible.'

CXXX. "More Light, Lord." Ezra ix. 8. *"That our God may lighten our eyes, and give us a little reviving in our bondage."*

Prayer supplies a leverage for the uplifting of ponderous truths. One marvels how the stones of Stonehenge could have been set in their places; it is even more to be inquired after whence some men obtained such admirable knowledge of mysterious doctrines: was not prayer the potent machinery which wrought the wonder? Waiting upon God often turns darkness into light. Persevering inquiry at the sacred oracle uplifts the veil, and gives grace to look into the deep things of God. A certain Puritan divine at a debate was observed frequently to write upon the paper before him; upon others curiously seeking to read his notes, they found nothing upon the page but the words, "More light, Lord," "More light, Lord," repeated scores of times: a most suitable prayer for the student of the word.

CXXXI. Washington at Prayer. Neh. i. 6. *"Let Thine ear now be attentive, and Thine eyes open, that Thou mayest hear the prayer of Thy servant."*

A gentleman narrates the following:

"I received the following anecdote of Washington, about fifty years ago, from the farmer referred to in the narrative. He was a member of the Society of Friends, who, from their peaceable habits, were lukewarm or opposed to the War of Independence. While the army lay in the neighbourhood of White Plains, a farmer, whose dwelling was near the camp, one morning at sunrise, while passing a clump of brush, heard a moaning noise. Thinking his ox or his ass had fallen into a pit, he, on approaching the spot, heard the voice of a human being engaged in prayer. He hid in the thicket, and listened, resolved to see the speaker. Having finished his aspirations to heaven, this man of God came forth from his hiding-place. It was George Washington. When the farmer entered his dwelling, he said to his wife: 'Martha, we must not oppose this movement any more. This work is from the Lord. I heard the man George Washington send to heaven such prayers for the cause and the country, and I know they will be heard.'

Thus Washington rose with the sun and prayed for his country; fought for it by day, and watched for it by night."

We would add to this, that whilst a student at Princeton we frequently heard a similar testimony from a venerable old man in that vicinity. He stated that he belonged for several months to Washington's bodyguard, and that it was his duty to stand guard from two until five o'clock each morning, and that it was invariably the general's custom to rise at four o'clock, and read the word of God and kneel down and pray in an audible voice for several minutes, after which he commenced the business of the day. He stated moreover that he uniformly reprimanded all profane swearing in those under his authority. The memory of the piety of such a man should be cherished as a rich legacy to the nation of which he was the father.

CXXXII. Found Off Guard. NEH. iv. 9. *"Nevertheless we made our prayer unto our God, and set a watch against them day and night, because of them."*

THE following illustration from Roman history is suggestive. Machærus was a fortress too impregnable to be taken by all the prowess of Rome. Among its defenders was a young man, whose strong arm had often scattered the assailants, and kept them back till his compatriots had regained their refuge after many a successful sally; but on one occasion he dallied just outside the gate. An unseen foe, of great strength, who had been lying in wait for such an opportunity, grasped him in his arms and bore him off to the Roman camp. There he was first mercilessly and ignominiously scourged, full in the view of those by whose side, but an hour before, he had been doing stern battle against the enemies of his country. Then a cross was brought forward, and preparations made to nail him to it. This was more than the defenders of the fortress could bear to witness. They inquired whether no ransom could avail to save their young hero's life. No; nothing short of the surrender of their place of impregnable strength, in defence of which his and their blood had been shed together. The sacrifice was made, and the conditions honourably observed by the Romans. But what was the life-long feeling of the young Eleazar? All his patriot spirit crushed, and a sense of shame ever burning on his cheek that no tears of repentance could ever cool. All this from one moment's imprudence. Found off guard did it all.

CXXXIII. The Bible in Iceland. NEH. viii. 8. "*So they read in the book, in the law of God distinctly.*"

DR. EBENEZER HENDERSON was sent to Iceland by the Bible Society to distribute the Icelandic Scriptures amongst the inhabitants. It was found by Henderson that there was a famine of the word of God in the island, often only one copy of the Scriptures in a whole parish.

During the course of his first and his two subsequent journeys, he disposed, or arranged for the disposal, by gratuitous distribution or by purchase, of 4,055 Bibles, and 6,634 New Testaments, and thousands of tracts, with which the Icelanders might beguile their long winter evenings more profitably than with their national *sagas* and oft-reiterated traditional tales. The rapture with which his gift of a New Testament was frequently hailed may be gathered from such an incident as the following:

He had sent, as was his custom, a notice round the neighbourhood where he travelled of the object of his journey. In response, a young man, amongst others, had been despatched by his poor and aged parents to learn the truth of the message they had heard. On receiving a Testament, it was hardly possible for him to contain his joy. As a number of the people had at the time collected around the door of the tent, he caused the young man to read the third chapter of the Gospel of John. He had scarcely begun when the people all sat down or knelt on the grass, and listened with the most devout attention. As he proceeded, the tears began to trickle down their cheeks, and they were all much affected. The scene was doubtless as new to them as it was to Henderson; and on his remarking, after the young man was done, what important instructions were contained in the Scripture that had been read, they all gave their assent, adding, with a sigh, that these truths were too little attended to. The landlady especially seemed deeply impressed with the truths she had heard, and remained some time after the others were gone, together with an aged female, who every now and then broke out into exclamations of praise to God for having sent "His clear and pure word" among them. "It is impossible," adds Henderson, "for me to describe the pleasure I felt on this occasion. I forgot all the fatigues of travelling over the mountains, and indeed, to enjoy another such evening, I could travel twice the distance. I bless God for having counted me worthy to be employed in this ministry, to dispense His holy word among a people prepared by Him for its reception, and to whom, by the blessing of His Spirit, it shall prove of everlasting benefit."

CXXXIV. God's Mercies to the Worst of Repenting Sinners. NEH. ix. 17. *"A God ready to pardon."*

A STORY is told concerning a bold rebel that had made a great party against one of the Roman emperors. A proclamation was therefore sent abroad, that whosoever could bring in the rebel, dead or alive, he should have a great sum of money for his reward. The outlaw, hearing of it, comes, and, presenting himself before the emperor, demands the sum of money proposed. The emperor bethinks himself that if he should put him to death, the world would be ready to say that he did it to save his money; and so he freely pardons the rebel, and gives him the money. Here now was light in a dark lantern, mercy in a very heathen. And shall such a one do thus that had but a drop of mercy and compassion in him, and will not Christ do much more that hath all fulness of grace and mercy in Himself? Surely His bowels yearn to the worst of sinners repenting; let them but come in, and they shall find Him ready to pardon, yea, One that is altogether made up of pardoning mercies.

CXXXV. The Pithiest Grace. NEH. xii. 31. *"Two great companies of them that gave thanks."*

LUTHER, Melanchthon, and Bugenhagen were close friends. One afternoon the three friends had supper with Camerarius, and it occurred to Luther to ask who could furnish the briefest and pithiest "grace." His own was "*Dominus Jesus, Sit potus et esus,*" "May the Lord Jesus be our drink and meat"; and it must have been accepted as both short and suggestive. Nothing can do justice to Bugenhagen's but his bluff Pomeranian: *Dit und Dat, Drocken und Natt, gesegne uns Gad,* "This and that, dry or wet, bless us, God." Melanchthon's was briefest, and surely pithiest and profoundest of all: *Benedictus benedicat,* "May the blessed One give His blessing"; and the sententious benediction is still familiar in many a college hall.

CXXXVI. Delusiveness of Earthly Glory.
ESTH. v. 13. *"Yet all this availeth me nothing."*

THIS is how Wellington wrote about the great victory at Waterloo: "I cannot express the regret and sorrow with which I contemplate the heavy loss I have sustained. Believe me, nothing except a battle lost is so terrible as a battle won. The glory arising from such actions is no consolation to me, and I cannot suggest it has any consolation to you."

CXXXVII. Card-playing. JOB i. 1. *"One that feared God, and eschewed evil."*

THOMAS SCOTT, rector of Aston Sandford, Buckinghamshire, was in youth exceedingly fond of card-playing; and after he became a clergyman he occasionally joined in a game, from an idea that too great preciseness might prejudice his neighbours, and being of opinion that there was no harm in the practice. He says however that he felt it a very awkward transition to remove the card-table, and introduce the Bible and family worship. But his fetters were completely broken in the following manner. Being on a visit to one of his parishioners, a person to whom his ministry had been useful, she said to him: "I have something which I wish to say to you, but I am afraid you will be offended. You know A. B.; he has lately appeared attentive to religion, and has spoken to me concerning the sacrament; but last night he, with some others, met to keep Christmas, and they played at cards, drank too much, and in the end quarrelled and raised a riot; and on remonstrating with him on his conduct, his answer was, 'There is no harm in cards; Mr. Scott plays at cards.'" This smote the minister to his heart, and fixed his resolution never to play at cards again.

CXXXVIII. A Singular Dream. JOB i. 6. *"Now there was a day when the sons of God came to present themselves before the Lord, and Satan came also among them."*

JOHN HUSS once had a singular dream. He thought that the powers of evil thronged his chapel of Bethlehem to obliterate the pictures of Jesus upon the walls. But angels of light on the other side with swift hands repainted them in colours richer, and in more entrancing beauty. Such are the powers that contend in the place of our assemblies. But fairer, tenderer, stronger shall the influence of Jesus grow under angel hands. The saints witness its triumphs. The faithful ministry paints Emmanuel with impassioned force and many a loving repetition, till every stone and beam seem eloquent of His story, and the whole place a monument to His incomparable name.

CXXXIX. Resignation to God's Will. JOB i. 21. *"The Lord gave, and the Lord hath taken away; blessed be the name of the Lord."*

RABBI MEIR was from home, and during his absence his two sons died. His wife laid them upon the bed, and spread a white covering over their bodies. On her husband's return she thus addressed him: "Rabbi, I would fain ask thee one question. A few days ago a person entrusted some jewels to my custody, and now he demands them back again; should I give him them?" "This is a question," said Rabbi Meir, "which you should not have thought it necessary to ask. Wouldest thou hesitate or be reluctant to restore to every one his own?" "No," she replied; "but yet I thought it best not to restore them without acquainting you therewith." She then led him to the bedside, and took off the covering from the bodies. "Ah! my sons, the light of mine eyes; I was your father, but you were my teachers." The mother too wept bitterly. At length she said, "Rabbi, we must not be reluctant to restore that which was entrusted to our keeping. See, the Lord gave, the Lord has taken away; and blessed be the name of the Lord." "Blessed be the name of the Lord," echoed Rabbi Meir; "and blessed be His name for thy sake too!"

CXL. Resignation. JOB i. 21. *"The Lord gave, and the Lord hath taken away; blessed be the name of the Lord."*

IN a beautiful letter of resignation, Scott, the famous commentator, thus writes of the death of his youngest boy:

"I have to inform you that it has pleased the Lord who gave also to take away from us our youngest boy, your husband's godson, and thereby to discharge both him and us from our trust. After a lingering and wasting disorder, he was released from this world of sin and sorrow, and I doubt not gained the blessed assembly above, to unite in their song of praise to Him that sitteth on the throne, and to the Lamb that was slain, and hath redeemed them to God with His blood. He died on September 25th. Nature will heave the anxious sigh, but faith looks within the veil, beholds the happy deliverance, approves, and rejoices; and I trust we both are enabled to say from our hearts, 'The Lord gave, and the Lord hath taken away; blessed be the name of the Lord.'"

CXLI. Going where All Problems will be Solved. JOB v. 9. *"Which doeth great things and unsearchable; marvellous things without number."*

WHEN Sir David Brewster lay on his death-bed, he was attended by his friend, Sir James Young Simpson, a man of kindred genius and of kindred Christian hopes. "The like of this I never saw," Sir James Simpson said to Mr. Cousin after he had left the dying chamber. "There is Sir David resting like a little child upon Jesus, and speaking as if in a few hours he will get all his problems solved for him." For in that supreme hour of dawning immortality his past studies were all associated with the name and person of the Redeemer. "I shall see Jesus," he said, "and that will be grand. I shall see Him who made the worlds," with allusion to those wonderful verses in the

Epistle to the Hebrews, which had formed the subject of the last sermon he had heard a few weeks before. Thus tracing all to the Creator and Redeemer, he felt no incongruity, even in these hours, in describing to Sir James Simpson some beautiful phenomena in his favourite science. Reference was made to the privilege he had enjoyed in throwing light upon "the great and marvellous works of God." "Yes," he said; "I found them to be great and marvellous, and I felt them to be His."

CXLII. Importunate Prayer. Job vi. 8. *"Oh that I might have my request; and that God would grant me the thing that I long for!"*

THE following answers to prayer are a warning to suppliants who utter requests which they feel *must* be answered, without any thought as to whether it be best in God's sight or not.

A child was very ill, and his father felt that he could not give him up. While others watched he prayed, and with such insistence that he recorded, "About six o'clock my anxiety was in a measure relieved, and in going to the sick room I found that the boy had fallen into a sleep, and from that hour he grew better." And yet, looking back after the lapse of years, it had been better and happier for parents and child, for others also, in later years, if the short life had then ended.

Again comes the history of a similar case, and one of the parents recorded, "Saved in answer to importunate prayer." The life was saved, but the nature seemed to be changed, and the boy grew to manhood a curse, a sorrow, and a burden to those most nearly connected with him. And yet he was the child of Christian parents, and was brought up as a Christian child.

CXLIII. Penalty of Reading the Bible. Job xiii. 15. *"Though He slay me, yet will I trust in Him."*

IN his "History of the Dutch Republic," Mr. Motley tells us of one Titelmann, a blood-red persecutor of the Netherlands. Upon any pretext would he put to death man, woman, or child.

There was a poor schoolmaster, Geleyn de Muler, of

Oudenarde. He had been suspected of Bible reading. Titelmann found him and his wife and four children, and told him that death by fire was his fate if he did not recant.

"Will you give me a trial?" said Muler.

"You are my prisoner, and are to answer me and none other," was the reply. Some questions were asked by Titelmann, and then Muler was demanded to recant. He was for some moments speechless.

"Do you not love your wife and children?"

"God knows," said the schoolmaster, "that were the heavens a pearl, and the earth a globe of gold, and were I the owner of all, most cheerfully would I give them all to live with my family, even though our fare be only bread and water."

It was enough. Muler was strangled, and his body burned. Such faith in God, how much is it needed in this world!

CXLIV. Dying Words of an Unbeliever. JOB xiv. 14. *"If a man die, shall he live again?"*

THE dying words of the late Harriet Martineau were: "I have no reason to believe in another world. I have had enough of life in one, and can see no good reason why Harriet Martineau should be perpetuated." What gloom and sadness! Now listen to St. Paul: "I have fought a good fight, I have finished my course, I have kept the faith; henceforth there is laid up for me a crown of righteousness, which the Lord, the righteous Judge, shall give me at that day." Who, in the light of such experiences, can refrain from exclaiming, "Let me die the death of the righteous, and let my last end be like his"?

CXLV. The Tomb Forgets No One. JOB xvi. 22.
"When a few years are come, then I shall go the way whence I shall not return."

VICTOR HUGO, when in the depth of severe affliction—the loss of his two sons—wrote the following lines:

"Patience. They have but gone before. It is just that the evening should come for us all. It is just that all should go up, one after the other, to receive their pay.

The exempts are such only in appearance. The tomb forgets no one."

CXLVI. True Wisdom. JOB xxviii. 28. *"Behold, the fear of the Lord, that is wisdom; and to depart from evil is understanding."*

WE are told in history how Edmund Rich, Archbishop of Canterbury, found his love of learning at Oxford bringing its troubles. "His Old Testament frowned down upon a love of secular learning, from which Edmund found it hard to wean himself." At last in a dream the form of his dead mother floated into the room where the teacher stood amidst his mathematical diagrams. "What are these?" she seemed to say; and seizing Edmund's right hand, she drew on the palm three circles interlaced, each of which bore the name of one of the Persons of the holy Trinity. "Be these thy diagrams henceforth, my son," she cried; and her figure faded away. And so Edmund Rich learned to put first things first.

CXLVII. Conscience a Gnawing Worm. JOB xxxiv. 18. *"Is it fit to say to a king, Thou art wicked? and to princes, Ye are ungodly?"*

HUGH LATIMER was very outspoken to King Henry VIII., feeling that he must tell him his duty. "You that be of the court, and especially ye sworn chaplains," he said long afterwards, "beware of a lesson that a great man taught me at my first coming to court. He told me for good will; he thought it well. He said to me, 'You must beware, howsoever ye do, that ye contrary not the king; let him have his sayings; follow him; go with him.' Marry! out upon such counsel! Shall I say as he says? *Say your conscience, or else what a worm shall ye feel gnawing!* What a remorse of conscience shall ye have when ye remember how ye have slacked your duty! Yet a prince must be turned not violently, he must be won by a little and a little. He must have his duty told him, but with humbleness, with request of pardon, or else it were a dangerous thing."

CXLVIII. Dr. Ryland and his Hymn. JOB xxxv. 10.
"*Where is God my Maker, who giveth songs in the night?*"

DR. RYLAND was the author of that beautiful hymn, which he wrote under singular circumstances:

> "O Lord, I would delight in Thee,
> And on Thy care depend;
> To Thee in every trouble flee,
> My best, my only Friend."

He was at Bristol Academy, engaged to be married to a young lady whom he fondly loved. She was taken with a dangerous sickness, from which it was feared she would not recover. Filled with anguish, he called to inquire about her, and was told by the servant if he would call in half an hour he would hear the opinion of the doctors, who were then holding a consultation on the case. He retired to an empty house, then under repair, sat down on a large stone, and taking a piece of slate wrote thereon that beautiful hymn, which has been the comfort of thousands of the tried children of God:

> "When all created streams are dried,
> Thy fulness is the same:
> May I with this be satisfied,
> And glory in Thy name!

> "No good in creatures can be found
> But may be found in Thee;
> I must have all things, and abound,
> While God is God to me."

He called, and received a favourable report. The lady recovered, they were married, and lived most happily together for seven years, when she was removed by death. Thus out of trial came a song, even as out of the lion came honey.

CXLIX. The Captive Set Free. JOB xxxix. 27. "*Doth the eagle mount up at thy command, and make her nest on high?*"

MANY years had a noble eagle been confined in such a manner that no one had seen it even attempt to raise a wing. Perfectly subdued, unconscious now of its native power, it remained inactive and apparently contented. But its owner was about to leave for a far country, never to return. He could not take the eagle with him. "I will do one act of kindness before I go," said he, and unloosed the chain from the captive bird. His neighbours and children looked on, with regret that they should see the eagle no more. A moment, and it would be gone for ever! But no; the bird walked the usual round, which had been the length of his chain, unconscious that he was free. The gazers looked on in wonder and in pity. The slow rustling of a wing was heard. It was stretched, and then folded. Anon it was stretched to its full expansion, and then folded softly again. Now, slowly and cautiously, the eagle expands both wings, and looks up into the blue sky. One effort to mount, then another, and the wings have found their lost skill; and upward, higher, and speedier he mounts his way, until lost to view.

Hast thou, O child of God, been pinioned long to the cares and toils of earth, so that thy wings of faith and love have lost all power to rise? Once thou couldst soar, and thou mayest soar again. His "grace is sufficient for thee."

CL. The Wheat and the Chaff. Ps. i. 4. *"The ungodly are not so: but are like the chaff which the wind driveth away."*

"WHAT is in yonder vessel?" I inquire of a passing stranger. "Chaff," he replies, turning a hasty glance in the direction to which I point, and passes on. His answer is all that you could expect him to give, and yet it is not correct. The vessel was filled with wheat and chaff, mingled together as they were thrashed from the sheaf; but it has been shaken from side to side for some time, and the wheat has all sunk to the bottom, while the chaff has all risen to the top. In like manner many real, though not perfect Christians, are set down as hypocrites by careless observers, because the things of the Spirit gravitate downward, lie unseen, while the vanities that perish in the using occupy almost all the visible surface of the life.

That which is Christlike in Christians should not be small, but large and full-grown; should not sink out of sight, but stand forth visible to all.

CLI.   Colour-blind. Ps. iv. 6.   *"Who will show us any good?"*

THERE is an optical peculiarity called Daltonism or colour-blindness. It is so common that nearly one in twenty have it. It consists in an inability to distinguish colours. Green is confounded with red. Those who suffer from this defect are unable, so far as the colour is concerned, to distinguish the petals of a rose from its leaves, or the blossom of the scarlet poppy from the unripe corn among which it is growing. The beautiful hues of sunset are a delusion to them; the faces of their friends wear a strange complexion; and the fair aspects of nature appear quite different from what they are to others. And yet the eye of the colour-blind seems the same as an ordinary eye. Its structure and appearance look precisely similar. The peculiarity is almost unknown or unrecognised by those who have it; and being ignorant of its existence themselves, they cannot easily be persuaded to believe it. And so are there not many coming to the Lord's house as His people come, worshipping the Lord as His people worship, making the same profession of religion, and walking in the same ways, presenting no apparent difference between themselves and true Christians, and yet who are colour-blind spiritually? The whole economy of redemption, the entire scheme of grace, is to them altogether different from what it is to those who know the power of godliness. The things that are spiritually discerned are to them uninteresting and incomprehensible. The colours of the heavenly landscape are confounded by them, and appear of one uniform dull hue. Christ Himself, who is the chiefest among ten thousand and altogether lovely, has no form or comeliness to them that they should desire Him. While the believer utters his rapturous song, "My Beloved is white and ruddy," they say, "What is thy Beloved more than another beloved?" They cannot see the beauties and glories of the world unseen; and in the very midst of them are crying out, "Who will show us any good?"

CLII. Praying for What we Do not Expect.

Ps. v. 3. *"My voice shalt Thou hear in the morning, O Lord; in the morning will I direct my prayer unto Thee, and will look up."*

"I WAS once," narrates Daniel Quorm, "staying with a gentleman who was a very religious kind of man; and in the morning he began the day with a long family prayer, that we might have a Christ-like spirit, and the mind that was also in Christ Jesus, and that we might have the love of God shed abroad in our hearts by the Holy Ghost given to us. A beautiful prayer it was, and I thought, What a good, kind man you must be! But about an hour after, I happened to be coming along the farm, and I heard him hallooing and scolding and going on, finding fault with everything. And when I came in the house with him he began again. Nothing was right, and he, I found, very impatient and quick-tempered. ''Tis very provoking to be annoyed in this way, Daniel. I don't know what servants in these times be good for but to worry and vex one with their idle, slovenly ways.' I did not reply for a minute or two. And then I said, 'You must be very much disappointed, sir.' 'How so, Daniel? Disappointed?' 'I thought you were expecting to receive a very valuable present this morning, and I see it has not come.' 'Present, Daniel?' and he scratched his head, as much as to say, 'Whatever can the man be talking about?' 'I certainly heard you speaking of it, sir,' I said quite coolly. 'Heard me speak of a valuable present! Why, Daniel, you must be dreaming. I've never thought of such a thing.' 'Perhaps not, but you've talked about it; and I hoped it would come whilst I was here, for I should dearly love to see it.' He was getting angry with me now, so I thought I would explain. 'You know, sir, this morning you prayed for a Christ-like spirit, and the mind that was in Jesus, and the love of God shed abroad in your heart.' 'Oh! that's what you mean, is it?' and he spoke as if that weren't anything at all. 'Now, sir, wouldn't you be rather surprised if your prayer was to be answered, if you were to feel a nice, gentle, loving kind of spirit coming down upon you, all patient and forgiving and kind? Why, I believe you would become quite frightened; and you'd come in and sit down in a faint, and imagine that you must be going to die, because you felt so heavenly-minded?' He did not like it very much, but I delivered my testimony, and learned a lesson for myself too. We should stare very often if the Lord were to answer our prayer."

CLIII. A Christian Philosopher. Ps. v. 12. *"For Thou, Lord, wilt bless the righteous; with favour wilt Thou compass him as with a shield."*

FARADAY stands out prominently as a Christian as well as a philosopher. Concerning his standing in science there is no dispute. He takes rank among the first of his contemporaries. Universities and learned societies were eager to do him honour.

His religious character appears to have been developed from a very early period. "When an errand-boy, we find him hurrying the delivery of his newspapers on a Sunday morning, so as to get home in time to make himself neat, to go with his parents to chapel; his letters, when abroad, indicate the same disposition; yet he did not make any formal profession of his faith till a month after his marriage, when nearly thirty years of age. Of his spiritual history up to that period little is known, but there seem to be grounds for believing that he did not accept the religion of his fathers without a conscientious inquiry into its truth. It would be difficult to conceive of his acting otherwise. But after he joined the Sandemanian Church, his questionings were probably confined to matters of practical duty; and to those who know him best, nothing could appear stronger than his conviction of the reality of the things he believed. In order to understand the life and character of Faraday, it is necessary to bear in mind that he was a Christian, but that he was a Sandemanian. From his earliest years that religious system stamped its impress deeply on his mind; it surrounded the blacksmith's son with an atmosphere of unusual purity and refinement; it developed the usefulness of his nature, and in his after career it fenced his life from the worldliness around, as well as from much that is esteemed as good by other Christian bodies. But his sympathies burst all narrow bounds. Thus the Abbé Moigno tells us that, at Faraday's request, he one day introduced him to Cardinal Wiseman. The interview was very cordial, and his eminence did not hesitate frankly and good-naturedly to ask Faraday if, in his deepest conviction, he believed all the Church of Christ—holy, catholic, and apostolical—was shut up in the little sect in which he bore rule. 'Oh, no,' was the reply; 'but I do believe, from the bottom of my soul, that Christ is with us!'"

CLIV. God's Anger Consistent with His Love.
Ps. vii. 11. *"God is angry with the wicked every day."*

THEON was one day reading in the Holy Scriptures when he suddenly closed the book, and looked thoughtful and gloomy.

Hillel perceived this, and said to the youth: "What aileth thee? Why is thy countenance troubled?"

Theon answered: "In some places the Scriptures speak of the wrath of God, and in others He is called Love. This appears to me strange and inconsistent."

The teacher calmly replied: "Should they not speak to man in human language? Is it not equally strange that they should attribute a human form to the Most High?"

"By no means," answered the youth; "that is figurative, but wrath——"

Hillel interrupted him, and said: "Listen to my story. There lived in Alexandria two fathers, wealthy merchants, who had two sons of the same age, and they sent them to Ephesus on business connected with their traffic. Both these young men had been thoroughly instructed in the religion of their fathers.

"When they had sojourned for some time at Ephesus, they were dazzled by the splendour and treasures of the city, and, yielding to the allurements which beset them, they forsook the path of their fathers, and turned aside to idolatry, and worshipped in the temple of Diana.

"A friend at Ephesus wrote of this to Cleon, one of the two fathers at Alexandria. When Cleon had read the letter, he was troubled in his heart, and he was wroth with the youths. Thereupon he went to the other father, and told him of the apostasy of their sons, and of his grief thereat.

"But the other father laughed, and said, 'If business do but prosper with my son, I shall give myself little concern about his religion.'

"Then Cleon turned from him, and was still more wroth.

"Now, which of these two fathers," said Hillel to the youth, "dost thou consider as the wiser and the better?"

"He who was wroth," answered Theon.

"And which," asked the preceptor, "was the kinder father?"

"He who was wroth," again answered the youth.

"Was Cleon wroth with his son?" asked Hillel.

And Theon replied, "Not with his son, but with his backsliding and apostasy."

"And what," asked the teacher, "thinkest thou is the cause of such displeasure against evil?"

"The sacred love of truth," answered his disciple.

"Behold then, my son," said the old man, "if thou canst now think divinely of that which is Divine, the human expression will no longer offend thee."

CLV. Daniel Webster's Knowledge of the Bible. Ps. viii. 1. "*O Lord our Lord, how excellent is Thy name in all the earth! who hast set Thy glory above the heavens.*"

THOUGH Webster's fame rests chiefly upon his oratorical powers, he was remarkable, too, for his familiarity with the Bible. In fact, his colleagues once nicknamed him, the Bible Concordance of the United States Senate.

While a mere lad, he read with such power and expression that the passing teamsters, who stopped to water their horses, used to get "Webster's boy" to come out beneath the shade of the trees and read the Bible to them. Those who heard Mr. Webster, in later life, recite passages from the Hebrew prophets and Psalms, say that he held them spellbound, while each passage, even the most familiar, came home to them in a new meaning. One gentleman says that he never received such ideas of the majesty of God and the dignity of man as he did one clear night when Mr. Webster, standing in the open air, recited the eighth Psalm.

Webster's mother observed another old fashion of New

England in training her son. She encouraged him to memorize such Scriptural passages as impressed him. The boy's retentive memory, and his sensitiveness to Bible metaphors and to the rhythm of the English version, stored his mind with Scripture. On one occasion the teacher of the district school offered a jack-knife to the boy who should recite the greatest number of verses from the Bible. When Webster's turn came, he arose and reeled off so many verses that the master was forced to say, "Enough." It was the mother's training and the boy's delight in the idioms and music of King James's version that made him the "Biblical Concordance of the Senate."

But these two factors made him more than a "concordance." The Hebrew prophets inspired him to eloquent utterances. He listened to them, until their vocabulary and idioms, as expressed in King James's translations, became his mother-tongue. Of his lofty utterances it may be said, as Wordsworth said of Milton's poetry, they are "Hebrew in soul." Therefore they project themselves into the future.

The young man who would be a writer that shall be read, or an orator whom people *will* hear, should study the English Bible. Its singular beauty and great power as literature, the thousand sentiments and associations which use has attached to it, have made it a mightier force than any other book.

CLVI. An Infidel and a Little Girl who was Sorry for Him. Ps. viii. 2. *"Out of the mouth of babes and sucklings hast Thou ordained strength, because of Thine enemies, that Thou mightest still the enemy and the avenger."*

THE celebrated Hume was dining at the house of an intimate friend. After dinner the ladies withdrew; and in the course of conversation, Mr. Hume made some assertion, which caused a gentleman present to observe to him, "If you can advance such sentiments as these, you certainly are what the world gives you credit for being, an infidel." A little girl, whom the philosopher had often noticed, and with whom he had become a favourite, by bringing her little presents of toys and sweetmeats, happened to be playing about the room unnoticed. She however listened to the conversation, and on hearing the above expression, left the room, went to her mother, and asked her, "Mamma, what is an infidel?" "An infidel, my dear!" replied her mother; "why should you ask such a question? An infidel is so awful a character that I scarcely know how to answer you." "Oh! tell me, mamma," returned the child; "I must know what an infidel is." Struck with her eagerness, her mother at length replied, "An infidel is one who believes that there is no God, no heaven, no hell, no hereafter." Some days afterwards Hume again visited the house of his friend. On being introduced into the parlour, he found no one there but his favourite little girl; he went to her and attempted to take her up in his arms, and kiss her as he had been used to do; but the child shrank with horror from his touch. "My dear," said he, "what is the matter? do I hurt you?" "No," she replied; "you do not hurt me; but I cannot kiss you, I cannot play with you." "Why not, my dear?" "Because you are an infidel." "An infidel! what is that?" "One who believes there is no God, no heaven, no hell, no hereafter." "And are you not very sorry for me, my dear?" asked the philosopher. "Yes, indeed, I am sorry!" returned the child with solemnity; "and I pray to God for you." "Do you, indeed? and what do you say?" "I say, O God, teach this man that Thou art." A striking illustration of the above text.

CLVII. Not Christianized, but Humanized.
Ps. x. "*The wicked in his pride doth persecute the poor.*"

I SAID last year to an old saint of ninety years, "Is the world better or worse than when you knew it first?" The old man turned thoughtfully to me, and said, "I will not say that, so far as I know it, it has been Christianized; but I *do say that it has been humanized*." Brutal sports trained men to count the defenceless as their prey, and made the sight of suffering too familiar a thing to be noticed. Here is a bit of testimony that I have met with from old people in many forms, and which will find its counterpart in Simon's story. A farmer who had hired a little lad began striking him before they were out of the "Church-town." The poor mother came up and pleaded for her son : " O sir, how would you like to see your little ones served like that ?" The man, with an oath, bade her be gone, saying, " *Thy* child is made o' cuse (coarse) clay ; but mine is made of fine." Was not some such sentiment as that general concerning the poor in the early part of the century ? One has even met with it lingering still in more modern dress. To-day, to be poor is a suspicion, almost a crime, with some few people.

CLVIII. Is there no God? Ps. xiv. 1. *"The fool hath said in his heart, There is no God."*

MISS MARTINEAU tells, in her Autobiography, that it was an unspeakable relief to her to arrive at the conclusion that there is no God. She went out of her house afterwards, she says, and looked up at the stars with a new sensation. And all the worries of life became less irritating to her on her being assured that she had no one to be ultimately responsible to but herself. On the other hand, it would certainly be to make for many this world a waste and howling wilderness, to deprive them of the comfort of believing that a Supreme Mind and Hand have been directing it through the ages.

CLIX. A Merchant Prince. Ps. xv. 4. *"He that sweareth to his own hurt, and changeth not."*

IT has been well said that he who gives to charity only on his death-bed may be said to be " rather liberal with that which is another man's, than of his own, and gives his wealth to the strong robber, Death, in no other sense than the traveller yields his purse to the highwayman." Samuel Fletcher, of Manchester, one of the merchant princes of that city, was one of those men whose delight it is to be their own almoners. He commenced business for himself in 1811, and in a few years, by constant honesty, perseverance, and self-denial, took his place among the foremost merchants of that great mercantile centre. A striking example of his integrity in business matters is given in the following :—An event of European interest (the battle of Leipsic) caused a revolution in the Manchester market, and suddenly and enormously enhanced the value of a certain class of goods, of which Mr. Fletcher had a quantity in stock, but which he had virtually promised to a customer at a lower price, before the news arrived of the battle. An enterprising speculator came in and offered to take the entire stock at the advanced prices, and even to advance on these. Mr. Fletcher told him that the goods were not his to sell. It was in vain that the usual casuistry of interest was used to shake the plain ethics of truth and honesty; it was in vain to urge that the bargain had not been formally ratified, etc. Mr. Fletcher contented himself with saying that, however vexatious the loss, he had really, if not formally, agreed to part with the goods at the price stipulated, and that "a just man, even though he swears to his own hurt, changeth not."

CLX. The Christian's Portion. Ps. xvi. 5. *"The Lord is the portion of mine inheritance and of my cup."*

EXCELLENT was the answer of Basil the Great to the Emperor Valens, who first essayed him with large proffers of honour and riches to draw him from Christ: "Offer these things to children—I regard them not." Then after threatening, he replied: "He who has but a few books and a wretched garment can suffer nothing from confiscation: banishment is nothing to one to whom all places are alike, and torture cannot be inflicted where there is not a body to bear it. Put me to death, and you do me a favour, for you send me earlier to my rest."

CLXI. It has been tried. Ps. xviii. 30. *"The word of the Lord is tried."*

BUILDING a bridge across the Niagara River, below the Falls, was once thought to be impossible. The banks are steep and high, the distance across nearly an eighth of a mile, and the river here boils and foams so that no boat can stand the fury of the torrent a moment. Sending piles and building arches, as with other bridges, was quite out of the question. Yet a bridge was built—a wire suspension bridge, so called because it had to be hung by cables driven into huge blocks of granite on each bank. The cables were made of twisted wire. The bridge looked like a spider's thread.

But would the cables hold? That had to be tried. How frightened the spectators were when the engineer drove the first carriage across! A terrible plunge would that be into the raging waters, two hundred and fifty feet underneath. But the bridge stood the trial. Then gales and storms tried it, and it stood. "I am afraid to trust it, it looks so slender," said one of a party, shrinking back, when visiting the Falls a year afterward. "It has been tried," said the guide; "there is no danger," and we crossed safely. The Bible tells us of something that is tried. "The word of the Lord is tried." Its declarations and promises are tried, and its threatenings also are to be relied on.

CLXII. God seen in His Works. Ps. xix. 1. "*The heavens declare the glory of God; and the firmament sheweth His handywork.*"

An Arab, a wild son of the desert, one more accustomed to fight than to reason, to plunder a caravan than to argue a cause, was asked by a traveller how he knew that there was a Deity? He fixed his dark eyes with a stare of savage wonder on the man who seemed to doubt the being of God; and then (as he was wont, when he encountered a foe, to answer spear by spear), he met the question by another: "How do I know whether it was a man or a camel which passed by my tent last night?" Well spoken, child of the desert! for not more plainly do the footprints in the sand reveal to thy eye whether it was a man or a camel that passed thy tent in the darkness of the night, than God's works reveal His power and being.

CLXIII. A Martyr's Legacy to his Children. Ps. xix. 10. "*More to be desired are they than gold, yea, than much fine gold.*"

John Penry, the Welsh martyr, was executed at St. Thomas-a-Watering, Surrey, as secretly as it could be done, for fear of a popular tumult. He died in the thirty-fourth year of his age, leaving a widow and four daughters, and a great host of Christians to deplore his untimely end. He had never meddled with politics. His sole offences were his exposures of the glaring abuses of the episcopal clergy in Wales, whereby souls of his countrymen were ruined, and his open confession of Nonconformity towards the close of his life. In a letter written a few days before his death, he thus counsels his children: "Although you should be brought up in never so hard service, yet, my dear children, learn to read, that you may be conversant day and night in the Word of the Lord. If your mother be able to keep you together, I doubt not that you shall learn both to write and read by her means. I have left you four Bibles, each of you one, being the sole and only patrimony or dowry that I have for you. I beseech you and charge you not only to keep them, but to read in them day and night; and before you read, and also in and after reading, be earnest in prayer and meditation, that you may understand and perform the good way of your God."

CLXIV. The "Speaking Leaves." Ps. xix. 10.

"More to be desired are they than gold, yea, than much fine gold: sweeter also than honey and the honeycomb."

ABOUT thirty years ago the people in the South Sea Islands had never seen a book, nor did they know that there was any way of getting or giving knowledge but by speech. Now they know the value of "speaking leaves," as they call tracts and books. Such is their desire for them that they will travel ten miles in a small canoe, in the open sea, to obtain a single copy, for which they offer fruit and native cloth. Many have come thirty or forty miles on land, carrying a burden all the way, that they might buy a book. One of these natives fenced off a plot of ground, planted it with arrow-root, and waited till it was ripe. He then prepared it for use, and getting with it into his canoe, spread its sail to the wind, and steered for a missionary station. After sailing for some miles, a sudden gust of wind filled the little sail, and upset the canoe. The poor fellow soon got his canoe right again, and himself safe in it, but the arrow-root had gone to the bottom of the sea. He turned his canoe round towards home, which he reached with a sad heart. But as soon as he got there, he planted a fresh plot of arrow-root, and waited until it was ready; then he set out once more, sailed again over the open sea, reached the station, and bought a book.

The next day he was on his return, full of joy that he had got what he had so long wished to possess.

CLXV. Happiness of doing Good. Ps. xix. 11.
" In keeping of them there is great reward."

As Henry Martyn was on his way to India, he was watchful, day and night, for opportunities of doing good to those on board the ship in which he sailed. He was especially attentive to the sick. One day, when the hatches were shut down in consequence of a gale, he went below to visit a sick sailor. As there was perfect darkness below, he was obliged to feel his way. He found the man swinging in his hammock, in darkness, and heat, and damp, without a creature to speak to him, and in a burning fever. " I gave him," says Martyn, " a few grapes which had been given to me, to allay his thirst. How great the pleasure of doing good, even to the bodies of men ! "

Martyn had large experience of the pleasure of doing good. His efforts to do good were unceasing, and they were made at the expense of self-sacrifice. They were thus of a kind to yield him the largest amount of pleasure.

Have you had experience of the pleasure of doing good ? especially of doing good to the souls of men ? There is no pleasure like it. He who labours in simplicity and in godly sincerity to do good, has his reward in a calm and enduring pleasure which no earthly prosperity, no wealth, nor honours can bestow.

How many seek for happiness from afar, when it can be had in its purest form by doing good to their neighbours ! To do good and communicate forget not, if you would be happy, if you would enjoy the Saviour's smile.

The manner in which Mr. Martyn became possessed of the grapes which he gave to the sick man is interesting and instructive.

The ship, after touching at the Cape of Good Hope, sailed thence on the Sabbath. On that day a boat came alongside with fruit ; " but," says Martyn, " I did not think it right to buy any, though I longed to have some to carry to sea." On the day on which he visited the sick man, a passenger who came on board at the Cape, and to whom he had scarcely ever spoken, sent him a plate of fruit, by which he was greatly refreshed, and enabled to relieve the sick man.

It is somewhat remarkable, that this seasonable present came on the very day on which Martyn entered in his common-place book the following sentiment, taken from an author he was reading: "If, from regard to God's Sabbath, I deny myself, He will more than make it up to me." In keeping God's statutes there is great reward."

CLXVI. Wild Faith. Ps. xix. 13. *"Keep back Thy servant also from presumptuous sins."*

JOHN BUNYAN says, in one of his many books, "Faith must be always in exercise. Only put not in the place thereof presumption. I have observed that as there are herbs and flowers in our gardens, so there are counterfeits in the field: only they are distinguished from the others by the name of wild ones. Why, there is faith, and wild faith: and wild faith is this presumption. I call it wild faith, because God never placed it in His garden—His Church: 'tis only to be found in His field—the world. I also call it wild faith, because it only grows up and is nourished where other wild notions abound."

CLXVII. The Traveller's Tree. Ps. xxiii. 5. *"Thou preparest a table for me in the presence of mine enemies."*

MR. ELLIS describes this wonderful tree, which grows in Madagascar, and is so called from its always containing, in the most arid season, a large quantity of pure fresh water, supplying to the traveller the place of wells in the desert. Being somewhat sceptical as to the truth of what he had heard, Mr. Ellis determined to see for himself. Coming to a clump of the trees, one of his bearers struck one of them with his spear, four or five inches deep, into the thick, firm end of the stalk of the leaf, and on drawing it back, a stream of pure clear water gushed out, about a quart of which was caught, and all drank of it on the spot. It was cool, clear, and perfectly sweet. Such a tree, so valuable to the thirsty traveller, forms no bad emblem of the ordinances of grace, prepared for the Lord's people in the wilderness of this world.

CLXVIII. Communion Sunday. PSALM. xxiv. 7.
"Lift up your heads, O ye gates."

THE father of the celebrated Principal Carstares was a man of warm devotional character, and suffered severely in the persecution time. Wodrow (*Analectic*) tells of him: "He was doing duty at the sacrament for a brother minister at Calder. Upon the Sabbath he was very wonderfully assisted in his first prayer, and had a strange gale through all the sermon, and there was a remarkable emotion among the hearers. Singing the 24th Psalm (see vers. 7-10), as he came to the tables, all in the assembly were marvellously affected, and glory seemed to fill that house. He served the first table in a kind of rapture, and he called some ministers there to the next, but he was in such a frame that none of them would come and take the work off his hands. He continued at the work with the greatest enlargement, and melting upon himself and all present, that could be, and served fourteen or sixteen tables. A Christian that had been at the table and obliged to come out of the church, pressing to be in again, stood without the door and said he was rapt in the thought of the glory that was in that house for near half an hour, and got leave scarce to think upon any other thing."

It seems to have been a movement similiar to that which took place at Kirk of Shotts under John Livingstone, and is evidence of the great wave of religious feeling which was then sweeping over Scotland, the tide-mark of which we can best see in Rutherford's "Letters."

CLXIX. The Wigtown Martyrs. Ps. xxv. 7. *"Remember not the sins of my youth."*

"My sins and faults of youth
  Do Thou, O Lord, forget;
After Thy mercy think on me,
  And for Thy goodness great,"

was the beginning of the song of Margaret Wilson as the sea was rising round her at the mouth of the water of Blednoch by Wigtown. She was twenty years of age, and along with an elderly woman, Margaret Lachlan, was condemned to be drowned for attending field and house conventicles, and for refusing the test. They were tied to stakes within tide-mark where the waters of the Solway come up swift and strong. The old woman was put farther in that the sight of her struggles might terrify the younger and lead her to conform, but she was faithful to the death.

> "O do Thou keep my soul;
> Do Thou deliver me;
> And let me never be ashamed
> Because I trust in Thee."

Desperate efforts have been made to cast discredit on the narratives in Napier's "Life of Claverhouse," and it has been made a test case along with the death of John Brown of Priesthill. The question has been set at rest by the book of Dr. Stewart of Glasserton. The two women are buried in Wigtown churchyard, and descendants of the family to which Margaret Wilson belonged are to be found in the neighbourhood of Glenvernock where she lived.

CLXX. A Song of Thanksgiving. Ps. xxvi. 8.
"Lord, I have loved the habitation of Thy house."

PINETON of Chambrun, one of the French Huguenots, who after fleeing by night and hiding in woods by day, escaped at length from France in the time of the *dragonnades* of Louis XIV., tells that, when he and his companions came in sight of Geneva, they burst into tears and sung for thanksgiving from ver. 8 of this Psalm to the end. "Lord, I have loved the habitation of Thy house, and the place where Thine honour dwelleth. . . . My foot standeth in an even place; in the congregations will I bless the Lord."

CLXXI. A Psalm of Comfort. Ps. xxvii. 1-14.
"The Lord is my light," etc.

WHEN India was still heaving with the groundswell of the terrible mutiny of 1857, the wife of Sir John Lawrence was called home to her children in England, and had to leave her husband worn out with the anxiety and labour which did so much for the preservation of the Indian Empire, unable to leave his post and surrounded by smouldering embers which might at any moment break out again into flame. She writes: "When the last morning—January 6, 1858—arrived, we had our usual Bible reading, and I can never think of the 27th Psalm, which was the portion we then read together, without recalling that sad time." In perusing the Psalm one can see what springs of comfort must have opened in every verse from the beginning, "The Lord is my light and my salvation; whom shall I fear?" to the close, "Wait on the Lord: be of good courage, and He shall strengthen thine heart: wait, I say, on the Lord."

CLXXII. A Message from Heaven. Ps. xxvii. 6. *"And now shall mine head be lifted up above mine enemies round about me."*

A BOY was brought to Christ when at a public school. It became known among his school-fellows, and one day, when he entered the play-ground, he found them drawn up in a body to meet him; and as soon as they had him in their midst, they assailed him with laughter and cries of contempt. He was taken completely by surprise; his face burned with shame and anger, and the ground seemed to be reeling beneath his feet. It was a Monday morning, and the first exercise, after they had entered the school, was to repeat some verses of a psalm. A pupil was called up to repeat them, and as the poor young Christian sat bewildered among his persecutors, the first words which fell on his ears were,—

> "And now even at this present time,
> Mine head shall lifted be,
> Above all those that are my foes,
> And round encompass me."

They seemed to be sent straight from heaven to him. They completely drove away his agitation, and made him calm and happy. He knew it was his Father saying to him, "Be strong, and of a good courage;" and sorely did he need this encouragement in his hour of confession.

CLXXIII. Lapse of Memory. Ps. xxx. 5. *"Weeping may endure for a night, but joy cometh in the morning."*

DR. LIEFCHILD relates the following anecdote regarding

this text:—"One Sabbath morning a singular lapse of memory befel me, which I had never before and have never since experienced. When I rose from sleep, I could not recollect any portion of the discourse which I had prepared on the day before, and what was most strange, I could not even remember the text of the prepared sermon. I was perplexed, and walked out before breakfast in Kensington Gardens. While there, a particular text occurred to my mind; and my thoughts seemed to dwell upon it so much, that I resolved to preach from that, without further attempting to recall what I had prepared—a thing which I had never ventured to do during all my ministry.

"From this text I preached, and it was, 'Weeping may endure for a night, but joy cometh in the morning.' I preached with great liberty, and in the course of the sermon I quoted the lines,—

> 'Beware of desperate steps! the darkest day—
> Live till to-morrow—will have passed away.'

"I afterwards learned that a man in despair had that very morning gone to the Serpentine to drown himself in it. For this purpose he had filled his pockets with stones, hoping to sink at once. Some passengers, however, disturbed him while on the brink, and he returned to Kensington, intending to drown himself in the dusk of the evening. On passing my chapel, he saw a number of people crowding into it, and he thought he would join them in order to pass away the time. His attention was riveted to the sermon, which seemed to be in part composed for him; and when he heard me quote the lines alluded to, he resolved to abandon his suicidal intention."

CLXXIV. A Martyr of the Netherlands. Ps. xxx. 5. *"For His anger endureth but a moment."*

AMONG those who suffered in the Netherlands during the fierce governorship of Alva was one John Herwin. "In prison," says the chronicler of the time, "he used to recreate himself by singing of psalms, and the people used to flock together to the prison door to hear him. At the place of execution one gave him his hand and comforted him. Then began he to sing the 30th Psalm. A friar interrupted him, but Herwin quickly finished his Psalm, many joining with him in singing of it. Then he said to the people, 'I am now going to be sacrificed; follow you me when God of His goodness shall call you to it.' And so he was first strangled and then burnt to ashes."

Ver. 5 was among the latest sayings of Dr. John Brown, the commentator, as he repeated it:—"His anger is for a moment; His favour is for a life: weeping may endure for a night, but joy cometh in the morning."

CLXXV. Closing Words. Ps. xxxi. 5. *"Into Thy hands I commit my spirit."*

This Psalm has furnished closing words to many a life, especially ver. 5. It was one of the seven sayings on the cross, and the last—"Father, into Thy hands I commend My spirit." It was the dying words of Stephen addressed to Christ, "Lord Jesus, receive my spirit." It was the parting word of Luther, and of Knox, of John Huss when he was burned at Constance in 1415, of Jerome of Prague, of Julian Palmer, one of the noted martyrs in the reign of the English Mary, of Francis Teissier, the first martyr of the "Desert," who ascended the scaffold in 1686 singing it, and of countless others. "The Lord Himself gave the word, and great has been the company of those that published it." No watchword of the Captain of salvation, made perfect through sufferings, has been taken up by so many sons whom He has led to glory through the valley of the shadow of death.

On a dark morning, December 22, 1666, it was the dying song of Hugh M'Kail—

> "Into Thy hands I do commit
> My spirit; for Thou art He,
> O Thou, Jehovah, God of truth,
> That hast redeemed me."

He was among those that came from the west before the fight at Pentland, but, wishful to enter Edinburgh on a mission to friends, he was taken at Braid's Craigs, and after suffering the torture of the boot, was condemned to death (see Ps. xvi., p. 192). "About two of the clock," says the narrative, "he was carried to the scaffold with five others that suffered with him, where he appeared to the conviction of all that formerly knew him with a fairer, better, and more staid countenance than ever they had before observed. Being come to the foot of the ladder, he directed his speech northward to the multitude, saying that 'as his years in the world had been few [he was twenty-six] so his words at that time should not be many.' Having done speaking to the people, who heard him with great attention, he sung a part of the 31st Psalm, and then prayed with such power and fervency as forced many to weep bitterly. Having ended, he gave his cloak and hat from him; and, when he turned himself and took hold of the ladder to go up, he said with an audible voice, ' I care no more to go up this ladder, and over it, than if I were going home to my father's house.' And as he went up, hearing a great noise among the people, he called down to his fellow-sufferers, ' Friends and fellow-sufferers, be not afraid. Every step of this ladder is a degree nearer heaven.' " His farewell address is known to all acquainted with Scottish history, and is one of the most rapt and seraphic of that fervid time. Death touched his lips with a live coal from the altar above before it closed them on earth.

CLXXVI. An Extempore Sermon. Ps. xxxi. 23.
"O love the Lord, all ye His saints: for the Lord preserveth the faithful."

THE famous William Grimshaw, of Haworth, was on one occasion cited before the Metropolitan. A complaint being lodged against his intrusion into other folds, his grace announced a confirmation service in Grimshaw's church, expressing a desire to have an interview with him. In the course of the conversation, the prelate, after stating the charge of his preaching where he had a mind, added, " And I learn that your discourses are very loose; that, in fact, you can and do preach about anything. That I may judge for myself of your doctrine and manner of stating it, I give you notice that I shall expect you to preach before me and the clergy present, in two hours hence, and from the text which I am about to name." The text being named, " Why, my lord," said Grimshaw, " should the congregation be kept out of the sermon for two hours? Send a clergyman to read prayers, and I will begin immediately." Prayers being read, Mr. Grimshaw ascended the pulpit, and commenced an extempore prayer for the archbishop, the people, and the young persons about to be confirmed; and so wrestled with God for His assistance and blessing, that the congregation, the clergy, and the prelate were moved to tears. After the sermon, when the clergy were gathered, expecting to hear the archbishop's reproof of Grimshaw's extemporaneous effusions, taking him by the hand, with a tremulous voice and faltering tongue he said, "I would to God that all the clergy in my diocese were like this good man." Grimshaw afterwards observed, "I did expect to be turned out of my parish on that occasion; but if I had, I would have joined my friend Wesley, taken my saddle-bags, and gone to one of his poorest circuits."

CLXXVII. The Favourite Psalm of St. Augustine. Ps. xxxii. 1-11.

THIS was the favourite Psalm of Augustine. With reference to it he says, "*Intelligentia prima est ut te nôris peccatorem*," "The beginning of understanding is to know thyself to be a sinner."

When Luther was once asked which were the best psalms, he replied, *Psalmi Paulini*, "the Pauline psalms;" and being asked to name them he gave the 32nd, 51st, 130th, and 143rd. These all belong, it will be observed, to the penitential psalms. Luther's frame of spirit, and his struggle for the truth of justification by faith, naturally disposed him to this view. But the best psalms may be said to be those which at the time we feel to be most needed. The heart feels the way to it in time of danger as David's hand to Goliath's sword. "There is none like that; give it me;" and God's word is like the sword at the gate of Eden—" it turns every way."

Ver. 2 was the spiritual aspiration which Izaak Walton set up for the model of his own life. In closing the life of Bishop Sanderson, he says: "Tis now too late to wish that my life may be like his, for I am in the eighty-fifth year of my age; but I humbly beseech Almighty God that my death may be, and I as earnestly beg of every reader to say Amen. 'Blessed is the man unto whom the Lord imputeth not iniquity, and *in whose spirit there is no guile.*'"

This Psalm was also the favourite of Alexander Peden,

of whom so many stories are told in the south of Scotland. He wandered for years with a life on the edge of death among the moors and mists, and died at last in bed. Men would call it "charmed"; he would have accounted for it by "snow and vapours fulfilling His Word." When hard pressed by the troopers and brought to a breathless stand, his accustomed prayer was that God would cast the skirt of His cloak over him, and more than once he was saved by the mist. He died without violence, but his persecutors took his body and hung it on a gibbet at Cumnock. There he lies buried, and the place has become *God's field*. "When the service was ended," says the story of his life, "he and others that were with him lay down in the sheep-house and got some sleep. He rose early, and went up by the burnside and stayed long. When he came in to them he did sing the 32nd Psalm from the 7th verse to the end—

> 'Thou art my hiding-place; Thou shalt
>   From trouble keep me free;
> Thou with songs of deliverance
>   About shalt compass me.
>
> * * * * *
>
> 'Ye righteous, in the Lord be glad,
>   In Him do ye rejoice;
> All ye that upright are in heart,
>   For joy lift up your voice.'

When he had ended, he repeated the 7th verse again, and said, 'These and what follow are sweet lines which I got at the burnside this morning, and I will get more to-morrow, and so shall we get daily provision.'"

CLXXVIII. An early Saint. Ps. xxxiv. 9. "*O fear the Lord, ye His saints: for there is no want to them that fear Him.*"

WHEN Columba felt that his departure was at hand, he desired to visit the corn-fields, and say farewell to the brothers at work amidst the green ears. Too infirm to walk, he was drawn in a car by oxen. Reaching the workers, he said, "I much wished to fall on sleep on Easter-day; but then I was fain to wait a little longer, that the glad festival might not be changed into a day of gloom for you." Then among the springing wheat the labourers wept bitterly, for they knew that they should see the beloved familiar face no more; but with tender, hopeful words, he comforted them; and, turning towards the East, he blessed the island and all its people.

On the following Saturday, supported by his faithful friend Diarmid, he proceeded to bless the granary belonging to the community. Seeing two large heaps of corn piled up, he exclaimed, "I rejoice to know that, when I leave them, my children will not suffer from want. To-day is Saturday, which in Holy Writ is called Sabbath, or rest. And truly to me it is Sabbath, for it is the last day of my mortal life. On this very night I shall go the way of my fathers. It is my Lord Jesus who deigns to invite me; and it is He who has made known that my summons will come to-night."

Then he began to wend his way to the monastery; but wearying with the journey, he rested by the wayside. Before him spread the bright and varied panorama he knew and loved so well. And as he gazed on isles, ocean, and cloud-capped mountain, he broke into the language of prophecy: "This place, apparently small and obscure, shall be largely honoured, not only by the Scottish kings and their people, but also by the chiefs of barbarous nations and their subjects; and it shall be held in reverence even by the holy men of other Churches." After this he returned to his cell, and occupied himself in his favourite work of transcribing the Psalms. On coming to the thirty-fourth Psalm, ninth verse, "They who fear the Lord shall want no manner of thing that is good," he laid aside his pen for the last time.

The saint then repaired to the church for vespers. Returning to his cell, he lay for some time on his bed with its stone pillow, and proceeded to give his final directions, that Diarmid might communicate them to his disciples:—
"Dear children, these are my last words. Live in peace and charity one with another, and God, who strengthens the good and comforts the just, will grant you all that is needful in this life, and will also bestow the everlasting joys which are reserved for all who keep this law." Then he lay in silent communing with the Master in whose service

he had spent his life; but in the dim dawn, as the bell rung its first matin chime, with a quick access of the old vigour he arose and entered the church alone.

The building, as the awe-stricken brethren approached, seemed filled by a dazzling radiance, which, however, passed away before Diarmid reached the spot. Groping in the darkness, the monk called out with tears, "Where art thou, O my father?" but the kindly voice, once swift to respond, was silent. Prostrate before the altar lay the venerable saint, and Diarmid, placing himself at his side, raised the honoured head upon his knees. The death scene recalls the past vividly, as might a picture of Rembrandt's. Again we see a crowd of weeping monks, holding their rude lanterns aloft; and, grouped round the central figures, all eyes are riveted to the beloved face over which the shadow of death is darkly stealing. Then the heavy eyes are opened, and for one moment they rest on the brethren with an expression of love and serenity, and raising the right hand, Columba makes the sign of blessing. A soft sigh escapes his lips, and the apostle of Caledonia enters into his rest; closing his career in the year of grace 597, and in the seventy-sixth year of his age.

CLXXIX. God does not Forget His Saints.
Ps. xxxiv. 10. "*The young lions do lack, and suffer hunger: but they that seek the Lord shall not want any good thing.*"

OLIVER HEYWOOD, ejected from Coley Vicarage by the Act of Uniformity, lived on a little stock of savings, until one day he and his children were at starvation point, and with no earthly prospect of another meal. They sang at family prayer—

> "When cruse and barrel both are dry,
> We still will trust the Lord Most High."

With empty purse and empty basket, their faithful old servant then set out from the house, and wandered through the streets of Halifax, thinking of the famishing children whom she loved like her own life, and wondering how God would give them this day their daily bread. Returning home, one of the tradespeople of the place, standing at his poor, knew her, called her in, and told her that he was just casting about for a messenger to take a remittance of five guineas just sent him from Manchester, for the master. On her arrival home with money and food, it looked like a miracle, and the father said, when they met at evening prayer—" The Lord hath not forgotten to be gracious. His word is true from the beginning. 'The young lions *may* lack, and suffer hunger : but they that trust the Lord shall not lack any good thing.'"

CLXXX. The Tongue. Ps. xxxiv. 13. "*Keep thy tongue from evil, and thy lips from speaking guile.*"

IN Grecian history we read how the Athenians erected to Laena's memory a bronze statue of a lioness without a tongue. She was put to the torture, but would not give the name of her lover, one of the conspirators who had helped to kill Hipparchus. Some say she bit out her tongue, lest she should, in a moment of agony, disclose anything.

CLXXXI. God's Readiness to Hear and Answer Prayer. Ps. xxxiv. 15. "*The eyes of the Lord are upon the righteous, and His ears are open unto their cry.*"

A MOTHER had been trying to soothe to sleep her sick boy, and the following conversation took place :—

"Oh, what if we should both fall asleep, and dear baby alone up in your room ?"

"Well, I intend to sleep, and I intend that you should sleep too. If baby does wake up, I'll hear her first cry."

"Would you ? How is that ? How do you hear so quickly ? "

"Well, dear, I think that verse helps us to know about it, 'His ear is ever open to their cry.' I feel that my ear is very open to my baby's cry. God made the mother's heart and the mother's ear, and 'He who made the ear, shall He not hear ?' Doesn't this help us to know that His ear must be very open to His children's cry ? Think often about this, dear boy, when you are left alone and in pain."

CLXXXII. Praising God. Ps. xxxv. 28. "*And my tongue shall speak of Thy righteousness and of Thy praise all the day long.*"

WE are told of Mr. Guthrie, of Fenwick (the author of the

well-known book "A Saving Interest in Christ"), that he, had a "most gaining way of conversing with people, and would have *stolen them off their feet to Christ before ever they were aware!*" He preached one day on the noble and seraphic exercise of praising God; and after he had pressed that duty as seriously as he could, he came to answer some objections that might be proposed. Among other things he put this objection: "And ye may praise God that get many mercies from Him; but what say ye to us that are under many miseries and wants, and get not mercies from Him?" Mr. Guthrie, looking out at the window of the kirk, and seeing very pleasant weather, presently says, "Yes; hast thou nothing to praise God for? Wilt thou not praise God, man, for good weather to the lambs?"

CLXXXIII. Early Years of Wickedness. Ps. xxxvi. 1. *"There is no fear of God before his eyes."*

THOMAS SCOTT, the famous commentator, was very wild in early youth. He says himself, referring to the years spent at school at Scorton, "My own conduct at this period was as immoral as want of money, pride, and fear of temporal consequences, and a natural bashfulness would allow it to be; except that in one thing I retained a sort of habit of my family, and never learned to swear, or to take the name of God in vain, unless sometimes when provoked to violent passion. There was no fear of God before my eyes.'

CLXXXIV. Educated Eyes. Ps. xxxvi. 6. *"Thy righteousness is like the great mountains: Thy judgments are a great deep."*

WHEN a traveller is fresh among the Alps, he is constantly deceived in his reckoning. One Englishman declared that he could climb the Righi in half an hour, but after several panting hours the summit was still ahead of him; yet when he made the boast, some of us who stood by were much of his mind—the ascent seemed so easy. This partly accounts for the mistakes men make in estimating eternal things: they have been too used to molehills to be at home with mountains. Only familiarity with the sublimities of revelation can educate us to a comprehension of their heights and depths.

CLXXXV. Accumulation of Money. Ps. xxxvii. 16.
"A little that a righteous man hath is better than the riches of many wicked."

MANY cases of individual conversion under Mr. Sherman's powerful ministry have come to light. One is told of a gentleman who was bent on accumulating money, and who, hearing of the minister's fame, strolled into Sherman's chapel. The text was Ps. xxxvii. 16: "A little that a righteous man hath is better than the riches of many wicked." He had gathered heaps of money, and supposed that happiness was to be found in its accumulation. The sermon put his thoughts on a new track. He learned a new lesson and went home thoughtful, and began questioning himself about the employment of his money for doing good to the souls of men. His house afterwards was always open to Mr. Sherman, who witnessed for himself the fruits of piety in this new friend and in his family, and found that home a "Bethel" for Christian devotion and intercourse. On what little pivots do the happiness and salvation of individuals often turn!

CLXXXVI. Cruelty to Animals. Ps. xxxvii. 26. *"The righteous is ever merciful."*

ONE of the many pleasant stories about General Grant shows his kindness to animals. One day, at City Point, he saw a soldier whipping a horse that could not pull a load out of a rut. He went and put his shoulder to the wheel and helped push the cart out, saying to the teamster, "If you would assist your horse instead of beating him, you would get along better." The soldier demanded to know who he was, but the general merely replied that he could find out at headquarters. A more frightened or ashamed man than this soldier when he found who it was that had taught him such a wholesome lesson is not often found.

CLXXXVII. One Eye Inward. Ps. xxxvii. 31. "*The law of his God is in his heart; none of his steps shall slide.*"

DR. PAYSON was accustomed to say, that "the Christian should always have, as it were, *one eye turned inward*, to keep watch over his feelings and motives; and thus the work of self-examination would be comparatively easy when it was engaged in more formally and deliberately. And it is evident that such a mode of living is not only useful and desirable, but *necessary*, if a man would be thoroughly acquainted with himself, and furnished against the wiles of Satan and the treachery of his own heart.

CLXXXVIII. Burdens. Ps. xxxviii. 4. "*For mine iniquities are gone over mine head : as an heavy burden they are too heavy for me.*"

THERE is a gateway at the entrance of a narrow passage in London, over which is written, "No burdens allowed to pass through."

"And yet we do pass constantly with ours," said one friend to another, as they turned up this passage out of a more frequented and broader thoroughfare. They carried no visible burdens, but they were like many who, although they have no outward pack upon their shoulders, often stoop inwardly beneath the pressure of a heavy load upon the heart. The worst burdens are those which never meet the eye.

There is another gate—one which we are invited to enter, and must enter, if we would ever attain to rest and peace, and over which is also inscribed, "No burdens allowed to pass through." This is the strait gate which leads to life; and by it stands One who opened the narrow way to which it leads, saying to each one of us, "Come unto Me, all ye that labour and are heavy laden, and I will give you rest."

CLXXXIX. The Use of Wool in the Ears. Ps. xxxviii. 13. "*I, as a deaf man, heard not.*"

"WE are told concerning Bernard of Clairvaux that, after he had given himself up entirely to contemplation and

walking with God, he met with a considerable difficulty in
the visits of those friends who were still in the world.
Their conversation brought back thoughts and feelings
connected with the frivolities which he had for ever forsaken ; and on one occasion, after he had been wearied
with the idle chit-chat of his visitors, he found himself
unable to raise his heart towards heaven. When he was
engaged in the exercise of prayer, he felt that their idle
talk was evidently the cause of his losing fellowship with
God. He could not well forbid his friends coming, and
therefore he prepared himself for their injurious conversation by carefully stopping his ears with little wads of flax.
He then buried his head deep in his cowl, and though
exposed for an hour to their conversation, he heard nothing,
and consequently suffered no injury. He spoke to each of
them some few words of edification, and they went their
way. We do not suppose that for any great length of
time he was much troubled with such visitors, for he must
have been an uncommonly uninteresting companion. If
people once discover that their clatter is lost upon you,
they are not quite so eager to repeat the infliction."

CXC. Meditation. Ps. xxxix. 3. *"While I was musing the fire burned."*

A WRITER of the present day says, "I remember Alma
Tadema, the great painter, saying to me that he sat down
every day at his easel. Sometimes he began without en-
thusiasm, and painted on with little interest. But after an
hour or so he surprised himself in a fit of absorption : the
fire had kindled within him as he worked.

CXCI. Brought back from Gates of Death. Ps. xxxix. 13. *"O spare me, that I may recover strength, before I go hence, and be no more."*

As Columba drew near the close of his laborious life, he
devoted more time than before to religious meditation and
prayer. According to Adamnan, many marvels announced
to the monks that they were soon to lose the good abbot.
His lonely cell was illumined nightly by a mysterious
lustre, and the voice of the apostle was heard uplifted in

unknown canticles. There is a glen on the west of the island, over whose walls hang wreaths and festoons of the ivy with which the monks wove together the walls of their rude huts, still called the "glen of the temple." This leads to an arable level, known now, as in Columba's time, by the name of *Machar*, or the sandy plain. Out of the midst of this plain rise two green hills. One morning Columba said to his attendants, "Let no one follow me to-day; I would be alone;" and he withdrew to the solitude of Machar. A monk, however, fearing that some accident might befall the aged man, followed at a distance, and climbing a rocky point, he saw Columba on the larger of the two hills, surrounded by a company of angels in white raiment. After the lapse of a thousand years, this eminence is still known as the '*Cnoc* Angel—the knoll of the angels. Two of the monks who were admitted into his intimate confidence, sitting one day in his cell, saw that he changed countenance; first, a glow as from excess of joy shone on his face, and then a pallid gloom, as though he were plunged into sorrow. With tender solicitude they asked what ailed him. Still he was silent. They threw themselves at his feet, and implored him not to conceal from his children the mysteries that had been revealed to him. "Dear children," he replied after a pause, "I would not afflict you. Know then that it is thirty years to-day since I began my pilgrimage in Caledonia. Long have I prayed God that with this thirtieth year my exile might terminate, and I might be recalled to the heavenly country. When you saw me so joyous, it was because I could see the angels who came in quest of my soul. But suddenly they halted, yonder, on that rock across our island strait, as if they would fain approach but were prevented—prevented because the Lord hath given less heed to my fervent prayer than to that of the many Churches which have prayed for me, and have obtained that I should linger in this body four more years. This is the reason of my sorrow. But in four years I shall die without previous illness; in four years the holy angels will return for me, and I shall take my blissful flight with them towards the Lord."

That such a vision may have risen in the mind of the aged saint, worn by work and watching, is highly probable.

CXCII. A Duke's Example. Ps. xl. 3. "*Many shall see it, and fear, and shall trust in the Lord.*"

IN a town in Bavaria, there is a little tumble-down church where the duke as often as he came that way used to go in and pray. If on coming out of the church he happened to meet any of the peasants, he loved to converse with them pleasantly. One day he met an old man, and after some talk, asked him whether he could do anything for him.

The peasant replied, "Noble sir, you cannot do anything better for me than you have already done."

"How so? I do not know that I have done anything for you."

"But I know it," said the man; "for how can I forget that you saved my son! He travelled so long in sinful ways, that for long he would have nothing to do with church or prayer. Some time ago he was here, and saw you, noble sir, enter this church. 'I should like to see what he does there,' said the young man scornfully to himself, and he glided in after you. But when he saw you pray so devoutly, he was so deeply impressed that he also began to pray, and from that moment became a new man. I thank you for it. This is why I said you can do me no greater favour than you have already done."

CXCIII. A Hymn. Ps. xl. 8. "*I delight to do Thy will, O my God.*"

THE late Henry Venn Elliot loved best of his sister Charlotte's hymns, " Thy will be done." For himself, he did not care so much for " Just as I am," though he often said he believed " she had done more good by that hymn than he had done in all his ministry."

CXCIV. Subjection of the Will. Ps. xl. 8. "*I delight to do Thy will, O my God.*"

THERE is a memorable passage in the history of St. Francis that may throw light on this subject. The grand rule of the Order which he founded, was implicit submission to the superior. One day a monk proved refractory. He must be subdued. By order of St. Francis, a grave was dug deep enough to hold a man; the monk was put into it; the brothers began to shovel in the earth; while their superior standing by looked on stern as death. When the mould had reached the monk's knees, St. Francis asked, "Are you dead yet? Is your will dead? Do you yield?" There was no answer; down in that grave there seemed to stand a man with a will as iron as his own. The signal was given, and the burial went on. Dead to pity and all the weaknesses of humanity, St. Francis stood ready to give the signal that should finish the burial. It was not needed, the iron bent; he was vanquished; the funeral was stopped. The poor brother said, "I am dead!"

CXCV. The Secret of a Preacher's Success. Ps. xl. 10. "*I have not hid Thy righteousness within my heart; I have declared Thy faithfulness and Thy salvation: I have not concealed Thy lovingkindness and Thy truth from the great congregation.*"

ONE of the secrets of the success of Sherman (who followed Rowland Hill at Surrey Chapel) as a preacher was the studied simplicity of his style, and his homely and forcible illustrations. "The glory of the gospel," he used to say, "is its simplicity. We never think of painting gold or diamonds." Whilst appreciating the value of literary art, he feared some might think "more of the polish than the material." One Sunday morning a learned doctor preached a very eloquent sermon, of which Mr. Sherman was a hearer. When the doctor came into the vestry after he left the pulpit, Mr. Sherman said, "Well, doctor, do you call this preaching the gospel?" The doctor hesitated and replied; "Well, I am sure I took a great deal of pains in the composition of my sermon! "I doubt not," Mr. Sherman replied; "but suppose, doctor, that a poor hungry soul had come into Surrey Chapel this morning, do you think there would have been anything for him to feed upon? Take my advice, and whenever you have such an opportunity as you had this morning, preach Christ and the plenitude of His grace. I suppose you had not fewer than 2000 hearers. What an opportunity of proclaiming the great salvation!"

CXCVI. Sick Rooms. Ps. xli. 3. *"The Lord will strengthen him upon the bed of languishing: Thou wilt make all his bed in his sickness."*

It has been well said that sick rooms should be like those wayside chapels we see abroad, with the tokens of the Passion within, where tired workers can turn in for a few moments and lay down their burthen, and find rest and refreshment of spirits. Beware, lest the wayside chapel be transformed into a drug shop, where an incessant talk of ailments forms only a new call to endurance on the part of those who set foot within them.

CXCVII. Duty of Hopefulness. Ps. xliii. 5. *"Why art thou cast down, O my soul? and why art thou disquieted within me? hope in God: for I shall yet praise Him, who is the health of my countenance, and my God."*

After a great disappointment in early life, Sir William Rowan Hamilton fell into deep despondence, and on one occasion was tempted to commit suicide. He thus writes to a friend: "I have once in my life experienced, in all but its last fatal force, the suicidal impulse. It was, as I full well remember, in the month of February, 1825, and when on my way from Dublin to this Observatory, for Dr. Brinkley had invited me to join a dinner party here. The grief which had recently fallen upon me was one which I feel even yet. I remember the exact spot where I thought for a moment of plunging, for death, into the water. A feeling of personal courage protected me, revolting against the imagined act, as one of cowardice. I would not leave my post; I felt I had something to do. Alas! what practical irreligion and real unbelief were shown in that complete and prostrate despondence! I am now deeply convinced that along with resignation and heavenly hope, it is a *duty* to cherish also, if possible, a spirit of hope, though not of anxiety, with respect to this earthly existence, for to a sinful and tremendous depth, at the thought of which I shudder now, I have sounded long ago the abysses of the opposite spirit, and through God's grace emerged."

CXCVIII. The Conversion of Count de Gasparin.

Ps. xlv. 5. "*Thine arrows are sharp in the heart of the king's enemies ; whereby the people fall under Thee.*"

ADOLPH MONOD, at Lyons, France, one Lord's day was preaching from the text, "God so loved the world," etc. He spoke of Christ as the true God-man, and announced that the next Sabbath he would show how men could be saved by faith in this God-man. But the authorities of this church were opposed to a doctrine so purely evangelical, and informed Monod that if he did not omit the sermon he had announced, they would have him arrested and brought before the Prefect, and dismissed from his office. Monod, notwithstanding, preached his sermon, and the authorities made their complaint. The Prefect demanded the two sermons, and Monod sent them to him.

The Prefect, Count de Gasparin, was a Catholic. He came home at evening to his wife, and found the sermons. He never liked sermons, especially evangelical sermons ; but he was a man who discharged faithfully the duties of his office. It was necessary that the sermons should be read. He came to his wife with the manuscripts in his hand, complaining that he would have to give up the whole evening to this irksome and protracted labour. She offered, as her husband's worthy helpmeet, to read them with him. They began. With every page they grew more interested. They forgot that it was evening and night. That which at first was an official duty became a service of the heart. They finished the first, and eagerly grasped the second. And what was the result ? As a magistrate, Gasparin was forced to deprive Monod of his place, because all the authorities demanded it. But he and his wife became evangelical Christians, living, joyful, and happy believers in Christ. They found that night "the pearl of great price," and it has remained in the family. Their son, Count Agenor de Gasparin, has long been the head and pillar of the evangelical party in France.

CXCIX. The Worth and Beauty of a Soul.

Ps. xlix. 8. "*For the redemption of their soul is precious.*"

IT is told of St. Catherine of Sienna that she set a true value on the individual soul, however defaced by sin, and exclaimed, of one sunk and degraded, to her Dominican Confessor Raymond, "Oh, father, could you but see the beauty of a rational soul, you would sacrifice your life a hundred times for its salvation.

CC. The Reconciliation Death. Ps. xlix. 8. *"The redemption of their soul is precious."*

THE death of Dr. Friedrich Schleiermacher, one of the greatest names of Germany, is worthy of record. Profound as his theological views may appear, and scientific beyond dispute as many deem them, they are in many respects only the gropings of a grand mind, which was self-relying and proud, after that truth which the Spirit of God has often made patent to babes. Upon his deathbed his sufferings were great, and he complained of a violent sensation of burning inwardly. "Dear children," he said, "you should now all of you go from the room, and leave me alone; I would fain spare you the woful spectacle." The perfect lineaments of death presented themselves; his eye appeared to have grown dim,—his death-struggle to have been accomplished. At this moment he laid his two forefingers upon his left eye, as he often did when reflecting deeply, and began to speak: "We have the reconciliation-death of Jesus Christ, His body and His blood." While thus engaged, he had raised himself up, his features began to grow animated, his voice became clear and strong, and he said with priestly solemnity, "Are ye one with me in this faith?" to which his friends replied with a loud "Yea!" "Then let us celebrate the Lord's Supper! But there can be no talk of the sacristan. Quick, quick! let no one stumble at matters of form!" After that which was necessary for the purpose had been fetched (his friends having waited with him, during the interval, in solemn silence), he began, with increasingly radiant features, and eyes in which there had returned a wonderful, indescribable brightness, nay, a sublime glow of affection, with which he looked upon those around him, to utter a few words of prayer and of introduction to the sacred service. After this, addressing in full and aloud, to each individual, and last of all to himself, the words of the institution, he first gave the bread and the wine to the others who were present, then partook of them himself, and said, "Upon these words of Scripture I abide; they are the foundation of my faith." After he had pronounced the benediction, his eye first turned once more towards his consort with an expression of perfect love, and then he looked at each individual with affecting and fervent cordiality, uttering these words, "Thus are we, and abide in *this* love and fellowship, *one!*" He laid himself back upon the pillow. The radiance still rested upon his features. After some minutes he said, "Now, I can hold out here no longer;" and again, "Give me another position." He was laid upon his side; he breathed a few times; life came to a stand. The children had entered the room in the meantime, and surrounded the bed, kneeling. His eye gradually closed.

It is amid scenes like these that the life is tested. It is there that men are detected whether they have been gambling regarding their eternity, and staking all on the throw of a die, or giving diligence to make their calling and election sure. Calmly to adjust the position of the body, and as calmly to wait for "the purchased redemption" of the soul—it is thus that we discern between the fine gold and the reprobate silver.

CCI. What Next! Ps. xlix. 17. "*When he dieth he shall carry nothing away: his glory shall not descend after him.*"

A PROFESSOR of great reputation for wisdom and piety was once accosted by a student just entering the university of which he was a professor. "My parents have just given me leave to study the law, which is the thing I have been wishing for all my life, and I have now come to this university on account of its great fame, and mean to spare no pains in mastering the subject." While thus he was running on, the professor interrupted him. "Well, and when you have got through your course of studies, what then?" "Then I shall take my doctor's degree." "And then?" answered the doctor. "And then," continued the youth, "I shall have a number of difficult cases to manage, which will increase my fame, and I shall gain a great reputation." "And then?" repeated the holy man. "Why, then there cannot be a question I shall be promoted to some high office or another; besides, I shall make money and grow rich." "And then?" the holy man gently interposed. "And then," replied the youth, "I shall live in honour and dignity, and be able to look forward to a happy old age." "And then?" was again asked. "And then, and then," said the youth, "I shall die." Here the holy man lifted up his voice and again inquired, "And then?" The young man could answer no more, but went away sorrowful.

CCII. "The Cattle on a Thousand Hills."
Ps. l. 10. "*For every beast of the forest is Mine, and the cattle upon a thousand hills.*"

MOTHER JOHNSON (as she was affectionately called) and her husband were real Christians, not ashamed of their Lord, and they took every opportunity which offered to speak a word for their Master. Being in charge of a small side station in the north of Scotland, they came often in contact with Highland drovers on their way to southern markets with their cattle. They used to talk faithfully to such, as they stopped at the cottage for refreshment and rest. By-and-by the husband died, and Mother Johnson went to a northern city, where she lived amongst the poorest—and still laboured for God as a Bible-woman. She was in no society's pay, but she read in her Bible that God would supply all her need, and she believed it.

One winter's evening, after a long day's work, she arrived at her humble lodging, her feet wet with melting snow, and on taking off her boots which were much worn, she literally talked with the Lord in some such words, "Ye ken, Lord, ye promised to supply all my need when I was on your business."

"The cattle on a thousand hills are Mine," came instantly into her mind.

"Ah, Lord, I ken naething aboot the cattle," and holding up her boots, she added, "See how holey they are; I need a new pair." "The cattle upon a thousand hills are Mine," was once more the answer.

This went on for some time, until the constant repetition of the apparently inappropriate passage almost annoyed her. Then a stranger came to her door, and knocked—a drover—who said as he came into her poor room, "Mother Johnson, mine had a gude time awa Sooth this year wi oor cattle, and some of the auld friends sent ye this," placing five pounds in her hands. Then, as she said to a lady visitor, "I kent a' aboot His cattle."

CCIII. A Pauline Psalm. Ps. li. 1-19.

THIS has had a manifold history, open and secret. It is one of the Pauline psalms which delighted Luther.

It was sung by George Wishart and his friends at the Laird of Ormiston's, in East Lothian, on the night when he was taken prisoner. "After suppar he held comfortable purpose of the death of Goddis chosen childrin, and mirrelie said, 'Methinks that I desire earnestly to sleep;' and therewith he said, 'Will we sing a psalm?' And so he appointed the 51st, which was put in Scotishe meter, and began thus,—

> 'Have mercy on me, God of might,
> Of mercy Lord and King;
> For Thy mercy is set full right
> Above all earthly thing,
> Therefore I cry baith day and night,
> And with my hert sall sing;
> To Thy mercy with Thee will I go.'"

The version of the Psalm is by John Wedderburn, of Dundee.

The Psalm was read to Lady Jane Grey and her husband, Guildford Dudley, when they were executed together, Aug. 22nd, 1553,—read to her in Latin, and repeated by her in English. It was read also at Norfolk's execution a few years later; it was the *Miserere* or dying psalm of the time.

When it was read to Henry V. of England as he was dying, the closing words, "Build Thou the walls of Jerusalem," seemed to fall on his ear as a reproach, and he murmured, "If I had finished the war in France, and established peace, I would have gone to Palestine to rescue the Holy City from the Saracens."

Crespin, in his "Martyrologie," tells of Pierre Milet, burned in 1550 on the Place Maubert, Paris, with the refinements of cruelty common at the time, that, being hoisted in the air, he began to sing the 51st Psalm, *Misericorde au pauvre vicieux*. When the fire was kindled it caught the straw which was put under his armpits and burned his hair. But not the less he continued the psalm when his limbs were consumed.

It was the last prayer of Œcolampadius, the close friend of Zwingli, whose untimely death, in 1531, aggravated a sickness he had, and brought him to his end. He called the ministers of the churches round him, exhorted them to fidelity and purity of doctrine, prayed earnestly with the words of David in the 51st Psalm, and soon after fell asleep.

Ver. 18. The first presbytery of the Irish Presbyterian Church was constituted in Carrickfergus by immigrants from Scotland, June 10th, 1662. There were five ministers and as many elders. The sermon was from Ps. li. 18, "Do good in Thy good pleasure unto Zion; build Thou the walls of Jerusalem." Two hundred years afterwards, in 1842, every minister of the Irish Presbyterian Church preached from this same text. There were then above five hundred.

CCIV. Caught by Guile. Ps. li. 13. *"Then will I teach transgressors Thy ways; and sinners shall be converted unto Thee."*

BILNEY, who afterwards became a martyr for the truth, fell in love with young Latimer, then a Roman Catholic priest. It was not safe then to preach the Gospel, so he said to Latimer, "I would like you to be my father confessor," and according to the usages of his Church, he dared not refuse. Afterwards Latimer told that when Bilney made his study a confessional, he poured forth such a tale of sin and grace that it gave him "a smell of the grace of God." Thus Latimer was caught by guile, and turned from that day.

CCV. An Old Hebrew Parable. Ps. li. 17. *"The sacrifices of God are a broken spirit: a broken and a contrite heart, O God, Thou wilt not despise."*

AN Israelite came to the door of the tabernacle with a lamb for a sin-offering. The priest took it from his hands, but found it maimed. He called the offerer: "Dost thou not know the law?" "But, my father, I am poor!" "Why then didst thou not bring two turtle-doves, as the law allows thee?" "Nay, my father, but the lamb is more valuable, and I was ashamed to bring so small a sacrifice to our God and before His people." "And dost thou think, my son, that God is pleased with the value of thy offering? The cattle upon a thousand hills are His. He demands obedience, and a spotless dove is more acceptable than an ox that is blemished. Go and subdue thy pride." The Israelite went his way, sorrowful and ashamed. The penitent in the Psalm of David was a part of the service of the temple for that day. A poor penitent came up to worship before the Lord who had just risen from a sick bed. He could now scarcely sustain his tottering limbs. The words of the Psalm were like a cordial to his sinking spirit. One after another brought his sacrifice, and was accepted; but the penitent had none. At length he drew near the priest, and said, "Last night a poor widow and her children came to me, and I had nothing to give her but the two pigeons which were ready for sacrifice." "Why then art thou come to me, my son?" I heard them sing, "The sacrifices of God are a broken spirit. Will He not accept mine? God be merciful to me a sinner!" The old priest was melted, and the tears started in his eye as he raised the poor penitent. He laid his hands on his head: "Blessed be thou, my son! Thine offering is accepted. It is better than thousands of rivers of oil. Jehovah make His face to shine upon thee, and give thee peace!"

CCVI. The Last Hours of Darnley. Ps. lv. 4.
"My heart is sore pained within me."

DARNLEY'S servants told of the last hours of his life that Mary's words at parting made him feel very uneasy. She left him at the house of the Kirk o' Field (near the site of the present University), and went to Holyrood that night to be present at the marriage of one of her maids of honour. On quitting him she said, "It is a year to-day since David Rizzio died." He could not sleep, and turned to read the lesson of the day, which was the 55th Psalm. Next morning he was found lying dead in the little garden beside the house. It was Sabbath evening, Feb. 9th, 1567.

Some of the verses sound like a knell on a sinful past, and a threatening of doom on the men of blood around. Well for poor Darnley if he got his heart into the closing words of the Psalm!

Ver. 4. "My heart is sore pained within me; and the terrors of death are fallen upon me."

Ver. 5. "Fearfulness and trembling are come upon me, and horror hath overwhelmed me."

Ver. 23. "But Thou, O God, shalt bring them down into the pit of destruction: bloody and deceitful men shall not live out half their days; but I will trust in Thee."

CCVII. My Wanderings. Ps. lvi. 8. "*Thou tellest my wanderings: put Thou my tears into Thy bottle: are they not in Thy book?*"

This verse was frequently in the mouth of Archbishop Ussher, who was driven to and fro through England and Ireland, amid the troubles and changes in Church and State. He was one of the best and most learned men of his time; born in 1580 in Dublin, he died at Reigate, in England, in 1655, and was a preacher of the gospel for fifty-five years.

CCVIII. An Exemplary Lady. Ps. lvi. 8. "*Put Thou my tears into Thy bottle: are they not in Thy book?*"

THERE is an old MS. of a sermon preached at the funeral of the Lady May Farewell, at Hill Bishops, near Taunton, in 1660, which was delivered by the good old Puritan, Mr. George Newton. The Lady Farewell had been a good friend to him, and he was always welcomed at her home. Part of the discourse runs as follows:—

"She lived not in pleasure, but in a strict performance (not of the easiest only, but) of the hardest and severest private duties, and in diligent attendance of the publique ordinances in her own and in the neighbour congregations, under which, while some were hardened, she melted, and closely dropt many a silent, secret tear (I speake it upon good assurance), which, though she covered, God observed and received into His bottle. Among many other graces which I have not room to mention, her humility was orient. She had exactly learned Bernard's golden rule, which he illustrates with a simile: 'As he that goes in at a little low door, it matters not how much he stoops, but if he beare himself one inch too high, he is in danger'; so she regarded not how low she stoopt, nor how far she condescended, in doing any office, or in bearing any burthen, wherein she might fulfil the law of love."

CCIX. Sin against God. Ps. lvii. 4. *"Against Thee, Thee only have I sinned."*

SCOTT, the commentator, was bound apprentice to a surgeon at Alford, near Brazloft, after he left school. Here he behaved in such a manner that his master dismissed him at the end of two months, and he returned home in deep disgrace. He says: "Yet I must regard this short season of my apprenticeship as always the choicest mercies of my life. My master, though himself irreligious, first excited in my mind a serious conviction of sin committed against God. Remonstrating with me on my misconduct, he said, 'I ought to recollect that it was not only displeasing to him, but wicked in the sight of God.' This remark proved the primary means of my conversion."

CCX. A Missionary of the Seventh Century. Ps. lx. 1-12.

THIS was the Psalm sung at the death of Cuthbert, March 20th, 687. It was in the order of service. This missionary of the seventh century is first heard of as a shepherd boy on the hills of Gala Water, then known as Wedale. Arrested by the religious feeling of the time, he settled first in Melrose under Boisil, who was head of the monastery. He became the apostle of the glens of the south of Scotland and north of England, and retired first to Lindisfarne, or Holy Island, then from love of solitude, which was a passion of the age, to the lonely, storm-beaten Ferne Islands, known to later generations through the heroism of Grace Darling. Numerous legends have gathered round his life, and the wanderings of his body after his death, till it reached its present resting-place in Durham Cathedral. The many churches that bear his name between the Forth and the Tyne are witnesses to the estimate of his work; and, in the midst of growing corruption of Christian truth, and the conflicts of contending races, Saxon and Briton, Pict and Scot, he sowed seed which took vital hold, and sprang up in after ages. The account of his death has been given by Bede, who received it from Herefrid, an eye-witness. He had retired to one of the Ferne Islands, and was known to be dying. A company of his brethren from Lindisfarne came to visit him, but only one was admitted to his death-bed. Meanwhile the others sang the 6oth Psalm. When Herefrid came out and announced his death, one of them mounted the high ground above the cell, and held up two lighted torches, one in either hand, a preconcerted signal to their friends in the Holy Isle that Cuthbert had departed. They were engaged in singing the same Psalm, and the wail was carried with it across the sea.

It was in the time of Cuthbert that the Pictish kingdom, after a great victory over the Saxons, crossed the Forth, occupied Edinburgh and the Lothians, and so made way for a separate nationality in the North of Britain which became the basis for an independent Scottish Church, the Church of Knox, of Melville, and of the Covenanting struggle.

The 6oth Psalm had a place in one of the incidents of that history. Robert Douglas gave it out when he preached the coronation sermon of Charles II. at Scone, January 1st, 1651, the Marquis of Argyll putting the crown on the head of the ungrateful monarch who afterwards sent him to the scaffold. The text was 2 Kings xi. 12, 17, the sermon very long, and filled with unpalatable and uncourtly truths. The Covenanters, intent on reconciling loyalty with liberty, were the dupes of the frivolous, selfish king; but there was a word of prophetic insight in the close of the sermon when the preacher quoted Neh. v. 13, which he said had been done before in the East Kirk of Edinburgh at the ratification of the Solemn League and Covenant: "Also I shook my lap, and said, So God shake out every man from His house, and from His labour, that performeth not this promise, even thus be he shaken out, and emptied."

Thirty years of broken pledges and oppression followed, but the threatening was made good.

The same Psalm had a memorable place in the history of the Secession Church of Scotland. When Ebenezer Erskine, in 1740, was driven from his church, he took his place with an immense multitude below the battlements of Stirling Castle, and sang the first five verses of this Psalm. Looking down on the field where the heroic Wallace gained a decisive victory for his country, the words have in them the ring of battle,—

> "And yet a banner Thou hast given
> To them who Thee do fear;
> That it by them because of truth
> Displayèd may appear.
>
> "That Thy beloved people may
> Delivered be from thrall,
> Save with the power of Thy right hand,
> And hear me when I call."

The Psalm of his friend Wilson of Perth, in the same circumstances, had a quieter tone though scarcely less appropriate: Ps. lv. 6–8 and 12–14. His text was fittingly chosen, Heb. xiii. 13. Both of these leaders were children of the Covenanters. When the Secession and Relief Churches joined in 1847, in Tanfield Hall, Edinburgh, to form the United Presbyterian Church, the 60th Psalm was again sung, and with it Ps. cxlvii. 1–3, division ending in reconstruction,—

> "God doth build up Jerusalem;
> And He it is alone
> That the dispersed of Israel
> Doth gather into one."

CCXI. The Morning Song of the Christian Church. Ps. lxiii. 1–11.

As early as the third century this was the morning song of the Christian Church.

Ver. 6, 7. In the life of Theodore Beza it is told that, beginning to be much troubled with want of sleep, he beguiled the time with holy meditations, and, speaking to his friends of it, used that speech, "When I remember Thee upon my bed, and meditate on Thee in the night watches. Because Thou hast been my help, therefore in the shadow of Thy wings will I rejoice." And also **Ps. xvi. 7,** "My reins also instruct me in the night seasons."

CCXII. The Lord's Prayer of the Old Testament. Ps. lxvii. 1-7.

THIS Psalm has been called by the ancient expositors "the Old Testament Lord's Prayer." It has, like it, seven divisions. The first three and last three are linked by a longer one in the middle, and the third and fifth are in the same words. It is by special distinction the missionary psalm.

In the year 1644 the Corporation of London invited the Houses of Parliament to a grand banquet, as proof of the union of their cause, and in celebration of their victory. The Westminster Assembly of Divines and the Scottish Commissioners were also invited, and the festival was after the manner of that of Solomon at the dedication of the temple. Stephen Marshall, a noted preacher of the day, selected for his text the appropriate words 1 Chron. xii., last three verses; and the spiritual provision seems to have reached a profusion not thought of in public feasts of our days. Baillie gives a full description of the rejoicings, and tells how the feast ended with the singing of the 67th Psalm, Dr. Burgess reading the line, that all might take part, "a religious precedent," says a chronicler of the time, "worthy to be imitated by all godly Christians in both their public and private meetings."

CCXIII. The Song of Battles. Ps. lxviii. 1-35.

As the sun rose from the German Ocean at the battle of Dunbar, September 3rd, 1650, and as the Scottish army left their strong position on the heights for a miserable defeat in a wretched cause, Cromwell pointed to the sun with the opening words, "Let God arise, let His enemies be scattered." The thanksgiving psalm sung by his army on the field was the 117th, known afterwards among the Puritans as "the Dunbar Psalm."

The 68th Psalm was known among the Huguenots as "the song of battles," and was raised by them in many a

bloody and despairing conflict. It often seemed to fail,
but in the end, and in the highest sense, it must succeed.

> "Que Dieu se montre seulement
> Et l'on verra soudainement
> Abandonner la place,
> Le camp des ennemis epars,
> Et ses haineux, de toutes parts
> Fuir devant sa face."

CCXIV. A Mediæval Saint. Ps. lxix. 1. "*Save me, O God; for the waters are come in unto my soul.*"

ST. CATHERINE of Sienna, like other mediæval saints, considered the body as a thing to be crushed. Her austerities were terrible. She deprived herself almost entirely of food, and for many of the last years of her brief life seems to have lived on a few raw vegetables and the sacred wafer. Three times a day she scourged herself with an iron chain, and she wore a spiked chain round her loins. She denied herself natural sleep, passing the whole night in prayer, till the matin bell of St. Dominic rang out clear in the early dawn, when she would lie down on her bed of planks for an hour's repose, satisfied that her brethren were carrying on the eternal hymn of love and adoration. No wonder that her poor disordered body became the seat of infernal visions, that her whole life became such a mingled web of visions, and realities, of truest service and strangest ecstasies. Like St. Antony, she cried, "Lord, where wert Thou when my heart was so troubled?" "I was in the midst of thy heart." "Ah, Lord," she replied, "Thou art everlasting Truth, and I humbly bow before Thy word; but how can I believe that Thou wert in my heart when it was filled with such detestable thoughts?" Then the Lord asked her, "Did these thoughts give thee pain or pleasure?" "An exceeding pain." "Thou wast in woe because I was hidden in the midst of thy heart; My presence it was which rendered these thoughts insupportable to thee."

CCXV. "My Psalm." PSALM lxxi. 1–24.

THIS was in his old age the favourite psalm of the Covenanter Robert Blair, which he was accustomed to call "my psalm." The Christian Father Origen used to put this same claim to passages of the Bible which came home to him—"this is my Scripture." Robert Blair was one of the most distinguished men of his day for ability, learning, and piety. He had in his early years a successful discussion with Dr. John Cameron, famous as a scholar in France and Scotland, professor in Saumur, and Principal of the University of Glasgow. His life was a very eventful one. He was forced to take refuge from persecution in Ireland, and was one of the chief founders of Presbyterianism there. Still pursued, he was half-way across the Atlantic to seek rest in New England, but was driven back by storm to continue his work. He died in 1666, near Aberdour, in Fife, where he lies buried.

This was the Psalm asked for on his death-bed by Philip de Morny, known as Plessis de Morny, a man of illustrious family, earnest piety, and chivalrous spirit, who cast in his lot with the Huguenots, and stood by them in every extremity. Prayer being ended, he desired they would read unto him the 71st Psalm, giving testimony of the infinite pleasure which he took in it, and of the application he made for his own consolation. He said he was persuaded of an eternal life by the demonstration of the Holy Spirit, more powerful, more clear, and more certain than all the demonstrations of Euclid, repeating two or three times the words of the psalmist—cxvi. 10, "I believed, therefore have I spoken."

CCXVI. Like Jesus. Ps. lxxii. 4. *"He shall judge the poor of the people, He shall save the children of the needy, and shall break in pieces the oppressor."*

MR. SHERMAN had an excellent Christian wife, greatly beloved by all who knew her, and especially so by the poor. A lady overheard some poor women speaking of her. "There she is," said one of them, "the dear creature; she is like Jesus Christ." "How so?" asked another. "I know she is very good; but why is she like Jesus Christ?" "Because," was the reply, "she never despises any one, and has always a smile and a kind word for the poor."

CCXVII. A Word of Refreshing. Ps. lxxiii. 1
"Truly God is good to Israel."

AFTER the defeat of Montcontour, as they were carrying away Coligny, nearly suffocated by the blood of three wounds, which was pouring into his closed visor, an old friend of his, who was wounded like himself, and carried beside him, repeated the first words of this Psalm—

"Si est ce que Dieu est tres doux"—

"Truly God is good to Israel." The historian adds, "That great captain confessed afterwards that this short word refreshed him, and put him in the way of good thoughts and firm resolutions for the future."

Ver. 26, "My flesh and my heart faileth," was the last verse on which the thoughts of Charles Wesley rested. When near his death, he called his wife to him and bade her write to his dictation. He died as he had lived. It was the last of 7000 hymns, some of them the finest in the English language, which had flowed from his heart in all the turns and changes of life.

> "In age and feebleness extreme,
> Who shall a sinful worm redeem?
> Jesus, my only hope Thou art,
> Strength of my failing flesh and heart.
> O could I catch a smile from Thee,
> And drop into eternity!"

CCXVIII. "Notwithstanding his Talents." Ps. lxxiii. 22. *"So foolish was I, and ignorant: I was as a beast before Thee."*

ON one occasion Sir David Brewster was listening to a brief memoir of a man of science, a medical man, of whom it was said that "notwithstanding his high talents and his great literary and scientific attainments, he received Christ as his Saviour." Brewster interrupted the reader with an exclamation of vehement disapproval. "*Notwithstanding his talents!* That disgusts me," he said. "A merit for a man to bow his intellect to the Cross! Why, what can the highest intellect on earth do but bow to God's word and God's mind thankfully?"

CCXIX. The Covenanters. Ps. lxxiv. 10. *"O God how long shall the adversary reproach?"*

> "How long, Lord, shall the enemy
>   Thus in reproach exclaim?
> And shall the adversary thus
>   Always blaspheme Thy name?
> Thy hand, even Thy right hand of might,
>   Why dost Thou thus draw back?
> O from Thy bosom pluck it out
>   For our deliverance sake."

This Psalm was sung by the Covenanters before the fight at Pentland (Rullion Green), November 28th, 1666. Goaded by oppression, they had come from the west country in arms to present a remonstrance to the Government. They approached Edinburgh in the hope of a hearing, and of support from their friends there; but a strong force had been collected to overawe them. A minute and interesting account is given by Veitch, in his memoir, of the retreat of the weary, discouraged, and half-armed remnant by Colinton, and along the east side of the Pentlands. They were intercepted by General Dalziel, through a pass in the hills near Glencorse, and sang this Psalm before the action. They made a brave resistance, successful at first, but were at last broken. The fugitives were slaughtered with great barbarity, the captured shut up in Greyfriars churchyard, without food or shelter, numbers executed and banished to the plantations. The graves of some of the slain may be seen on the hillside where they fell, and a monument which has faith and truth in its lines if rude in rhyme :—

> "A cloud of witnesses lie here,
>   Who for Christ's interest did appear;
> And to restore true liberty,
>   O'erturned then by tyranny,
> These heroes fought with great renown,
>   By falling got the martyr's crown."

CCXX. Made Perfect through Suffering. Ps. lxxiv. 16. *"The day is Thine, the night also is Thine."*

JULIANA HORATIA EWING, the favourite writer of children's stories, suffered greatly before her death. She was seldom able in her illness to concentrate her attention on solid works, and for religious exercise chiefly relied on what was stored in her memory. She liked to repeat the alternate verses of the Psalms when the others were read to her. After one night of great suffering, in which she had been repeating George Herbert's poem, "The Pulley," she said that the last verse had helped her to realize what the hidden good might be which underlay her pain :—

> "Let him be rich and weary : that at least
> If goodness lead him not, yet weariness
> May toss him to my breast."

She had each week a calendar written out, with a text chosen by herself at the top, and as each day passed it was struck through by her pencil. One week she had, "In patience possess ye your souls." For the text of another week she had, "Be strong, and of a good courage," as the words had been said to her by a dear friend to cheer her just before undergoing the trial of an operation. Later still, she chose,—"The day is Thine, the night also is Thine."

CCXXI. Earth's Dark Places. Ps. lxxiv. 20. *"The dark places of the earth are full of the habitations of cruelty."*

INFANTICIDE was fearfully common among the Hawaiian islanders before the introduction of Christianity. We are told of an old woman who was seen on the outskirts of a Sunday-school celebration, beating her breast and wailing. A missionary went to her, and said, "What is the matter that you should weep over such a beautiful sight? You should be happy to see such a sight, for you can remember when things were very different among our people." And the poor soul cried out in anguish, "Why didn't the missionaries come before? These hands are stained with the blood of my twelve children, and not one of my flesh to rejoice here to-day!" And again she wailed,—"Oh, why didn't the missionaries come before?"

CCXXII. Religion a Stepping-stone to Worldly Success. Ps. lxxxiii. 3. *"Thy hidden ones."*

GOD has many hidden ones. The following extract from the will of the late distinguished mathematician, Professor De Morgan, will serve to suggest the consoling thought that the life-long faith, which so happily found expression at the end of life, may have existed in the case of many other reserved and conscientious persons, whose lives were hid with Christ in God, though they died and made no sign:—" I commit my future destiny, with hope derived from experience, to Almighty God, who has been through my life, and will be hereafter, my Guide and support: to God the Father of our Lord Jesus Christ, of whom I believe in my heart that God has raised Him from the dead, and whom I have not confessed with my mouth in the sense usually attached to these words, because such confession has been, in my time, the only way up in the world."

CCXXIII. A Servant Girl at the Scaffold. Ps. lxxxiv. 4–12. *"Blessed are they that dwell in Thy house."*

MARION HARVEY, a servant girl in Borrowstounness, twenty years of age, was executed at Edinburgh in 1681, for hearing Donald Cargill, and for helping his escape at South Queensferry. When annoyed by the Bishop on the way to the scaffold, who wished to thrust the prayers of his curate on her and her fellow-sufferer, she said, "Come, Isabel, let us sing the 23rd Psalm," which they did; and, having come to the scaffold, and sung the 84th Psalm, she said, "I am come here to-day for avowing Christ to be the Head of His Church and King in Zion. Oh seek Him, sirs; seek Him, and ye shall find Him."

Isabel Alison, who suffered with her, belonged to Perth, and lived very privately till she was apprehended for having heard Donald Cargill, and for refusing the test. On the scaffold she said, "Farewell all created comforts. Farewell sweet Bible, in which I delighted most, and which has been sweet to me since I came to prison. Farewell Christian acquaintances. Now into Thy hands I commit my spirit, Father, Son, and Holy Ghost." Whereupon the hangman threw her over.

No execution of those cruel times seems to have excited a deeper interest and sympathy throughout the country. Lord Fountainhall, a judge of the time, twice notices their end, and tries to excuse the sentence. In his "Observes," he says, "There were hanged at Edinburgh two women of ordinary rank for their uttering treasonable words and other principles and opinions contrary to all our government. They were of Cameron's faction. At the scaffold, one of them told, so long as she followed and heard the curates, she was a swearer, Sabbath breaker, and with much aversion read the Scriptures, but found much joy upon her spirit since she followed the Conventicle preaching."

CCXXIV. The Brothers De Witt. Ps. lxxxvi. 7.
"In the day of my trouble I will call upon Thee."

THE Word of God has been the comfort of very many in the prospect of sufferings and death. We are told of the brothers De Witt, the renowned Dutch statesmen, that when their assassins found them, the brothers heard them approach without alarm. Cornelius de Witt, broken down by the agonies of torture, was lying on his bed, and John was seated before a table reading the Bible to his brother, to strengthen him against the fear of death and the anguish of the last hour of life.

CCXXV. Deliverance from Evil. Ps. lxxxvi. 13.
"For great is Thy mercy toward me: and Thou hast delivered my soul from the lowest hell."

THE late J. H. Evans, of St. John's Chapel, London, was in early youth a student of Wadham College, Oxford. This College was notorious as gay and dissolute, and the men there sought every means to destroy young Evans. Speaking after the manner of men, their success was certain; but God did not leave him to himself. Conscience was not silent, and in the midst of the most hilarious scenes, it told him that this was not true happiness; and he has been heard to tell in after life, that when the last reveller of the jovial party had left, he has often looked round on the vacant seats and empty glasses, laid his head upon the table, and wept bitterly. A great check applied to him to keep him from open sin was the power of a mother's love. Once, led on by designing companions, he was induced to enter a place of peculiar temptation; but the thought of his mother's distress darted into his mind, and filled him with indescribable awe. He rushed from the house, and neither raillery nor entreaty could ever lead him again into similar temptation. In late life he spent some hours in Oxford, and went over his old College, and sitting in Wadham Gardens, he dwelt on the scenes he had passed through, and at length, with deep emotion, repeated the text, "Great is Thy mercy towards me: and Thou hast delivered my soul from the lowest hell."

CCXXVI. Never be too Tired to Pray. Ps. lxxxviii. 9.
"Lord, I have called daily upon Thee, I have stretched out my hands unto Thee."

A MUSSULMAN, when on a journey, was joined by a Hindu, and the two marched on together till darkness overtook them. Passing the night at some halting-place, they resumed their journey on the morrow, travelled in company till the day wore away, and again halted for the night. The Hindu, as was his custom, said his prayers, *then* took his meal, and lay down to rest. In the early morning he arose, washed his hands and face, performed his devotions, and was ready to start. But he had not seen his companion the Mussulman engaged in any act of devotion for the two days they had been together, and at this he wondered greatly. Wishful to ascertain the truth of the matter, he waited for a third night, and watched him closely, but saw and heard nothing of the Mussulman's prayers.

At length, addressing his fellow-traveller, he said: "Oh, Mussulman, what kind of conduct is this of yours? Do you not worship God day or night?"

The Moor answered, "Yes, it is binding on Mussulmans to worship God five times a day."

"Then," said the Hindu, "what sort of Mussulman are you? For three days I have not seen you say your prayers."

"What can I do?" answered the Moor. "I am marching along all day, and am so tired that I cannot pray."

"But," asked the Hindu, "are you too tired to eat twice a day? If you are too weary to serve God, your Maker and Provider, I am afraid to journey in your company. To look in the face of a man like you in the early morning, will bring some calamity or other upon me. For whoever is too listless to serve God, will sooner or later be visited by some misfortune."

Was not this heathen Hindu traveller wiser than many who bear the Christian name? Let us learn from him that we must *never be too tired to pray*.

CCXXVII. "I have called Thee Father." Ps. lxxxix. 26. "*He shall cry unto Me, Thou art my Father, my God, and the Rock of my Salvation.*"

JOHN WOOLMAN, on an errand of mercy, was struck down by the plague, and he suffered protracted agonies.

"In my great misery," he cried on the third day, "I remember that I have called Thee *Father*." After that he had great stillness and peace. Some of his descendants still preserve a manuscript record, kept by the godly friends who nursed him, of his prayers and broken words as he passed through the last days of torture. They are simple and tender as a child talking to a father in the dark. The weak body yielded at last, and John Woolman was "at home."

CCXXVIII. God the Father Almighty. Ps. lxxxix. 26. "*Thou art my Father, my God, and the Rock of my Salvation.*"

LUTHER was one day catechising some country people in a village in Saxony. When one of the men had repeated these words, "I believe in God the Father Almighty," Luther asked him what was the meaning of "Almighty." The countryman honestly replied, "I do not know." "Nor do I know," said the catechist; "nor do all the learned men in the world know. However, you may safely believe that God is your Father, and that He is both able and willing to save and protect yourself and all your neighbours. Almighty God is the lovely Father of mankind."

CCXXIX. "An Hour or two sooner to Bed." Ps. xc. 12. "*So teach us to number our days, that we may apply our hearts unto wisdom.*"

THE following is a letter from Robert Leighton to his brother-in-law, Edward Lightmaker, a "word of comfort" on the death of a dear son; and it reveals the warmth and tenderness of the saintly man. When his brother-in-law died, Leighton said, as he returned from his funeral, "Fain would I have thrown myself into the grave with him."

"I am glad of your health and recovery of your little ones; but indeed it was a sharp stroke of a pen that told me your pretty Johnny was dead; and I felt it truly more than, to my remembrance, I did the death of any child in my lifetime. Sweet thing, and is he so quickly laid to sleep? Happy he! Though we shall have no more the pleasure of his lisping and laughing, he shall have no more the pain of crying, nor of being sick, nor of dying; and hath wholly escaped the trouble of schooling and all the sufferings of boys, and the riper and deeper griefs of riper years; this poor life being all along nothing but a linked chain of many sorrows and many deaths. Tell my dear sister she is now much more akin to the other world; and this will quickly be passed to us all. John is but gone an hour or two sooner to bed, as children use to do, and we are undressing to follow. And the more we put off the love of this present world and all things superfluous beforehand, we shall have the less to do when we lie down."

CCXXX. Hidden and Safe. Ps. xci. 1. "*He that dwelleth in the secret place of the Most High, shall abide under the shadow of the Almighty.*"

ONE morning a teacher went, as usual, to the schoolroom, and found many vacant seats. Two little scholars lay at their homes cold in death, and others were very sick. A fatal disease had entered the village, and the few children present that morning at school gathered around the teacher, and said, "Oh, what shall we do? Do you think we shall be sick, and die too?"

She gently touched the bell as a signal for silence, and observed, "Children, you are all afraid of this terrible disease. You mourn for the death of our dear little friends; and you fear that you may be taken also. I only know of one way of escape, and *that is to hide.*"

The children were bewildered, and the teacher went on: "I will read to you about this hiding-place," and read Psalm xci.: "He that dwelleth in the secret place of the

Most High shall abide under the shadow of the Almighty."
All were hushed and composed by the sweet words of
the Psalmist, and the morning lessons went on as usual.

At noon a dear little girl sidled up to the desk and said,
"Teacher, are you not afraid of the diphtheria?"

"No, my child," she answered.

"Well, wouldn't you be if you thought you would be
sick and die?"

"No, my dear, I trust not."

Looking at the teacher for a moment with wondering
eyes, her face lighted, as she said, "Oh, I know! you are
hidden under God's wings. What a nice place to hide!"

Yes, this is the only true hiding-place for old, for young,
for rich, for poor—for all.

Do any of you know of a safer or a better?

CCXXXI. The Lord a Sanctuary. Ps. xci. 2. *"I will say of the Lord, He is my refuge."*

A HEATHEN could say, when a bird (feared by a hawk)
flew into his bosom, "I will not betray thee unto thine
enemy, seeing thou comest for sanctuary unto me." How
much less will God yield up a soul unto its enemy, when
it takes sanctuary in His Name, saying, "Lord, I am
hunted with such a temptation, dogged with such a lust;
either Thou must pardon it, or I am damned; mortify it,
or I shall be a slave to it; take me into the bosom of Thy
love, for Christ's sake; castle me in the arms of Thy everlasting strength; it is in Thy power to save me from, or
give me up into, the hands of my enemy; I have no confidence in myself or any other; into Thy hands I commit
my cause, my life, and rely on Thee." This dependence
of a soul undoubtedly will awaken the almighty power of
God for such a one's defence: He hath sworn the greatest
oath that can come out of His blessed lips, even by
Himself, that such as "flee for refuge" to hope in Him
shall have "strong consolation."

CCXXXII. Heavenwards. Ps. xci. 15. *"He shall call upon Me, and I will answer him : I will be with him in trouble : I will deliver him, and honour him."*

A PLEASURE party, made up of a family and some friends,

put out in a small boat to an island a little distance off.
After staying awhile there, they all put out a short distance
seaward, with the exception of one lady and the boatman's
little boy. A sudden dense fog shortly afterwards fell,
and the boat tried in vain to make its way back to the
island. After beating about for hours, they were almost
despairing, when they thought they heard the faint echoes
of a childish voice calling something. Listening intently,
the father's quick ear recognised the voice of his boy
calling, "Steer this way, father; steer this way." Guided
by the sound of the voice, the father soon locked his boy
in his arms, and the whole party rejoiced in deliverance
from their peril.

A father and mother, whilst visiting friends in England,
heard of the death of their only daughter, in New York.
Bitter indeed was the cup, and yet amid the fogs of affliction and bereavement the voice of the angel-child calls
from the battlements of the jasper walls, "Steer this way,
father; steer this way." And following the well-known
voice, they expect to lay down the oars of life, and embrace
their child on the shores of that glorious land where storms
never rise and fogs never fall.

CCXXXIII. A Prophecy Fulfilled. Ps. xciv. 2. *"Lift up Thyself, Thou Judge of the earth: render a reward to the proud."*

MR. NORMAN, a Nonconformist minister, was brought
before Judge Foster for trial at Taunton Castle. Joseph
Alleine was tried at the same time and place. The judge
treated him very roughly, and poured unmeasured contempt
on other Nonconformist ministers. Mr. Norman "with
great gravity told him that their learned education in the
university, and holy calling in the ministry, not stained
with any unworthy action, merited good words from his
lordship, and better usage from the world." This simply
enraged the judge, and after another tempest of invective,
the prisoner said, "Sir, you must ere long appear before a
greater Judge, to give an account of your actions, and for
your railing on me, the servant of that great Judge."

Perhaps Mr. Norman saw the shadow of coming death
on the poor old judge's face; but when the judge died

suddenly a month afterwards, people remembered these words, and called it a prophecy.

CCXXXIV. Silence. Ps. xciv. 17. "*My soul had almost dwelt in silence.*"

HENRY PERREYOE, in a letter to a friend, describes with astonishment the life of the Bernardine Sisters, whom he had visited in their convent, a life unequalled for the rigour of its discipline, even in the Church of Rome. The Bernardines give their time to the direction of fallen women who have repented, and whose highest reward is to become Bernardines themselves at last. They live amongst the dreary deserts of sand that stretch along the southern coasts of France, like the first anchorites in the deserts of Africa. They eat black bread, drink water, and *never speak—never*. A sister of Chartreux may speak once in every week, a Bernardine is silent as the dead.

CCXXXV. Neptune's Cup. Ps. xcv. 5. "*The sea is His, and He made it, and His hands formed the dry land.*"

THE Rev. Joseph Cook, in one of his lectures, spoke of the difficulty of believing in a world without a directing Mind, and used the following beautiful illustration:—

"Almost imperceptible creatures in the sea build in the Indian Ocean a goblet. It is called 'Neptune's cup.' Sometimes it has a height of six feet and a breadth of three. It is erected solely by myriads of polypi. They have no consultation with each other. Each works in a separate cell; each is as much cut off from communication with every other as an inmate of a cell in the wards of Charlestown prison yonder is from his associates. They build the stem to the proper height, and then they begin to widen it. Everything proceeds according to a plan. Is the plan theirs, or does it belong to a Power above them, and that acts through them? As these isolated creatures build Neptune's cup, so the bioplasts, isolated from each other in the living tissues which they produce, build the rose and the violet and all flowers, the pomegranate and the cedar, the oak and palm and all trees, the eagle and all birds, the lion and all animals, the human brain and all men. Neptune's cup alone strikes us dumb. But what shall we say of the mystic structures built by the bioplasts? There is the cup; it is a fact; and the eye is another Neptune's cup; and the hand another Neptune's cup; and all this universe is another Neptune's cup: and out of such cups I, for one, drink the glad wine of Theism!"

CCXXXVI. Deadness of Heart. Ps. xcv. 7, 8.
"To-day if ye will hear His voice, harden not your heart."

AN intelligent and excellent minister was once called to visit a man then, on his deathbed, who had been for many years engaged in the African slave-trade. He had been a commander of a swift and successful ship, but had been often compelled to throw his poor captives to the sharks and the sea to save his vessel from the cruisers, or to lighten it in the storm; and had passed through the various terrible scenes incident to the prosecution of that infamous traffic. And now he was dying, in the full maturity of his powers, and in the midst, if we remember rightly, of pecuniary prosperity and social comfort. The minister spoke to him of repentance. "Repentance!" was his reply, "I *cannot* repent! You have seen many sorts of men, sir, and perhaps you think you have seen the most wicked and desperate among them. But I tell you that you do not know anything about an African slave-trader. His heart is *dead*. Why, sir, I know perfectly well—I understand it fully—that I shall die in spite of everything; and I know that I shall go to hell. There is no possible salvation for me. It is *perfectly impossible* but that I shall be damned. And yet it don't move me in the least. I am just as indifferent to it as ever I was in my life." And so he died, with despair perfected into insensibility and DEATH, the very fires of Divine wrath, as they flashed upon his face, not starting a sigh or a pulse of emotion. His heart *was* "DEAD!"

It is fearful to think that in all sin lies the tendency to just such spiritual death. When it is ripened and finished, it brings it forth, one sin leading to another, and that to another, and these to others, and moral insensibility coming in upon the soul, and all crimes becoming possible to it, and perfect despair, and the deadness of all affection and hope at last engulfing it—a deadness to be terribly consummated and rewarded hereafter, amid the gloom of the future, and beneath the punishments of God. There is an old fable of a man who fell asleep in a Grecian cavern; and the drops from above continually falling upon him, turned him, particle by particle, into coldness and rock; and though the soul still lived, it could not use or move the body. And so the influences of little sins, dropping on us continually, the influences even of the mere worldliness that is all about and over us, except they be resisted, will at last petrify the spirit. They harden it to all but the consciousness of loss, and the agony of remorse. They may leave it sensible of duty, aware of doom, but *unable* to flee from it.

CCXXXVII. The Pilgrim Fathers. Ps. c. 1. *"Make a joyful noise unto the Lord, all ye lands."*

LET us look into the magic mirror of the past, and see the harbour of Cape Cod on the morning of the 11th of November, in the year of our Lord 1620, as described to us in the simple words of the Pilgrims: "A pleasant bay, circled round, except the entrance, which is about four miles over from land to land, *compassed about to the very sea* with oaks, pines, junipers, sassafras, and other sweet weeds. It is a harbour wherein a thousand sail of ship may safely ride."

That small, unknown ship was the *Mayflower*: those men and women who crowded her decks were that little handful of God's own wheat which had been flailed by adversity, tossed and winnowed till every husk of earthly selfishness and self-will had been beaten away from them and left only pure seed, fit for the planting of a new world. It was old Master Cotton Mather who said of them, "The Lord sifted three countries to find seed wherewith to plant America."

Hark now the hearty cry of the sailors, as with a plash and a cheer the anchor goes down, just in the deep water inside of Long Point! and then, says their journal: "Being now passed the vast ocean and sea of troubles, before their preparation unto further proceedings as to seek out a place for habitation, they fell down on their knees and blessed the Lord, the God of heaven, who had brought them over the vast and furious ocean, and delivered them from all perils and miseries thereof."

Let us draw nigh and mingle with this singular act of worship. Elder Brewster, with his well-worn Geneva Bible in hand, leads the thanksgiving in words which, though thousands of years old, seem as if written for the occasion of that hour.

As yet, the treasures of sacred song which are the liturgy of modern Christians had not arisen in the Church. There was no Watts and no Wesley in the day of the Pilgrims; they brought with them in each family, as the most precious of earthly possessions, a thick volume containing, first, the Book of Common Prayer, with the Psalter appointed to be read in churches; second, the whole Bible in the Geneva translation, which was the basis on which our present English translation was made; and third, the Psalms of David, in metre, by Sternhold and Hopkins, with the music notes of the tunes adapted to singing. Therefore it was that our little band were able to lift up their voices together in song, and that the noble tones of Old Hundred for the first time floated over the silent bay and mingled with the sound of winds and waters, consecrating the American shores.

> "All people that on earth do dwell,
>   Sing to the Lord with cheerful voice,
> Him serve with fear, His praise forth tell;
>   Come ye before Him and rejoice.
>
> The Lord, ye know, is God indeed;
>   Without our aid He did us make;
> We are His flock, He doth us feed,
>   And for His sheep He doth us take.
>
> O enter then His gates with praise,
>   Approach with joy His courts unto:
> Praise, laud, and bless His name always,
>   For it is seemly so to do.
>
> For why? The Lord our God is good,
>   His mercy is for ever sure;
> His truth at all times firmly stood,
>   And shall from age to age endure."

This grand hymn rose and swelled and vibrated in the still November air; while in between its pauses came the warble of birds, the scream of the jay, the hoarse call of hawk and eagle, going on with their forest ways all unmindful of the new era which had been ushered in with those solemn sounds.

CCXXXVIII. Signs of Death. Ps. cii. 20. *"To hear the groaning of the prisoner."*

A MAN was in great distress about his soul; he thought he was lost, could never be saved, and he was in despair. He set off to a good old Christian who lived in the town, and told him all his heart, and finished with these words: "Now, David, I'm dead—quite dead." "Well, Jamie," said the old man, "go away home and pray. Ye're no dead yet. No, no; there's nae groans comes frae the grave."

Groans over deadness and coldness felt are not altogether signs of death.

CCXXXIX. A Martyr for Christ. Ps. ciii. 1. *"Bless the Lord, O my soul: and all that is within me, bless His holy name."*

DURING the persecution in the reign of Queen Mary, one of the martyrs was fastened with a chain to a post in the Smithfield Market of London, and when the wood piled about him was lighted, and the fire burning his clothes and frizzling his flesh, he cried, "Bless the Lord, O my soul: and all that is within me, bless His holy name."

CCXL. Blessing the Lord in the Depth of Sorrow. Ps. ciii. 1. *"Bless the Lord, O my soul: and all that is within me, bless His holy name."*

THE value and beauty of family worship in the time of bereavement are illustrated by an incident in the life of the Rev. J. A. James, which has almost a touch of the sublime. It was his custom to read at family prayer on Saturday evening the hundred and third psalm. On the Saturday of the week in which Mrs. James died, he hesitated, with the open Bible in his hand, before he began to read; but, after a moment's silence, he looked up and said, "Notwithstanding what has happened this week, I see no reason for departing from our usual custom of reading the hundred and third psalm—'Bless the Lord, O my soul: and all that is within me, bless His holy name.'" What must be the effect upon a household of such a scene! What a picture is thus presented of holy resignation and thankfulness—the greatest sufferer recognising, as the head of the family, the hand that has smitten his home and made it desolate, and in the depth of his sorrow blessing the name of the Lord!

CCXLI. Grace should Permeate the Entire Man. Ps. ciii. 1. "*All that is within me, bless His holy name.*"

IN the camphor tree every part is impregnated with the precious perfume; from the highest twig to the lowest root the powerful gum will exude. Thus grace should permeate our whole nature, and be seen in every faculty, every word, every act, and even every desire. If it be "in us and abound," it will be so. An unsanctified part of our frame must surely be like a dead branch, deforming and injuring the tree. "Bless the Lord, O my soul: and *all that is within me*, bless His holy name." When praise is truly spiritual, it pervades the whole man.

CCXLII. Old Age. Ps. ciii. 5. "*Who satisfieth thy mouth with good things; so that thy youth is renewed like the eagle's.*"

JOHN FOSTER has a stirring passage in one of his sermons on old age:—

"The old age of the wise and good resembles the winter in one of its most favourable circumstances, that the former seasons improved have laid in a valuable store; and they have to bless God that disposed and enabled them to do so. But the most striking point in the comparison, after all, is one of *unlikeness*. Their winter has no spring to follow it—in this world. It is to close, not by an insensible progression into summer season, but by a termination absolute, abrupt, and final; a consideration which should shake and rouse the most inveterate insensibility of thoughtless old age. But the servants of God will say: '*That* is well!' They would not make a gradation into a spring of moral existence if it could be put in their choice. Their winter, they say, is quite the right time for a great transition. It was in nature's winter (or toward that season) that their Lord came to the earth; it was in the winter that He died for their redemption; and the winter of their life is the right time for them to die, that their redemption may be finished. And there is eternal spring before them! What will *they* not be contemplating of beauty and glory, while those who have yet many days on earth are seeing returning springs and summers?"

CCXLIII. A Lover of the Psalms. Ps. civ. 34.
" My meditation of Him shall be sweet."

THOMAS À KEMPIS was supremely happy in his convent life. He spent much time in striving to soar above the things of sense into communion with God; and this not without the occasional application to his flesh of the scourge. He could not have survived, however, to the great age of ninety-one, if his bodily mortifications had been fanatical and excessive. The Holy Scripture was much in use by him, and he transcribed it from beginning to end, in four beautifully written volumes, which were long preserved in the monastery, as a memorial of his pious diligence. Especially did he love the Psalms, and join in chanting them with all his heart. His fellow monks, accordingly, perpetrated a miserable joke upon him, which is preserved, by honest Franciscus, to the honour certainly of Thomas à Kempis, and to the letting in of a curious light on the character and tastes of his companions at Mount St. Agnes, which were plainly of an earthlier sort. "He is as fond of the *Psalms*," they said, "as if they were *salmon*," which, as Brother Franciscus adds within brackets for the information of the ignorant reader, "is a most delicate kind of fish!" Brother Franciscus says that there existed in his time a portrait of Thomas à Kempis, almost wholly effaced from the canvas, but with this characteristic inscription legible still, "Everywhere have I sought rest but nowhere have I found it, unless in solitude and books (*in Hoexkens ende Boexkens.*)" He found it there, because in his solitude and among his books, he found and communed with the Lord, in whom he rested, on whom he meditated, and of whom he wrote.

CCXLIV. A Patriot. Ps. cv. 26. "*He sent Moses his servant.*"

PRESENTING a noble contrast to the proverb long common in Italy, *Dolce far niente*, "It is sweet to indulge in idleness," the old Roman sang, *Dulce et decorum pro patria mori*, "It is sweet and graceful to die for one's country;" and one of these old Romans is said, when it was only by such a sacrifice that Rome could be spared, to have rode out of its gates full armed in sight of weeping thousands, and taking brave farewell of brothers, friends, and countrymen, to have spurred his steed into the gulf that closed its monstrous jaws on horse and rider. The lofty patriotism of the poet may be only the sentimentalism of song, and the hero of the gulf only such a fable as adorns traditionary lore. But Moses was a patriot of that type.

How we extolled the conduct of the Americans in China, when, though not bound to mingle in the bloody fray, they felt it impossible to look on, mere spectators, where our flag was flying, and our guns were flashing, and our men were falling amid the smoke of battle! "Blood is thicker than water!" It was in such another act that Moses' patriotism first burst out into flame. Neither his rank as the adopted son of Pharaoh's daughter and probable successor to her father's throne, nor his education as a prince of Egypt, nor the pride, and pomp, and pleasures of a palace had made him ashamed of his race, or indifferent to their cruel sufferings. In the words of St. Paul, "By faith Moses, when he was come to years, refused to be called the son of Pharaoh's daughter; choosing rather to suffer affliction with the people of God, than to enjoy the pleasures of sin for a season; esteeming the reproach of Christ greater riches than the treasures in Egypt.

CCXLV. A Besieged Town. Ps. cvii. 1. "*O give thanks unto the Lord, for He is good: for His mercy endureth for ever.*"

IN the year 1642 Taunton was besieged by the Royalist forces. It was defended by heroic steadfastness by Robert Blake. When food had risen to twenty times its market-value, when many of the inhabitants had died of starvation, when half the streets had been burnt down by a storm of rockets and mortars, the defenders still held their ground, and Blake announced to the besiegers his grim resolve not to surrender "until he had eaten his boots." At last, in July, 1645, the besiegers were obliged to withdraw. Many sermons were preached on the occasion of the anniversary of the town's deliverance. In one preached before Parliament, the preacher said :—

"O give thanks unto the Lord, for He is gracious: and His mercy endureth for ever :
Who remembered us at Naseby, for His mercy endureth for ever;
Who remembered us in Pembrokeshire, for His mercy endureth for ever ;
Who remembered us at Taunton, for His mercy endureth for ever."

CCXLVI. The Pale Horse. Ps. cvii. 18. *They draw near unto the gates of death.*"

THE following is a closing passage of a sermon on death by Dawson. The preacher has been speaking of those to whom the blow of the rider on the pale horse brings no terror. The Christian sees his Father's servant on his Father's pale horse, and he knows he has been sent for to come home. And he closed his sermon with this passage: "I well remember the time when the pale horse and his rider approached *Sammy Hick*, 'the village blacksmith.' He was nearer to him than I thought him to be. I was with him on the Wednesday, and he died upon the Monday. The pale horse overtook him on the Monday. There was a young man said on Sunday night (he did not sleep with him, but watched with him) that such a night he did not expect to see again. They were singing and praising God ; and he said the place seemed filled with the glory of God. The pale horse and his rider approached, and poor Sammy's speech began to falter and his breath to fail. But, glory be to God, he was not afraid of seeing the pale horse at all. No ; it was joy, and peace, and love. Two or three neighbours came in, and thought they would sing him over the river. And when all the power of language failed,

'Joy beaming through his eyes did break,
And meant the thanks he could not speak.'

They saw his eyes sparkle ; they saw the joy of his soul

as he went along, and the thanks he could not speak. And just before he took his last step out of time into glory, the poor soldier waved his hand, crying, "Victory! victory!'"

CCXLVII. The little Ships and the great Sea.
Ps. cvii. 23. *"They that go down to the sea in ships, that do business in great waters."*

THE following is the prayer of the Breton fishers: "Mon Dieu, protégez moi—mon navire est si petit, et votre mer est si grande" (My God, protect me—my ship is so little, and Your sea is so great.)

> O God! my ship is small, Thy sea so wide,
> How shall I sail across in bark so frail?
> What may my oars against its waves avail,
> Or can I ever reach the farther side,
> If any shore bound that unmeasured tide?
> O endless waves! O feeble quivering sail!
> O great Eternity! I faint and fail,
> And dare not go, and may not here abide:
> My bark drives on, whither I do not know.
> My God! remember me, that I am dust—
> The way is too far for me, when I go;
> Yet will I leave the land and trembling trust.
> Thou who didst walk on stormy Galilee,
> Let me not sink in Thine unfathomed sea!

CCXLVIII. Timely Succour.
Ps. cvii. 43. *"Whoso is wise, and will observe these things, even they shall understand the lovingkindness of the Lord."*

SCOTT, the commentator, suffered from frequent attacks of illness, and after one long and dangerous sickness, which had occasioned heavy additional expenses, he found himself in debt to the amount of £10. His wife, though seldom distrusting Providence, lamented this exceedingly. His answer was the following: "Now observe if the Lord do not, in some way, send us an additional supply to meet this expense, which it was not in our power to avoid." He goes on to relate how, in the afternoon of the same day, when visiting his people, Mr. Higgins called at his house, and left a paper, which, he said, would entitle me to £10 from the sum of money left for the relief of poor clergymen. This relief he had never before received. "Whoso

CCXLIX. The 119th Psalm. Ps. cxix.

JOHN RUSKIN says that of all the pieces of the Bible which his mother taught him, that which cost him most to learn, and which was to his child's mind chiefly repulsive—the 119th Psalm—has now become of all the most precious to him, in its overflowing and glorious passion of love for the law of God.

CCL. Don't use a Crooked Ruler. Ps. cxix. 9.

"Wherewithal shall a young man cleanse his way? by taking heed thereto according to Thy word."

"THE Bible is so strict and old-fashioned," said a young man to a grey-haired friend, who was advising him to study God's Word if he would learn how to live. "There are plenty of books written now-a-days that are moral enough in their teaching, and do not bind one down as the Bible."

The old merchant turned to his desk, and took out two rulers, one of which was slightly bent. With each of these he ruled a line, and silently handed the ruled paper to his companion.

"Well," said the lad, "what do you mean?"

"One line is not straight and true, is it? When you mark out your path in life do not take a crooked ruler!"

CCLI. Hiding the Bible in the Heart. Ps. cxix. 11.

"Thy word have I hid in my heart, that I might not sin against Thee."

THE late excellent Rev. Dr. James W. Alexander was, in many respects, a model Christian man and minister. One important secret of it lay in some of his habits. One of these was that of taking, every morning, a verse or passage from the Bible for his meditation during the day, and with the view, he said, of having his entire life filled with its spirit and influence. David said to God: "Thy word have I hid in my heart, that I might not sin against Thee."

CCLII. Pulpit Reflectors. Ps. cxix. 46. *"I will speak of Thy testimonies also before kings, and will not be ashamed."*

THE eminent Lyman Beecher used to say that the reason why his ministry was so blessed to the salvation of men, was that he had so many pulpit reflectors in the Christians who lived out and diffused in every practical way the gospel which he proclaimed. A light placed alone scatters its beams on every hand, but a number of well-placed reflectors can concentrate and reflect its rays, and cause them to reach places where the direct rays of light would never go; so these pulpit reflectors, these Christians who take the gospel up in their lives, and who talk it, and act it, and live it from day to day, multiply the preacher's usefulness a hundredfold, and carry down into the deep and hidden corners, where sin and darkness lurk, those beams of light which, without their aid, would never reach the souls that sit in the shadow of death.

We need more pulpit reflectors. Let the ministers of the gospel preach with all fidelity, and then let the Christians on every hand take up the words of life which he proclaims, and reflect and re-echo them, and bear them to the souls which walk in darkness, and yet long to behold God's marvellous light, even the light of the knowledge of the glory of God, in the face of Jesus Christ.

CCLIII. About to Migrate. Ps. cxix. 54. *"The house of my pilgrimage."*

WE are told that the late authoress Juliana Horatia Ewing had hung over her hearth the motto: "Ut migraturus habita" (As one about to migrate), to temper her joys in the comforts of home, and to remind her that "here have we no continuing city, but we seek one to come."

CCLIV. The Decision of a Moment. Ps. cxix. 59. *"I thought on my ways, and turned my feet unto Thy testimonies."*

AT an unlooked-for moment we may decide the whole course of our lives settling the question of for Christ or against Christ. A young man in Oakland, Cal., was walking with a friend. "Let's go to a saloon," said the friend. Just then the young man looked up and saw on a sign, "Young Men's Christian Association." "No, I'll go up here," was the reply. "Oh, you baby!" sneered his companion; but he went up, and that step led to his giving himself to God and entering on the Christian life. But how about him who kept on his way in the life of sin?

CCLV. The Mellowing Power of Affliction.
Ps. cxix. 83. *"For I am become like a bottle in the smoke."*

IT was a custom of the ancients to hang skins of wine in the smoke of a fire to refine and mellow it by the warmth, and so the sooner to bring it to perfection. So the Psalmist says "that is what God has put me in the furnace of trial for, to refine me."

CCLVI. Persecution. Ps. cxix. 86. *"They persecute me wrongfully; help Thou me."*

THE pious Romaine, the well-known author of the "Triumph of Faith," suffered much for the truth's sake. What a picture is presented of the solitary witness of the truth, when we are told that, in his own Church of St. Dunstan's at Aberford, he had often to preach by the light of a single candle, *which he held in his hand*, as the churchwardens would neither light the church nor suffer it to be lighted!

CCLVII. "The Fulness of the Scriptures."
Ps. cxix. 97. *"O how love I Thy law! it is my meditation all the day."*

"I ADORE the fulness of the Scriptures," was the exclamation of Tertullian,—"in which posture of holy admiration," said Dr. Owen, "I desire my mind may be found while I am in this world."

"What do I not owe to the Lord," writes Henry Martyn, "for permitting me to take a part in the translation of His word? Never did I see such wonders, and wisdom, and love, in the blessed book, as since I have been obliged to study every expression; and it is a delightful reflection, that death cannot deprive us of he pleasure of studying its mysteries."

The same testimony was given by a kindred spirit employed in the same work. Shortly before his death, Dr. Buchanan, giving to a friend some details of his laborious revisions of his Syriac Testament, suddenly stopped, and burst into tears. On recovering himself he said, "I am not ill, but I was completely overcome with the recollection of the delight which I have enjoyed in this exercise. At first I was disposed to shrink from the task as irksome, and apprehended that I should find even the Scriptures pall by the frequency of this critical examination. But so far from it, every fresh perusal seemed to throw fresh light on the word of God, and to convey additional joy and consolation to my mind." "How delightful," observes his biographer, "is the contemplation of a servant of Christ thus devoutly engaged in his heavenly Master's work, almost to the very moment of his transition to the Divine source of light and truth itself!"

CCLVIII. A Heathen Convert and his Bible.
Ps. cxix. 97   "*O how love I Thy law.*"

AN aged convert from heathenism, a native of one of the Hervey Islands, some years ago received as a present a copy of the Bible. A few pages or chapters only had been given him before this, and he was greatly pleased in becoming the owner of the volume. After receiving it, he said, "My brethren and sisters, this is my resolve: The dust shall never cover my new Bible; the moth shall never eat it; the mildew shall not rot it. My light! My joy!"

CCLIX. A Surety. Ps. cxix. 122.   "*Be surety for Thy servant for good.*"

FOR many months James Sherman, who became the famed minister of Surrey Chapel, London, was in great darkness, inquiring and seeking after God. He says, "Day by day I read the Scriptures, to see if God spake to me by His promise, but no promise brought me relief." But after twelve months of wrestling and seeking, the day of deliverance came. Mr. King, of Doncaster, came to preach at Tottenham Court-road Chapel, and Sherman went to hear him. "All the way," he says, "I watered the pavement with my tears, and sent up my cries to Heaven. I heard him with emotion and some pleasure, yet my faith did not seem sufficiently strong to bring home to myself the blessing. I bent my steps homeward, but, as I was crossing from Bedford Street to Montague Place, I seemed to hear a voice saying to me, 'I am thy surety.' I turned round involuntarily, half imagining that some one was speaking to me. After a moment's pause, I said to myself, 'It is the voice of my Saviour.' And a flood of light was poured into the prison-house of my poor soul, and at once converted it into the temple of God."

CCLX. Dissatisfied with Myself. Ps. cxix. 130.
" The entrance of Thy words giveth light."

ONE of the neatest of the neat compliments for which Louis XIV. was famous was addressed to Massillon, the famous Court preacher: "Father," said the King, "I have listened in my chapel to many great preachers, and I have been very well satisfied with them; but as often as I hear you, I am very ill-satisfied with myself."

CCLXI. A Japanese Convert. Ps. cxix. 130. *" The entrance of Thy words giveth light."*

SIX Japanese girls were sent over to America to be educated. One of them took a situation as governess in a family, where she read the English Bible. She wrote under deep conviction to her father, urging him to procure a copy of the Bible and read it. He, thinking it was a whim of his child, dismissed the subject from his mind, and destroyed the letter. This was ten years ago. Some seven years later he went as Commissioner for Japan to the Austrian Exhibition. There he saw the Bible Stand, and was impressed with wonder that so much should be made of any single book, and that it should be thought worth translating into so many languages. He purchased a copy in Chinese, and read it with curiosity. Curiosity deepened into interest, and by degrees he became convinced of the truth of all the Book taught. In his journey through Europe he made his own observations of the three prevailing forms of Christianity—the Romish, Greek, and Protestant faiths. He was satisfied that the last of these came nearest to the teaching and spirit of the Book itself. On his return to Yeddo he applied to the American missionaries for baptism. Hearing of the step he had taken, his daughter wrote to him from America to suggest that, as he had the means at his disposal, he should purchase a heathen temple for purposes of Christian worship. He did so, and in the temple thus purchased the Christian missionaries now meet for worship.

CCLXII. A Peacemaker. Ps. cxx. 7. "*I am for peace.*"

It is said of the late Henry Venn Elliot, of Brighton, that he did everything heartily and with all his strength. He was very firm. Twice he put a stop to men fighting in the streets, thrusting himself between the combatants and saying, "If you want to fight, fight me," and he rebuked the crowds for encouraging the fights. "You call yourselves Christians," he said, "and yet delight to see your fellow-creatures fighting like wild beasts! Do you not know your bodies were made for God's service?" The mob dispersed at once. The home circle would never have known it from himself but spots of blood on his shirt betrayed the affair.

CCLXIII. Home, Sweet Home! Ps. cxxii. 2. "*Our feet shall stand within thy gates, O Jerusalem.*"

One night on the banks of the Potomac, as the Confederate and the Union armies lay opposite each other, the Union bands played, "The Star-spangled Banner," "Hail, Columbia!" and other Union songs; and the Confederates in contest played "Dixie," and other pieces of their side. It seemed that each would play the other down. By-and-by a band struck up "Home, Sweet Home!" The conflict ceased. The bands on the other side struck up, "Home, Sweet Home!" and voices from opposite sides of the river joined the chorus, "There is no place like home."

CCLXIV. Durie's Psalm. Ps. cxxiv. 1-8.

This is known in Scotland, in its second version and with its bold marching melody, as *Durie's Psalm*. James Melville, in his diary—date 1582—gives, in his own quaint way, an account of the incident which gave rise to the name. John Durie had been banished from his pulpit and from Edinburgh for his boldness of speech in criticising some of the acts of James VI., but the feeling in his favour was so strong that his sentence had to be reversed. The tune and the man can be best understood by giving James Melville's own words, spelling and all: "Within few days after the petition of the nobility, Jhon Durie gat leave to ga haim to his ain flock of Edinbrugh: at whase returning there was a great concours of the haill toun, wha met him at the Nether Bow; and going up the street, with bare heads and loud voices, sang to the praise of God, and testifying of great joy and consolation, the 124 Psalm—'Now Israel may say, and that trewly'—, till heaven and earth resoundit. This noise, when the Duc (of Lennox) being in the toun, heard, and ludging in the Hiegate looked out and saw, he rave his beard for anger, and hasted him off the toun." John Durie was a minister of mark in his time, and very popular with the citizens of Edinburgh. He was fearless and devout—a man of the people, and also a man of God; and the description of him is so graphic that it is worth giving: "Jhone Durie was of small literature, but had seen and marked the warks of God in the first Reformation, and been a doer baith with toung and hand. He had been a diligent hearer of Mr. Knox, and observer of all his ways. He conceived the grounds of matters weil, and could utter them fully and manfully with a mighty spirit, voice, and action. The special gift I marked in him was holiness, and a daily, careful, continual walking with God in meditation and prayer. He was a verie gude fallow, and took delyt as his special comfort to have his table and house filled with the best men. These he would gladly hear, with them confer and talk, professing he was but a buik-bearer, and would fain learn of them; and getting the ground and light of knowledge in any gude point, then would he rejoice in God, praise and pray thereupon, and urge it with a clear and forcible exhortation in assembly and pulpit."

The learned and pious Dr. Tholuck, of Halle, used to tell an anecdote of the death-bed of his father-in-law. He had been once a Roman Catholic, and as it happens that, though the mind may have been entirely emancipated, sometimes the fear of dying without priestly absolution returns, his son-in-law asked him if he had any such feeling. He expressed his confidence in the great High Priest, and, giving his hand a wave of triumph, said,—

"Strick ist entzwei, und wir sind frei."

The words are from Luther's version of this psalm, made in 1525, corresponding to—

"Broke are their nets, and thus escaped we."

The biographer of M'Cheyne, giving an account of his death, says: "Next day he continued, sunk in body and mind, till about the time when his people met for their usual evening prayer-meeting, when he requested to be left alone for half an hour. When his servant entered the room again, he exclaimed with a joyful voice, 'My soul is escaped as a bird out of the snare of his fowler; the snare is broken, and I am escaped.' His countenance, as he said this, bespoke inward peace; and ever after he was observed to be happy."

Ver. 8. With this verse the French Protestant Church always begins its public worship—words which well become the children of the Huguenots.

CCLXV. Interposition of Providence. Ps. cxxiv. 2.

"If it had not been the Lord who was on our side, when men rose up against us: then they had swallowed us up quick, when their wrath was kindled against us."

ON one occasion, the Prince Condé and Admiral Coligny —the leaders of the Huguenot party—had been driven from their homes by their opponents, who had attempted cruelly to massacre them; they took to flight accordingly, with their helpers and terrified families. "The Prince of Condé set out silently," says Matthieu, an eye-witness of the events he narrates, "but his situation touched all hearts with pity when they saw the first prince of the blood setting forward in the intensest heat, with his wife on the point of giving birth to a child, and three little children borne after them, followed by the now motherless family of Coligny, of whom only one was able to walk. The wife of D'Antelot, too, was there with her little girl only two years old, and several other ladies. The only escort for this troop of helpless women and children was one hundred and fifty soldiers, headed by two brave and affectionate fathers.

"They journeyed on as rapidly as possible, for their only hope of safety lay in crossing the Loire before they could be overtaken, and then seeking shelter in Rochelle; but the whole country was filled with hostile troops, and the bridges over the Loire were already occupied. They therefore determined to attempt a ford not commonly known, and arrived at it when the river, usually broad and furious, was so far diminished by the long drought that they crossed without difficulty, the prince carrying his youngest infant on his arm, clasped to his bosom.

"Scarcely had they reached the southern bank, when, turning round, they discovered the cavalry of their enemies in full pursuit, crowding rapidly upon the opposite side.

"An event now happened certainly very remarkable. Without any apparent cause, a sudden swell of waters came foaming and rushing down the stream, and in an instant filling the channel, rendered the ford impassable, and the defenceless company were thus rescued from the jaws of their destroyer.

"Can we wonder that men taught to rest upon Providence, and to discern the Almighty hand in the events of their agitated lives, should have regarded this as a signal interposition in their favour, and an undoubted sign that His arm was extended for their protection?"

CCLXVI. Almost drowned. Ps. cxxiv. 4. *"Then the waters had overwhelmed us."*

THE following anecdote relates to one of Mr. Wesley's early visits into Cornwall: "I was born," says old Peter Martin, "at Helstone, and baptized on the 12th of May, 1742. My wife is 94 years old; our united ages amount to 191 years. I have been sexton of this parish, Helstone, 65 years. I remember Mr. Wesley well. I first heard him preach in the street near our market-house 74 years ago. I have also seen him at Redruth, and had an adventure with him while I was ostler at the London Inn, then kept by Henry Pemberthy. Mr. Wesley came there one day in a carriage driven by his own servant, who, being unacquainted with the road farther westward than Redruth, he obtained my master's leave for me to drive him to St. Ives. We set out, and on our arrival at Hayle we found the sands between that place and St. Ives, over which we had to pass, overflown by the rising tide. On reaching the water's edge, I hesitated to proceed, and advised Mr. Wesley of the danger of crossing ; and a captain of a vessel, seeing us stopping, came up and endeavoured to dissuade us from an undertaking so full of peril, but without effect. Mr. Wesley was resolved to go on ; he said he had to preach at St. Ives at a certain hour, and that he must fulfil his appointment, and looking out of the carriage window, he called loudly to me, 'Take the sea! take sea!' In a moment I dashed into the waves and was quickly involved in a world of waters. The horses were now swimming, and the carriage became overwhelmed with the tide, as its hinder wheels became not unfrequently merged into the deep pits and hollows in the sands. I struggled hard to maintain my seat in the saddle, while the poor affrighted animals were snorting and rearing in the most terrific manner, and furiously plunging the opposing waves. At this awful crisis I heard Mr. Wesley's voice. With difficulty I turned my head towards the carriage, and saw his long, white locks dripping the salt sea down the rugged furrows of his venerable countenance. He was looking calmly forth from the windows, undisturbed by the tumultuous war of the surrounding waters, or by the danger of his perilous situation. He hailed me by a tolerably loud voice, and asked, 'What is your name, driver?' I answered, 'Peter.' 'Peter,' said Mr. Wesley,—'Peter, fear not; you shall not sink.' With vigorous spurring and whipping I again urged on the flagging horses, and at last got safely over ; but it was a miracle, as I shall always say. We continued our journey, and reached St. Ives without further hindrance."

CCLXVII. A Favourite Song of Scottish Reformation. Ps. cxxv. 1-5.

THIS psalm used to be sung frequently in early Scottish Reformation times. The tune which accompanied it was "St. Andrew." It was often sung, too, by the French Protestants, when hiding from the *Dragonnades* of Louis XIV., and fleeing to the frontiers for escape. Every verse, every word seems made for such emergencies.

CCLXVIII. A Sudden Death. Ps. cxxvi. 5. "*They that sow in tears shall reap in joy.*"

THIS was a favourite verse of Philip Henry, who used to say that weeping should not hinder sowing. His death was in accordance with it, It took place suddenly on the morning of a fast for public danger, when he was to have preached. Some wished to defer the service, but this text was quoted for going forward with it. His son Matthew Henry spoke from 2 Kings xiii. 20: "And Elisha died, . . . and the bands of the Moabites invaded the land."

CCLXIX. A Chosen Psalm of Catherine de Medici. Ps. cxxviii.

ALONG with Psalms vi. and cxlii., this was chosen for herself by Catherine de Medici. She could scarcely have selected any more unsuitable.

CCLXX. Philip Henry. Ps. cxxviii. 2. "*Blessed is every one that feareth the Lord: that walketh in His ways. For thou shalt eat the labours of thine hands; happy shalt thou be, and it shall be well with thee.*"

WHEN Philip Henry was settled at Worthenbury, he sought the hand of the only daughter and heiress of Mr. Matthews, of Broad Oak. The father demurred, saying that though Mr. Henry was an excellent preacher and a gentleman, yet he did not know from whence he came. "True," said the daughter; "but I know where he is going, and I should like to go with him." Mr. Henry records in his diary, long after, the happiness of the union, which was soon after consummated:—"April 26, 1860.

This day we have been married twenty years, in which time we have received of the Lord twenty thousand mercies—to God be glory!" Sometimes he writes—"We have been so long married, and never reconciled, *i.e.* there never was any occasion for it" His advice to his children, with respect to their marriage, was—"Please God, and please yourselves, and you will please me;" and his usual compliment to his newly-married friends—"Others wish you all happiness. I wish you all holiness, and then there is no doubt but you will have all happiness."

CCLXXI. A Psalm Beloved by Luther. Ps. cxxx.

By a curious unfitness, this Psalm with xxxii. was the choice of Diana of Poitiers; and yet may there not be a sense of deep fitness which comes at moments to the souls of the most frivolous? We can understand better Luther's love of it, with Psalm li. These Psalms are the nearest approach in the Old Testament to the 8th chapter of the Romans. One of his great psalm-hymns which penetrated to the inmost heart of the German people was formed on this 130th. If the 46th furnished the major, this gives the minor key in the songs of the Reformation of Germany:—

"*Aus tiefer Noth schrei ich zu Dir.*"
"Lord, from the depths to Thee I cry."

It was written in 1524, and has its own history. On the 6th of May of the year in which it was made, a poor old weaver sang it through the streets of Magdeburg and offered it for sale at a price that suited the poorest. He was cast into prison by the burgomaster, but 200 citizens marched to the Town Hall, and would not leave till he was freed. "So mightily grew the word of the Lord, and prevailed." And Psalms and music were chosen weapons of the time. "The ransomed of the Lord returned, and came to Zion with songs." This prayer-psalm had its comforting power on the singer. When Luther, during the Augsburg Diet, was at the Castle of Coburg, and had to suffer much from inward and outward trials, he fell into a swoon. When he awoke from it, he said, "Come, and in defiance of the devil, let us sing the Psalm, 'Lord, from the depths to Thee I cry;' let us sing it in full chorus and extol and praise God." In the first days of the Reform it was frequently employed as a funeral song. It was sung at the interment of the great friend and protector of Luther, Frederick the Wise, in 1525. When the body of Luther was on its way from Eisleben, where he died, to Wittenberg, where he lies buried, it rested for a night, Feb. 20th, 1546, in the church in Halle of which Justus Jonas, the bosom friend of Luther, was pastor (*Liebfrauenkirche*). This Psalm was given out by Jonas, and sung by the thousands who thronged and wept round Luther's coffin.

Dr. John Owen gives an account of the way in which he was led to write his commentary, or rather series of discourses, on this Psalm. "Mr. Richard Davis," he says, "who afterwards became pastor of a church in Rowel, Northamptonshire, being under religious impressions, sought a conference with me. I put the question to him, ' Young man, pray, in what manner do you think to go to God ?' 'Through the Mediator, sir,' Mr. Davis answered. 'That is easily said,' I replied, 'but I assure you, it is another thing to go to God through the Mediator than many who make use of the expression are aware of. I myself preached Christ some years, when I had but very little, if any, experimental acquaintance with access to God through Christ; until the Lord was pleased to visit me with sore affliction, whereby I was brought to the mouth of the grave, and under which my soul was oppressed with horror and darkness : but God graciously relieved my spirit by a powerful application of Psalm cxxx. 4 : "But there is forgiveness with Thee, that Thou mayest be feared," from whence I received special instruction, peace and comfort in drawing near to God through the Mediator, and preached thereupon immediately after my recovery.'" This is no doubt the reason why nearly three-fourths of Owen's treatise is occupied with this verse.

It was the 130th Psalm, sung in St. Paul's, May, 1738, and heard by John Wesley with deep emotion, which prepared him for the truth of justification by faith, which he embraced shortly afterwards through reading Luther on the Galatians. His conversations with Peter Bohlen, of the Moravian Brethren, also aided him greatly, and helped to preserve him from the mystic Arminianism of *Law's Serious Call*, to which he was at one time inclined. So far as we can see, Wesley's strength and that of the world-wide movement which has come from him would have failed in the birth, but for this decision. It is interesting, also, to mark the glimpses we get of souls touching one another age after age through the hidden life which springs from the Word of God,—David, Paul, Luther, Owen, Zinzendorf, Wesley, moving and being moved by the secret currents of that same spirit of which we hear the sound, but cannot tell whence it comes or whither it goes. When the veil is lifted that is spread over all nations, it will be as pleasant to trace the intertwining of the roots of the tree of life, as to look on its blossoms and admire its fruit.

Ver. 6. Jonathan Edwards, in his *Journal*, says, "In Sept., 1725, was taken ill at Newhaven; and endeavoured to go home to Windsor; was so ill at the North Village that I could go no further, where I lay sick for about a quarter of a year. And in this sickness, God was pleased to visit me again with the sweet influences of His Spirit. My mind was greatly engaged there on divine pleasant contemplations and longings of soul. I observed that those who watched with me would often be looking out for the morning, and seemed to wish for it; which brought to my mind the words of the Psalmist's, which my soul with sweetness made its own language: 'My soul waiteth for the Lord more than they that watch for the morning.' And when the light of the morning came, and the beams of the sun came in at the windows, it refreshed my soul from one morning to another. It seemed to me to be some image of the sweet light of God's glory."

CCLXXII. A Song of Christian Assemblies.
Ps. cxxxiii.

THIS Psalm has opened and closed many a Christian assembly, but has not yet found its way to the inmost heart of the Church of Christ. In 1638, it was sung at the termination of the famous Assembly held in Glasgow, of which Alexander Henderson was Moderator. That meeting was the tide-mark of the second Reformation—a bright morning that was soon obscured by clouds and storm, but it opened a day which is still advancing.

CCLXXIII. "Let us with a Gladsome Mind."
Ps. cxxxvi.

THIS Psalm was the foundation of John Milton's " Let us with a gladsome mind"—written when he was fifteen—the only one of his psalms which has found a responsive note in the songs of the Church, though no one felt more than he did the height of the Psalmist's great argument!

> "Their songs,
> Thin sown with aught of profit or delight,
> Will far be found unworthy to compare
> With Sion's songs to all true tastes excelling,—
> Where God is praised aright, and godlike men,
> The Holiest of holies, and His saints,—
> Such are from God inspired."
>
> *Paradise Reg.*, iv.

CCLXXIV. A Patriotic Psalm. Ps. cxxxvii.

THIS Psalm has struck the key to many a song of the love of country.

> "Yes! I may love the music of strange tongues,
> And mould my heart anew to take the stamp
> Of foreign friendships in a foreign land;
> But to my parched roof's mouth let cleave this tongue,
> My fancy fade into a yellow leaf,
> And this oft-pausing heart forget to throb,
> If Scotland! thee and thine, it e'er forget."
>
> GRAHAME.

The Abbé Curci, a great Oriental scholar, and author of a translation of the Old Testament into Italian, one of the few clergymen who have taken the side of Italy and freedom against the Pope, lectured to an immense assembly in Rome (1883), and expressed his special love to the 137th Psalm. He said it was the first and grandest patriotic song which was ever written—linking God and country together. Camoens, the national poet of Portugal, has paraphrased the 137th Psalm in a sonnet as the Psalm of "pious, patriotic memory."

It may be considered, in a higher point of view, as the spring of the Jerusalem songs, which, in all ages of the Church, looked away from a state of exile to the final home:—

"For thee, O dear, dear country,
  Mine eyes their vigils keep;
For very love, beholding
  Thy happy name, they weep:
E'en now, by faith, I see thee,
  E'en now thy walls discern;
To thee my thoughts are kindled,
  And strive, and pant, and yearn."

CCLXXV. A Distressed Church. Ps. cxxxvii. 3, 4. *"They that wasted us required of us mirth, saying, Sing us one of the songs of Zion. How shall we sing the Lord's song in a strange land?"*

IT has often been said that the first Nonconformists were a gloomy generation. "But," asks one of their advocates, "is it fair to ruin us, and then reproach us for not being merry? They that wasted us required of us mirth. . . . But how shall we sing the Lord's songs in a strange land and what other songs can we sing? Shall we set the Five-Mile Acts to music, and make merry with our sorrows?" Some degree of gloom was natural. One poor woman exclaimed to a Nonconformist minister, "I wonder how any one can laugh when God's Church is in such distress."

CCLXXVI. The Lord's Song. Ps. cxxxvii. 4. *"The Lord's song in a strange land."*

IN one of his recent letters from Shanghai, Archdeacon Moule describes an incident of his journey to Hangchow which shows Christian ideas are spreading. He was awakened, so he tells us, early on a Sunday morning as he lay in his boat hearing the younger boatman in his song, sung to beguile the toil of paddling, repeat the words, "Jesus is our best Friend: I love thee, my Saviour." The lad, when questioned, said he had never been in a Christian church or school himself, but had learned the words from a friend. Round Shanghai one may often hear snatches of prayer and hymns chanted by the boatmen at their work. Often those who sing have no idea of the true meaning of the words, but the hymns of the new faith upon heathen lips prophesy and promise a glorious victory.

CCLXXVII. In God's Hands. Ps. cxxxix. 12. "*The darkness and the light are both alike to Thee.*"

IRENÆUS PRIME mentions the following incident in one of his letters:—

"When I was about forty years old, and sitting at my work in the office in New York, a stranger entered, and without introduction or even mentioning his name, said to me: 'I have come in to see you whom I know very well, though you do not know me. About forty years ago I was going up the Hudson River on a sloop, for in those days there were no steamboats or railroads. When we were in Tappan Sea we were overtaken by a violent storm, and the passengers, of whom there were several on board, were greatly alarmed lest we should be capsized. In the midst of the excitement a young and beautiful woman stood in the midst of us and said: "In God's hands we are as safe on the water as on the land." Those words calmed the excitement, and we waited in hope till the storm abated. The lovely woman who thus proved our comforter in danger, afterward became your mother! Her words have been my motto all the years since. I have watched your life and marked every step you have taken, always keeping in mind the lesson I learned from the lips that taught your infant lips to pray.'

"Having said these pleasant words, the stranger left me, and I have never to my knowledge seen him or heard from him since. I asked my mother about it, and she remembered the time, the voyage, the storm, the excitement, but her own composure was so habitual that it was not memorable."

CCLXXVIII. The Evening Song. Ps. cxli.

THIS Psalm was the evening song of the early Christian Church.

CCLXXIX. Watching the Lips. Ps. cxli. 3. "*Set a watch, O Lord, before my mouth: keep the door of my lips.*

THE old Greeks tell us a story about the death of Hercules. That strong hero had shot his enemy Nessus, with a poisoned arrow, and the garment of the slain man was all stained with poisoned blood. Before he died, Nessus gave his clothing to the wife of Hercules, telling her that it would make her husband love her always. It came to pass after a time that she gave the fatal garment to her husband, and no sooner had he put it on, than the poison seized upon him; and when in his agony he tried to tear it off, it clung the closer, and so he died killed by his own poison. So it is with the man who clothes himself with the garment of cursing or bad talk, it clings to him and poisons him, soul and body.

CCLXXX. Fear of Death Overcome. Ps. cxliii.

THOMAS BILNEY, burned in the reign of Henry VIII., had, at first, fear of death, but he rose above it, and his behaviour at the stake made a great impression on the people: "He made his private prayer with such earnest elevation of his eyes and hands to heaven, and in so good and quiet behaviour, that he seemed not to consider the terror of his death; and ended at last his private prayers with the Psalm beginning, 'Hear my prayer, O Lord! consider my desire!' And the next verse he repeated in deep meditation thrice: 'And enter not into judgment with Thy servant, for in Thy sight shall no man living be justified.' And so, finishing that Psalm, he ended his prayers."

CCLXXXI. An Irish Bishop. Ps. cxliv.

FROM this Psalm, being the Psalm for the day, Bishop Bedell preached, Jan. 30th, 1642, in the midst of the Irish Rebellion, and died a few days afterwards. He was one of the best men of his time—humble, devout, self-sacrificing. The Bible which, with great labour, he got translated into the Irish language, was for a long time the one chiefly in use among the Scottish Highlanders; it was not till the beginning of the present century that it found much entrance into Ireland. All classes of the Irish had a great regard for him. His last sermon was preached in the house of a converted priest, to which he was allowed to retire from Castle Oughterard, County Cavan, where he had been kept a prisoner. He lies in a corner of Kilmore Churchyard, close to a large sycamore tree which he himself had planted.

CCLXXXII. The Te Deum of the Old Testament.
Ps. cxlv.

THE tradition about the *Te Deum* is that it was sung by Ambrose and Augustine, through a kind of inspiration—in 387—when they met at Milan, and when Augustine was baptized by Ambrose. The truth in this is that this hymn, which has been sung in so many countries and through so many centuries, had its commencement in a responsive Christian song which Ambrose introduced from the Eastern into the Western Church. It was a morning psalm of praise, and began, " Every day will I bless Thee, and praise Thy name for ever and ever." This 145th Psalm may be looked on, therefore, as having in it the germ of the wide-spread Christian hymn, and as being itself the *Te Deum* of the Old Testament. The Jews were accustomed to say that he who could pray this Psalm from the heart three times daily was preparing himself best for the praise of the world to come.

CCLXXXIII. Christ's Everlasting Kingdom. Ps. cxlv. 13. *" Thy kingdom is an everlasting kingdom."*

VOLTAIRE said, "In twenty years Christianity will be no more. My single hand shall destroy the edifice it took twelve apostles to rear." Some years after his death, his very printing press was employed in printing New Testaments, and thus spreading abroad the Gospel. Gibbon, who, " with solemn sneer," devoted his gorgeous history to sarcasm upon Christ and His followers, his estate is now in the hands of one who devotes large sums to the propagation of the very truth Gibbon laboured to sap.

CCLXXXIV. A Good Man of the Olden Time.
Ps. cxlvi.

N 1574 died David Home of Wedderburn, a gentleman of good account in Berwickshire, and father of David Home of Godscroft, author of the " History of the House of Douglas." He died in the 50th year of his age, of consumption, being the first of his family for a long period who had died a natural death—all the rest had lost their lives in the defence of their country. He was a man remarkable for piety and probity, candour and integrity. He had the Psalms, and especially some short sentences of them, always in his mouth, such as, "It is better to trust in the Lord than in the princes of the earth," "Our hope ought to be placed in God alone." He delighted particularly in the 146th Psalm, and sung it, playing on the harp, with the most sincere and unaffected devotion.

CCLXXXV. The Dairyman's Daughter. Ps. cxlviii. 8. *"Wind and storm fulfilling His Word."*

AMONG the voices of God's providence are the howling storm and the roaring sea. A pious chaplain, detained by contrary winds at the Isle of Wight over the Sunday, preached that day in one of the churches of the island. In the congregation there was a thoughtless girl who had come to show her fine clothes. The word of God arrested her, and she was converted. The story of her conversion is the narrative of the "Dairyman's Daughter," which has gone all round the world, and the fruit of the sermon is a hundredfold.

CCLXXXVI. A Pulpit Beggar. Ps. cxlviii. 17. *"Who can stand before His cold?"*

THE successor of Rowland Hill at Surrey Chapel was the famous James Sherman. Mr. Sherman was one of the most skilful and successful of pulpit-beggars. Give him a good cause, and he never failed to get money. At a Friday morning service, on one occasion, it was most bitterly cold, and very few people were present. The intensity of the cold had suggested his text—Psalm cxlviii. 17: "Who can stand before His cold?" In the course of his remarks, he alluded to the pitiable condition of the poor immediately around the chapel; and reminded his audience that if, in their comfortable homes, and so warmly clothed, they felt it so difficult to "stand before His cold," what must it be with the homeless and the half-naked? The appeal was so pertinent and so resistless that a considerable contribution was offered on the spot! Measures were devised for the relief of the poor, a brewhouse was turned into a soup-kitchen, and for months effectual relief was afforded to thousands.

CCLXXXVII. Three Lessons for Children. Prov. i. 8. *"And forsake not the law of thy mother.*

JOHN RUSKIN, in counting up the blessings of his childhood, reckoned these three for first good—Peace: he had been taught the meaning of peace in thought, act, and word; had never heard father's or mother's voice once raised in any dispute, nor seen an angry glance in the eyes of either, nor had ever seen a moment's trouble or disorder in any household matter. Next to this he estimates obedience—he obeyed word or lifted finger of father or mother as a ship her helm, without an idea of resistance. And lastly Faith—nothing was ever promised him that was not given; nothing ever threatened him that was not inflicted, and nothing ever told him that was not true.

CCLXXXVIII. Unconscious Danger. Prov. i. 27. *"When your destruction cometh as a whirlwind."*

THERE is an account of the defeat, forty years ago, of the troops of a distinguished general in Italy. Having taken their stand near Terni, where the waters of the river Velino rush down an almost perpendicular precipice of three hundred feet, and thence toss and foam along through groves of orange and olive trees toward the Tiber, into which it soon empties, they attempted, when pressed by the Austrians, to make their escape over a bridge which spanned the stream just above the falls. In the hurry of the moment, and all unconscious of the insufficient strength of the structure, they rushed upon it in such numbers that it suddenly gave way, and precipitated hundreds of the shrieking and now despairing men into the rapid current below. There was no resisting such a tide when once on its bosom. With frightful velocity they were borne along toward the roaring cataract and the terrific gulf whence clouds of impenetrable mist never ceased to rise. A moment more, and they made the awful plunge into the fathomless abyss, from which, amid the roar of the waters, no cry of horror could be heard, no bodies, or even fragments of bodies, could ever be rescued. The peril was wholly unsuspected, but none the less real, and ending in a "destruction" none the less "swift."

May we not see in this the picture of a great throng of

immortal men in respect to their *moral* end? It seems
generally to be assumed that, in our relations to eternity,
there is no danger except that of which we are distinctly
conscious,—which we see, or hear, or feel. But there cannot
be a greater delusion. It would be equally rational
for the blind man, who wanders among pit-falls, or on the
trembling brink of some frightful precipice, to infer that
there is no danger because he sees none. Insensibility to
danger is, in fact, one of the most startling characteristics
of the sinner's condition by nature, just as insensibility in
a mortal disease is one of the most alarming symptoms of
the disease itself.

CCLXXXIX. A Providential Escape. Prov. ii. 8
"He preserveth the way of His saints."

MR. J. HIBBS, a Methodist preacher, had once a providential
escape, which he tells as follows:—"When I was
stationed in Swansea, in the year 1836, I was appointed
delegate to the District Meeting held at St. Ives, Cornwall.
One Captain Gribble offered me a passage in his
vessel. I accepted the offer, and said, 'When are you
going out?' He replied, 'We have got our cargo, and
shall go to-morrow if the wind is fair.' I went to the
dock on Monday, Tuesday, and Wednesday; the wind
was still against him. He then advised me to take the
packet to Bristol, as he said it was quite uncertain when
he should be able to go to sea. I took the packet on the
Thursday morning. We had a very rough passage.
Through mercy we arrived safe in Bristol next morning. I
took coach for Exeter. A very heavy snow fell that day.
(It was on Good Friday; the district meetings were held
in April.) Saturday, took coach for Hayle. On our way,
in going up a certain hill, the horses ran back into a ditch
and upset the coach. It was fortunate that there was a
deal of snow, so that no one was hurt. I arrived at Hayle
between one and two o'clock on Sunday morning. I then
walked to St. Ives, a distance of five miles. I went to
Mr. Driffield's. When he saw me he said, 'Is Joseph yet
alive?' I answered, 'Yes.' He further said, 'We were
informed you were coming with a sailing vessel, and it
appears she is lost, for some of the wreck is come on shore.

We have gone through the stationing, and left you without a station.' I was given to understand that on the morning I left for Bristol the vessel went out. The wind was fair, but after being two hours at sea, all went to the bottom, captain and crew."

CCXC. A Good Man's Diary. Prov. ii. 20.
"Walk in the way of good men, and keep the paths of the righteous."

From an examination of Edwards' diary, we can account, humanly speaking, for his eminence as a Christian. Take these extracts for example:—

"*Resolved*,—Never to lose one moment of time, but to improve it in the most profitable way I possibly can.

"*Resolved*,—To live with all my might while I do live.

"*Resolved*,—To live so at all times, as I think best in my most devout frames, and when I have the clearest notions of the things of the gospel and another world.

"*Resolved*,—To study the Scriptures so steadily, constantly, and frequently, as that I may find, and plainly perceive, myself to grow in the knowledge of the same.

"*Resolved*,—To ask myself at the end of every day, week, month, and year, wherein I could possibly in any respect have done better.

"*Resolved*,—Never to give over, nor in the least to slacken my fight with my corruption, however unsuccessful I may be.

"*Resolved*,—After afflictions, to inquire what I am the better for them; what good I have got by them; and what I might have got by them.

"I think it a very good way to examine dreams every morning when I awake; what are the nature, circumstances, principles, and ends of my imaginary actions and passions in them, in order to discern what are my prevailing inclinations, etc.

"How it comes about I know not, but I have remarked it hitherto, that at these times when I have read the Scriptures most, I have evermore been most lively and in the best frame.

"Determined, when I am indisposed to prayer, always to premeditate what to pray for, and that it is better that the prayer should be of almost any shortness than that my mind should be almost continually off from what I say.

"I have loved the doctrines of the gospel; they have been to my soul like green pastures. The way of salvation by Christ has appeared in a general way glorious and excellent, most pleasant and most beautiful. It has often seemed to me that it would in a great measure spoil heaven to receive it in any other way.

"There are very few requests that are proper for an impenitent man that are not also, in some sense, proper for the godly.

"Though God has forgiven and forgotten your past sins, yet do not forget them yourself; often remember what a wretched bond-slave you were in the land of Egypt.

"One new discovery of the glory of Christ's face will do more toward scattering clouds of darkness in one minute than examining old experience, by the best marks that can be given through a whole year."

CCXCI. Giving a Tenth to the Lord. PROV. iii. 9. *"Honour the Lord with thy substance, and with the first-fruits of all thine increase."*

MRS. ISABELLA GRAHAM had received £1,000 unexpectedly, and, true to the godly habit which she had maintained through days of affluence and days of straitness, she put £100 at once into the bag, which had never received so large a sum before. The circumstance was never mentioned by her; but after her death this entry was found in her diary: "Quick, quick, before my heart gets hard."

CCXCII. In the Far Country. PROV. iv. 14. *"Enter not into the path of the wicked, and go not in the way of evil men."*

THE following is a strange incident in the early life of John Welch, who became one of the saintliest of Scotland's Reformed pastors. When a youth, he was sent to the grammar-school, probably at Dumfries; but so deeply fixed had his early unsettled habits become, that he proved insubordinate, and running away from school, joined himself to some robbers, whom he accompanied on their moss-trooping expeditions to the English border.

It is strange to find one afterwards so eminent for grace in such a connection. The bold fiery spirit he then evinced continued through life, but softened by deep communion with his Master, and turned into other and better channels. His youthful dreams of freedom and plenty, as is usual in parallel cases, came to a speedy conclusion. The expeditions, so far as he was concerned, were barren of success, and his clothes were at length worn to rags. The rough camp-life, with its exposure to all weathers, involuntary fastings, and sudden alarms, did not prove so agreeable in reality and in prospect, and like his prototype, the prodigal of the parable, he began to turn relenting and longing thoughts to his father's house. Indeed, he appears really to have been visited in that far country of famine by powerful workings of the Spirit of God. It seems that while he came to himself, he began to turn towards God as well as his father's house. It was the critical turning-point, the Hercules' choice, that sooner or later, and in some form, comes to every youth. Young Welch made a sudden and decided resolve, really, we think, through the grace of God, whom he had previously despised. He escaped from his robber-companions for good and all, and set out with all speed for his father's house. But the elder Welch was not a man to be trifled with, and that his son well knew, and the difficulty of facing him grew more formidable the nearer he came to his house. At length, arrived at the town of Dumfries, that lay on his way, he betook himself to the house of his aunt, Agnes Forsyth, to whom he communicated his sad plight. There he stayed for some days, not daring to return home. Meantime his father arrived on business in Dumfries, and having called on his cousin, Mrs. Forsyth, they sat and talked a while. At length she said, "Have you ever heard any news of your son John?"

"O cruel woman!" exclaimed the father with a burst of sorrow, "how can you name him to me? The first news I expect to hear of him is that he is hanged for a thief."

"Many a profligate boy," she answered, "has become a virtuous man."

But the father refused all the comfort she continued to

give, and at length suspecting something, he asked whether she knew his lost son was yet alive.

She answered, Yes, he was, and she hoped he should prove a better man than he was a boy; and with that she called upon him to come to his father. He came with every mark of heartfelt grief; and weeping, he kneeled and besought his father for Christ's sake to pardon his misbehaviour, and engaged to become a new man. His father, however, received him with reproaches and threats; but at length, through the importunate mediation of his cousin, and his own paternal relenting feelings, he was persuaded to receive him back to favour.

CCXCIII. Running from Sin. PROV. iv. 15. *"Avoid it, pass not by it, turn from it, and pass away."*

A LITTLE girl, in the days when the conversion of children was not the subject of as much prayer as now, applied for membership in a Baptist Church. "Were you a sinner," asked an old deacon, "before this change of which you now speak?" "Yes, sir," she replied. "Well, are you now a sinner!" "Yes, sir; I feel I am a greater sinner than ever." "Then what change is there in you?" "I don't quite know how to explain it," she said; "but I used to be a sinner running after sin, and now I hope I am a sinner running from sin." They received her, and for years she was a bright and shining light, and now she lives where there is no sin to run from.

CCXCIV. A Contrast. PROV. iv. 18. *"The path of the just is as the shining light, that shineth more and more unto the perfect day."*

WILLIAM WILBERFORCE, in his old age, meeting one of the companions of his youth whom he had not seen for many years, went up to him and said, "You and I, my lord, were well acquainted formerly." "Ah, Mr. Wilberforce!" he replied, cordially; and then added, "you and I are a great many years older now." "Yes, we are," returned the aged disciple of Christ; "and for my part I can truly say that I do not regret it." "Don't you!" exclaimed the nobleman, with an eager and almost incredulous voice, and a look of wondering dejection.

How affecting and characteristic the contrast. The aged Christian cheerful, the aged nobleman sad; the heaven-born child of God hopeful, the high-born child of earth desponding; the one gladdened by the bright and brightening glory of his faith and love, the other dismayed to find light after light going out, and darkness thickening around; the one rejoicing in the hope of being ever with the Lord, the other trembling at the very thought of the world to come.

CCXCV. Boys' Temptations. PROV. iv. 27. "*Remove thy foot from evil.*"

FULLER was only a boy of sixteen when he became known as a professed follower of Jesus Christ. The temptations, therefore, which assailed him at the outset, were boys' temptations. For example, as the spring of 1770 came on, the young people of the town met as usual in the evenings for youthful exercises; and on the occasion of a wake or a feast, there were special "on-goings." In these the young disciple had formerly taken his part. Now, however, he shunned them as injurious to his spiritual "interests;" and he tells us, that to avoid being drawn into them, or being harassed by even the sound of them reaching his ears, he began a practice which he continued with great peace and comfort for several years. "Whenever a feast or holiday occurred, instead of sitting at home by myself, I went to a neighbouring village to visit some Christian friend, and returned when all was over. By this step I was delivered from those mental participations in folly which had given me so much uneasiness. *Thus the seasons of temptation became to me times of refreshing from the presence of the Lord.*" This was, indeed, being more than a conqueror—turning what might have been an occasion of sin into a means of grace. It was a walking in the Spirit, that he might not be seduced into fulfilling the lusts of the flesh.

CCXCVI. The Wild Huntsman. PROV. v. 22. "*His own iniquities shall take the wicked himself, and he shall be holden with the cords of his sins.*

THE Germans have an ancient mythical legend which, with its fearful imagery, teaches an impressive lesson. A nobleman, with horse and hounds, sets forth on the Sabbath for a hunting excursion. The church bells, sounding out on the air their invitations to worship, call him in vain, as he passes. On his right a shadowy rider, on a white horse, attending him, pleads with him to desist from his madness; while on the left a black-visaged companion, bestriding a black steed, urges on the chase. So on he dashes, over highway and field, trampling down harvests and flocks, scoffing at the cries of the husbandman, till invading the sacred seclusion of a holy man, he is doomed *to continue the hunt for ever.* Then suddenly the glare of an unearthly light flashes on field and grove. The heavens darken with storm-clouds overhead, and the earth opens beneath. Demon fingers reach up from below toward the terrified rider; while howling hell-hounds spring from yawning abysses to pursue him. So, with ghastly face, ever turned backward in horror, amidst curses resounding through all the air, he rides, from age to age, the race of death.

It is but a feeble and shadowy image of the meaning of those words of Biblical forewarning: "His own iniquity shall take the wicked himself, and he shall be holden in the cords of his sins." How often an infatuated worldling is startled for a moment, half resolved to break from the bondage of sin; then, yielding to the old fascination again, he rushes on, and "the last state of that man is worse than the first."

CCXCVII. The Fatal Grasp. Prov. vi. 15. "*Without remedy, suddenly shall he be broken.*"

Travellers who visit the Falls of Niagara are directed to a spot on the margin of the precipice over the boiling current below, where a gay young lady a few years since lost her life. She was delighted with the wonders of the unrivalled scene; and ambitious to pluck a flower from a cliff where no human hand had before ventured, as a memorial of her own daring, she leant over the verge and caught a glimpse of the surging waters far down the battlement of rocks, while fear for a moment held her motionless. But there hung the lovely blossom upon which her heart was fixed, and her arm was outstretched to grasp the beautiful flower. The turf yielded to her pressure, and with a shriek she descended like a fallen star to the rocky shore, and was borne away gasping in death.

Every hour life's sands are sliding from beneath incautious feet; and, with sin's fatal flower in the unconscious hand, the trifler goes to his doom.

CCXCVIII. The Ochre Spring. PROV. vi. 27, 28. *"Can a man take fire in his bosom, and his clothes not be burned? Can one go upon hot coals, and his feet not be burned?"*

ON the moors of Yorkshire there is a stream of water, which goes by the name of the "Ochre Spring." It rises high up in the hills, and runs on bright and sparkling for a short distance, when it suddenly becomes a dark and muddy yellow. What is the reason of this? Why, it has been passing through a bed of ochre, and so it flows on for miles, thick and sluggish, useless and unpleasant. The world is full of such "beds of ochre." Fairs and races, sinful companions, bad books—all such things are just like beds of ochre; *connection with them is pollution.*

CCXCIX. Purity of Character. PROV. vii. 1. *"My son, keep my words, and lay up my commandments with thee."*

THERE grows a bloom and beauty, over the beauty of the plum and apricot, more exquisite than the fruit itself—a soft, delicate flush that overspreads its blushing cheek. Now, if you strike your hand over that, it is gone for ever; for it never grows but once. The flower that hangs in the morning impearled with dew, arrayed as a queenly woman never was arrayed with jewels: once shake it so that the beads roll off, and you may sprinkle water over it as you please, yet it can never be made again what it was when the dew fell silently on it from heaven. On a frosty morning you may see panes of glass covered with landscapes—mountains, lakes, and trees, blended in a beautiful, fantastic picture. Now, lay your hand upon the glass, and by a scratch of your finger, or by the warmth of your palm, all the delicate tracery will be obliterated. So there is in youth a beauty and purity of character which, when once touched and defiled, can never be restored—a fringe more delicate than frostwork, and which, when torn and broken, will never be re-embroidered. He who has spotted and soiled his garments in youth, though he may seek to make them white again, can never wholly do it, even were he to wash them with his tears. When a young man leaves his father's house, with the blessing of a mother's tears still wet upon his brow, if he once lose that early purity of character, it is a spot that he can never make whole again. Such is the consequence of crime. Its effects cannot be eradicated; it can only be forgiven.

CCC. A Young Man Void of Understanding.
PROV. vii. 7. "*I discerned among the youths a young man void of understanding.*

THE late Rev. Dr. Bedell, father of Bishop Bedell, of Ohio, was a very excellent Episcopal preacher in the city of Philadelphia. He was full of love for Christ and the souls of men, and under his preaching many were turned to righteousness who are now stars in his crown of rejoicing. As the crowd in his church one evening were waiting for the sermon, and the glowing-hearted minister stood in the holy place ready to begin, a young stranger entered the door of the church just in time to catch the words of this text. He was a wild, thoughtless, wicked youth, who had been invited to go and hear Dr. Bedell. But he had refused, with the profane remark that he would not go to church to hear Jesus Christ himself. This evening he was walking by the church, and an impulse, sudden and irresistible, urged him in. As he stood inside of the door, Dr. Bedell announced as his text, "I discerned among the youths a young man void of understanding."

The text was a sermon. It was the word of God, sharper than a two-edged sword. It discerned the thoughts and intents of his heart. The Spirit of God sent it home to his conscience. He had been an unbeliever and despiser of the gospel; but the eyes of his mind were opened. He had been a profligate; his sins were set in order before him. He was struck through as with a dart, when the folly and madness of his past life were revealed in the light of the gospel. The faithful preacher unfolded the exceeding foolishness of a life of sensual pleasure, idleness, frivolity, and the inevitable end of such a career. It is recorded of this young man that he became a regular attendant on the ministry of Dr. Bedell, a member of his Church, and a useful Christian.

CCCI. A Pious Son. Prov. viii. 17. *"I love them that love Me; and those that seek Me early shall find Me."*

This incident is found in the life of Reginald Heber, Lord Bishop of Calcutta. "One day when Reginald was at the age of fourteen, his mother missed her 'Companion to the Altar.' Search was made for it among all the servants, but it was nowhere to be found. After three weeks' fruitless inquiry, it was given up as lost, till at length she happened to mention it to Reginald, who immediately brought it to her, saying it had deeply interested him; and he begged permission to accompany his mother to the altar when the sacrament was next administered. Penetrated with gratitude to God for giving her so pious a son, Mrs. Heber burst into tears of joy as she cheerfully assented to his request.

CCCII. A Successful Life. Prov. x. 7. *"The memory of the just is blessed."*

Early in life the late Earl Cairns' interest in spiritual things began, and his love for the Bible and the means of grace. There was all through his life a gradual growth in grace, "going and growing" "from strength to strength;" "the path of the just is as the shining light, that shineth more and more unto the perfect day." When a little boy, he wrote for the *Church Missionary Gleaner*. One treatise on Psalm xiv. was considered very remarkable, in which he went into details on the spiritual meaning of the verses. When twenty-three he always rose at four a.m., in order to give time to God's Word and prayer before his legal work at six. For years after his marriage he conducted family prayers at 7.45 a.m. His invariable rule was to rise one hour and a half before that time to read the Bible and pray. This early rising continued during his busy life at the Bar, and in the House of Commons, though often not more than two hours in bed. What a lesson this is to us all! Surely this was the secret of his successful life, that he would allow nothing to come between him and God, and would not lose the quiet time alone with his Father in the early morning. His life was a life of prayer and dependence upon God. Before any work which required more than the usual effort and wisdom he spent time in special prayer. He never went to a Cabinet Council or spoke on any important matter without first waiting upon God in private and earnest prayer.

In his dying hours he showed the power which the Gospel exercised upon his soul. He conversed with those around him up to the last moment almost, in a calm and peaceful tone, indicating the depth of his trust in Christ as his Saviour.

CCCIII. Acorn Shells. PROV. x. 4. *"The hand of the diligent maketh rich."*

ON many parts of our coasts, between high-water and low-water marks, the rocks and stones are to be found encrusted all over with a peculiar little shell-fish. It has no power, like the limpet and other such creatures, to move about from place to place in search of food, at least in this the perfect stage of its existence; but wherever it first settles and begins to grow, there it must remain rooted to the spot. But like every other living thing, it waits not in vain upon God, who, in accordance with the nature and habits He has given it, sends it also its meat in due season.

When the tide is out and the rocks are left dry, the little acorn shell is closed and motionless; but when the advancing water begins to wash over it, immediately the jointed shell is opened, and rapidly and regularly the little creature casts forth its silver net into the tide, seeking diligently to gather the provision which the open and liberal hand of the great Creator brings within the reach of the tiniest of His creatures.

It is a beautiful sight on a calm summer day, to look down through the still, clear water, on the side of a rock covered with acorn shells, at the busy little hands waving and grasping in all directions with the utmost grace and agility.

CCCIV. Waiting upon God. PROV. xi. 18. *"To him that soweth righteousness, shall be a sure reward."*

A CHRISTIAN minister was holding a revival meeting in

Edinburgh several years ago, when the president of an infidel society came into the place and tried not only to ridicule what was going on, but to prevent persons coming forward to ask prayer. The minister went up to the man and said, "Are you a Christian?" He replied, "No, I am not." "Do you want to be a Christian?" The man gruffly answered, "No, I do not." The minister was touched, and affectionately said, "Well, shall we kneel down and pray together?" The man exclaimed, "What is the good? I do not believe in prayer!" The minister gently replied, "Well, but allow me to kneel down and pray for you." "You may do so if you like, but it will be of no benefit, for I do not believe in it." The minister knelt down and prayed, and after prayer the infidel president said, "I do not feel any different." The minister replied as he left him, "Ah, wait a while! God sometimes takes His own time."

Two years afterwards the minister met the same man, who exclaimed, "You see, I am just the same; I am not different; your prayer was no use!" The minister said, "Ah, my friend, we will still wait upon God!" Well, some time afterwards, the president of the infidel society was convinced of his error, and entered a religious meeting, and when it was asked, "Does any person present desire our prayers?" he stood up, and in heart-broken tones desired them to pray to God for his soul. The same day he gave his heart to God, and became a devout and exemplary Christian.

CCCV. Dynamite. Prov. xi. 19. *"He that pursueth evil pursueth it to his own death."*

An American minister, towards the close of his sermon, introduced a very powerful and dramatic illustration. "Down by Hell Gate" (in allusion to some well-known place where certain blasting was to be carried out), "the rock is tunnelled, and deep under the solid masses over which men walk with such careless security, there are now laid trains of explosive powder. All seems so safe and firm outwardly, it is hardly possible to imagine that those solid masses will ever be shaken; but the time will come when a tiny spark will fire the whole train, and the mountain will be in a moment rent in the air and torn to atoms. There are men," he said, looking round—and a kind of shudder went through the assembly—"there are men here who are tunnelled, mined; their time will come, not to-day or to-morrow, not for months or years perhaps, but it will come; in a moment, from an unforeseen quarter, a trifling incident, their reputations will be blown to atoms, and what they have sown they will reap—*just that*. There is no dynamite like men's lusts and passions."

CCCVI. No Deaths from Benevolence. PROV. xi. 24. *"There is that scattereth, and yet increaseth; and there is that witholdeth more than is meet, but it tendeth to poverty."*

AN eminent layman, in making a platform missionary speech said, "I have heard of Churches starving out from a saving spirit; but I have never heard of one dying of benevolence. And if I could hear of one such, I would make a pilgrimage to it, by night, and in that quiet solitude, with the moon shining and the aged elm waving, I would put my hands on the moss-clad ruins, and gazing on the venerable scene would say, "Blessed are the dead who die in the Lord."

CCCVII. A Small Offering. PROV. xi. 24. *"There is that witholdeth more than is meet, but it tendeth to poverty."*

DR. HALL tells the story of a Scotchman who sung most piously the hymn,—

"Were the whole realm of nature mine,
That were a present far too small,"

and all through the singing was fumbling in his pocket to make sure of the smallest piece of silver for the contribution-box.

CCCVIII. The Widow and the Sovereign. PROV. xi. 24. *"There is that scattereth, and yet increaseth."*

AT a missionary meeting held soon after the accession of our present Queen, one of the speakers related an anecdote concerning the Duchess of Kent and her royal daughter, which well illustrates how comfort and profit may attend giving liberally to the Lord. About fifty years ago there was a lighthouse on the southern coast, which was kept by a certain godly widow, who, not knowing how otherwise to aid the missionary cause, resolved that during the summer season she would place in the box the total of one day's gratuities received from visitors. Among the callers on a particular day was a lady attired as a widow accompanied by a little girl; and it appears that the two widows, drawn together as it were by common sympathy, conversed on their bereavements, tears mingling with their words. On leaving, the lady left a sovereign with her humble friend, and that day was the one set apart for placing all receipts into the missionary-box! The widow was thrown into a state of perplexity, poverty seeming to plead on the one hand, while her pledged word confronted her on the other. After thinking about the thing for some time, she put half a crown in the box; but on retiring to rest, found conscience sufficiently lively to deprive her of sleep. To obtain relief, she now rose, took back the silver and surrendered the gold, after which rest returned to her eyelids, and in the morning she felt comforted and refreshed. The matter occasioned no further trouble, but a few days afterwards the widow received a franked letter containing £20 from the elder lady above mentioned, and £5 from the younger; the first turning out to have been the Duchess of Kent, and the other the Princess Victoria, who now occupies the British throne.

CCCIX. How to Win Souls. PROV. xi. 30. "*He that winneth souls is wise.*"

TWO clergymen were settled in their youth in contiguous parishes. The congregation of the one had become very much broken and scattered, while that of the other remained large and strong. At a ministerial gathering, Dr. A. said to Dr. B., "Brother, how has it happened that while I have laboured as diligently as you have, and preached better sermons, and more of them, my parish has been scattered to the winds, and yours remains strong and unbroken?" Dr. B. facetiously replied, "Oh, I'll tell you, brother. When you go fishing, you just get a great rough pole for a handle, to which you attach a large cod line and a great hook, and twice as much bait as the fish can swallow. With these you dash up to the brook and throw in your hook with, 'There, bite, you dogs!' Thus you scare away all the fish. When I go fishing, I get a little switching pole, a small line, and just such a hook and bait as the fish can swallow. Then I creep up to the brook and gently slip them in, and I twitch them out till my basket is full."

Said the poet Cowper in a letter to Rev. J. Newton, "No man was ever scolded out of his sins. The heart, corrupt as it is, and because it is so, grows angry if it be not treated with some management and good manners, and scolds again."

CCCX. Kindness to Animals. PROV. xii. 10. "*A righteous man regardeth the life of his beast; but the tender mercies of the wicked are cruel.*"

FRANCIS of Assisi was a passionate lover of nature. Each living thing was a brother or sister to him in a sense where almost ceased to be figurative. Birds, insects, fishes wich his friends and even his congregations; doves were his especial favourites. He gathered them into his convents, and taught them to eat out of his hand, and laid them in his bosom. "My dear sisters," he exclaimed to some starlings who chattered round him as he preached, "you have talked long enough: it is my turn now. Listen to the word of your Creator, and be quiet!" His biographer, Bonaventura, gives the very sermon addressed by the Saint to this audience. "My little sisters," it began, "you should love and praise the Author of your beings who has clothed you with plumage and given you wings to fly when you will. You were the first created of all animals; you sow not, neither do you reap. Without any care of your own He gives you all. Therefore give praise to your bountiful Creator!

The well-known instinct by which animals discover and attach themselves to their rational friends was exhibited whenever Francis came abroad. The leveret did not seek to escape his notice. The half-frozen bees crawled to him in winter time to be fed. A lamb followed him even into the city of Rome. The wild falcon wheeled and fluttered round him.

CCCXI. A Wise Father. Prov. xiii. 1. *"A wise son heareth his father's instruction."*

Mr. Haweis, in "Winged Words," counsels fathers to make friends of their children, and relates this anecdote: "A young man said to me the other day, 'Father's old-fashioned; he doesn't know how money's made now. In his day people went slow in order not to lose. Now we go fast and win.'

"'So,' I said, 'I am glad to hear that; but are you quite sure?' and the young fellow laughed and went away. Some weeks after I met the father; he said, 'John has lost me £1,000.' 'How is that?' 'He has had his lesson, but I have had to pay for it,' said the father. 'He thought he knew better than I did, and could make money fast: "Give me a thousand, and I will turn it over in a week, father." "My dear boy," I said, "I saw through this scheme twenty years ago!" But John would not be convinced. So I thought—well, I can afford to lose £1,000, and the lesson may be worth more than that to John. So I gave him the money, and said, "John, you will lose it." A week later he comes to me: "Father, it's gone! all gone!" and he sits down and breaks out sobbing. He thought I should be very angry, but I only said, "I'm right glad to hear it," and I said no more. John has learnt his lesson, and is not going to speculate any more.'"

CCCXII. Slow to Wrath. Prov. xiv. 29. *"He that is slow to wrath is of great understanding: but he that is hasty of spirit exalteth folly."*

Giacomo Benincasa, the father of that fairest of pre-Reformation Saints, St. Catherine of Sienna, was a just and upright man, ruling his spirit in the fear of God, and with a temper as even as a calm. If he saw any of his household vexed and jarred, he would say cheerfully, 'Now then, don't put yourself out, or give way to unkindness, and God will bless you." And once when brought to the brink of ruin by an enemy, he still preserved his sweetness of spirit, and would calm his wife's complaints by saying, "Let him alone, dear; let him alone, and God will bless you, and show him his error."

CCCXIII. Impatience. PROV. xiv. 29. *"He that is slow to wrath is of great understanding: but he that is hasty of spirit exalteth folly."*

REV. THOMAS SCOTT, having gone on board a packet on one occasion when it did not sail at all punctually to the time which had been named, sat down to read in the cabin. A gentleman who had expressed much impatience and displeasure at the delay, at length addressed himself to him, observing that his quietness was quite provoking; that he seemed ready to put up with anything. His reply was: "Sir, I dare say I shall get to the end of our voyage just as soon as you will!"

CCCXIV. A Soft Answer. PROV. xv. 1. *"A soft answer turneth away wrath; but grievous words stir up anger."*

A LITTLE Sister of the Poor, who went about begging for money and broken food and cast-off clothing for the needy, one day asked help from one who was rich and by position at least a gentleman. He had a great dislike to being asked for alms, and after roughly refusing her, at last even struck the Sister. She only said gently, "That was for myself; now won't you give me something for my poor?" And the man was so ashamed of himself that he gave her a liberal subscription.

CCCXV. The Painted Eye. PROV. xv. 3. *"The eyes of the Lord are in every place beholding the evil and the good."*

SOME years ago there lived in an old-fashioned square on the "south side" of Edinburgh, a widow lady, who, in order to eke out her slender means of subsistence, let part of her house to lodgers. Her husband, who had been a portrait-painter of some note, had but lately died, and left her a nicely-furnished house, though but little means to support it.

A few sketches of his art still remained, and among others which she highly valued was a beautifully-painted eye. At the period in which the painter lived, it was not an uncommon thing among a few eccentric persons to have one of their eyes copied, and presented to a friend as a token of affection.

The painting in question was a remarkable production; the eye being so exquisitely painted, that to an imaginative beholder it seemed to reflect his own feelings, and to respond to them in sorrow or in joy; to flash with anger, or beam with tenderness.

In course of time it happened that a young man, sadly given to evil courses, became the tenant of the widow's parlour where hung the painted eye. A year or two previously he had left his distant home to attend the university, where he was now studying for the medical profession. The parting counsel of his father had been, to remember at all times, and under all circumstances, that *the eye of God was upon him.* He promised, and at first sincerely intended to let this thought regulate his conduct; but trusting to his own strength, and meeting with companions whose love of pleasure and sinful ways too well suited the natural corruption of his unrenewed heart, he plunged recklessly into excess of riot, and almost succeeded in banishing from his mind the recollection that there was a God above, to whom all his ways were known. Judge, then, of his discomfiture and annoyance to see an eye gazing at him from the wall of his new chamber! He tried, but in vain, to hide from its view by sitting with his back towards that part of the room. But the consciousness that it was there, that it was fixed upon him, so disturbed his mind that he could not rest. Remorse and terror seized upon him, and with a desperate effort he rushed to the picture and turned its face to the wall!

The good widow, little surmising that a picture she so highly valued could be in any way distasteful to her lodger, duly turned it round again; and much she wondered when the curious accident occurred again and again; for the unfortunate youth tried in vain to bear the sight of the eye, which now seemed to flash with anger, or again, to gaze upon him with tender reproach. He could not bear it. But he hardened his heart, and finally quitted his lodging.

How is it with thee? Does the remembrance that *God's eye is ever upon thee* rejoice thy heart and influence thy conduct in everything? Art thou working as under the eye of thy Master, who seeth in secret, and will reward thee openly?

CCCXVI. A Word in a Railway Carriage. Prov. xv. 23. *"A word spoken in due season, how good is it!"*

A RETIRED naval officer was once travelling by rail in Lancashire. When the train stopped at some station, a number of cattle-dealers and drovers entered the carriage. They were all excited, and it was soon evident that one of the company was being made a laughing-stock by the rest, and at last he was irritated, and uttered some oaths. The officer put his hand on his shoulder, and said, "Sir, you must not swear." The man looked at him and said, "And pray who made you, sir, a conductor over this carriage?" "No one," replied the officer; "but I am your friend, and you will say so before night." "Indeed I won't," retorted the angry man; "there's many a bad one that goes to meetings." "Too true," replied the officer, "but there's never a swearer that goes to heaven." This caused deep thought, and little more was said; but when the train stopped, the man, much softened, took the officer by the hand, and with real feeling said, "I don't like ye the less for what ye said to me."

CCCXVII. The Word in Season. Prov. xv. 23. *"A word spoken in due season, how good is it!"*

A PENNSYLVANIA family, which need not be named, consisted of father, mother, and two little girls—the elder, Ida, in her ninth year, and Katie, a little over six. The mother had found an interest in Christ four or five months before. Being advised by her pastor to institute family prayer with her two children, she did so every evening. The children usually prayed as well as the mother, and soon satisfied their friends that they had met a spiritual change. Little Katie became deeply interested in her father, and one evening, when about to engage in family devotion, entreated him to come and kneel with them in prayer. He gently replied, "No, Katie; I will lie here on the lounge, and you can pray for me." And they did pray, each in her own simple way, "Lord, help papa, and make him a good man." Shortly after that, when at the table, little Katie said,

"Papa, you must pray before you eat;" but he replied, "Katie, dear, I don't know how to pray." Then she went to him, and putting his hands together in the childish form, told him to pray, "Our Father who art in heaven." By this time he was pretty well broken down, as most any father would have been. He soon became deeply in earnest in seeking Christ, and one day while he was praying, Katie came, and putting her arms around his neck said, "Papa, can't you love Jesus?" One night the father, not being able to sleep, went downstairs to pray. This movement awakened Katie, and she followed him, and putting her arms around his neck, prayed for him most tenderly. With the aid of so loving and faithful a helper, he soon realized a change. He found his Saviour, and openly united with the Church. Who can estimate the joy of that household, and what an illustration it furnishes of the reward which comes from saying the "Word in season"!

CCCXVIII. Greedy of Gain. Prov. xv. 27. *"He that is greedy of gain troubleth his own house."*

A YOUNG man once picked up a sovereign lying in the road. Ever afterwards, as he walked along, he kept his eye steadfastly on the ground, in hopes of finding another. And, in the course of his long life, he did pick up at different times a good amount of gold and silver. But all these days, as he was looking for them, he saw not that the heaven was bright above him, and nature was beautiful around. He never once allowed his eye to look up from the mud and filth in which he sought the treasure; and, when he died a rich old man, he only knew this fair earth of ours as a dirty road to pick up money as we walk along.

CCCXIX. Preaching and Praying. Prov. xv. 29. *"He heareth the prayer of the righteous."*

THERE is a legend to this effect: A certain preacher, whose sermons converted men by scores, received a revelation from heaven that not one of the conversions was owing to his talents or eloquence, but all to the prayers of an illiterate lay brother, who sat on the pulpit steps, pleading all the time for the success of the sermon. It may, in the all-revealing day, be so with us. We may discover, after having laboured long and wearily in preaching, that all the honour belongs to another builder, whose prayers were gold, silver, and precious stones, while our sermonisings being apart from prayer, were but hay and stubble.

CCCXX. A Last Farewell. PROV. xv. 33. *"Before honour is humility."*

ON the occasion of a Welsh minister's death, Mr. Matthew Henry preached the funeral sermon, and thus describes the heavenly frame in which he closed his life on earth: "His solemn farewell to his children and pupils, the good counsel he gave them, the blessing with which he blessed them, and the testimony he bore with his dying lips to the good ways of God wherein he had walked, I hope they will never forget, and that particularly we should remember and practise the last thing he recommended—humility. 'It is,' said he, 'one of the brightest ornaments of a young minister to be humble.' The words of God, which he had made his songs in the house of his pilgrimage, were his delightful entertainment when his tabernacle was in taking down."

CCCXXI. A Bishop's Veneration for Whitefield. PROV. xvi. 7. *"When a man's ways please the Lord, He maketh even his enemies to be at peace with him."*

THE Countess of Huntingdon was converted through the means of her sister, Lady Margaret Hastings, who herself had been converted through the preaching of the lay Methodists.

The Countess sent a message to the Wesleys, avowing her great change, and identifying herself with their religious movements. Her husband, the Earl of Huntingdon, an excellent and pious man, was concerned at this, and recommended her to converse with Dr. Benson, Bishop of Gloucester, his former tutor. The Bishop cautioned her against "Evangelical Methodism;" but the Countess pressed him so hard with the Articles and Homilies of his own Church, that at length he got angry, and abruptly left her, expressing his regret that he had ever laid hands upon George Whitefield, to whom he attributed this change. "My Lord," she replied, "mark my words: when you come upon your dying bed, that will be one of the few ordinations you will reflect upon with complacency." The prediction was singularly verified; for when near his death, the Bishop sent ten guineas to Whitefield, as an expression of his great veneration for his character and work, with a request to be remembered by him in his prayers.

CCCXXII. An Enemy turned into a Friend. Prov. xvi. 7. "*When a man's ways please the Lord, He maketh even his enemies to be at peace with him.*"

DURING Luther's journey, a noble knight of the vicinity, learning that he was to tarry at a certain place, and yearning for the honours and emoluments that would accrue could he be safely caught up and transported to Rome, resolved to hazard the attempt. He ordered his armed retinue to prepare hastily, for there was no time to be lost, the aspiring noble being urged and commended to the task by his confessor, who assured him that he would be doing a good work, and would save many souls. He set out at early dawn, making his way along the picturesque *Berg-Strasse*, or mountain road, that skirts the forest of the Odenwald, between Darmstadt and Heidelberg. Arriving at the gates of Miltenberg in the evening, he found the city illuminated, and the town itself full of people, who had come thither to hear and see Luther.

More indignant than ever was the noble knight; indignation grew to rage when, arriving at his hotel, the host greeted him, "Well, well, Sir Count, has Luther brought you here too? Pity you are too late. You should have heard him. The people cannot cease praising him." In no mood for eulogy, the knight sought the privacy of his room. Awakened in the morning by the matin bell of the chapel, sleep had assuaged his ire, and his thoughts were at home, where he had left an infant daughter at the point of death. As he drew aside his curtain, he saw the flicker of a candle in the window opposite, and waiting a moment heard a deep, manly voice utter the words, "In the name of the Father, and of the Son, and of the Holy Ghost. Amen." He heard the voice further continuing in a strong, fervent petition for the whole Christian Church, and the victory of the holy gospel over sin and the world.

Being a devout man, his interest was aroused, and donning his armour, he inquired of the landlord who that earnest man was that he heard across the street. "That earnest man," responded the landlord, "is the arch heretic Luther himself. Has your grace a message for him?" "Ay," said the knight, "but I will deliver it with my own lips," and with a dubious shake of the head he crossed the street, entered the house, and in a moment stood before the object of his search. Luther instinctively rose from his chair, surprised and not a little disconcerted by the sudden appearance of a stalwart armed knight, perhaps having an unpleasant suspicion of his errand. "What is the object of this visit?" inquired Luther. Twice and thrice he repeated his question before received a reply. At length the knight, having recovered somewhat from the spell upon him, said, "Sir, you are far better than I. God forgive me for intending to harm you. I came here to make you a prisoner; you have made a prisoner of me instead. It is impossible for a man to pray as you pray to be an enemy of the holy Church, a heretic." "God be praised," said Luther, now relieved from his suspicions; 'it is His word and Spirit that has subdued you, not mine, though I may have been chosen to bring His word to honour in Christendom. Go now your way, therefore, in peace, my lord. He that hath begun a good work in you will perform it to Christ's coming. If it be God's will, you shall yet behold miracles; how the Lord will break many swords like yours, and cut the spear in sunder, as He has to-day." Convinced and confirmed, the knight lost no time in making his way homeward, attended by his retinue, now still more curious to know the object of this hasty expedition. Arriving at the bedside of his daughter, he found her now convalescent and out of danger, and falling on his knees he thanked God for all that had happened. A few years later, when Luther confessed his faith before Charles V., among the assembled nobles who stood on Luther's side was this knight, who had once thought to overthrow and destroy him.

CCCXXIII. A Kind Tone of Voice. Prov. xvi. 24.
"*Pleasant words are as an honeycomb, sweet to the soul, and health to the bones.*"

THE law of kindness may be violated in the tones of the voice. "Not so much what my mother said to me, as the way she said it," was once remarked by a despairing young man, who had sadly strayed from the precepts of the parental roof. "Oh," said he, as the tears coursed down his cheeks, "the way my mother said that last thing to me!" Whitefield says, "I carefully sought out those acceptable tones that were like a spell upon the heart, even when the words were unremembered." So wonderfully modulated was Whitefield's voice, that Garrick said "he could make men either laugh or cry by pronouncing the word Mesopotamia."

"Mother," said a little girl, "I like our preacher when he comes to see us, but I don't like to hear him preach." On being asked why, she said, "His preaching sounded like scolding all the time."

CCCXXIV. The Ways of Death. Prov. xvi. 25.
"*There is a way that seemeth right unto a man, but the end thereof are the ways of death.*"

ON the Lake of Geneva there stands a gloomy castle, where prisoners used to be confined, and in it there was a dark dungeon, with a dreadful staircase called the "*oubliettes.*" Sometimes the keeper went to a poor prisoner, and told him that now he was to obtain his life and liberty, and requested him to follow him. The prisoner went along thankful and glad, with visions of home and happiness. He reached the staircase, and was told to go down, step by step, in the darkness, that he might reach the castle gate, and so be free. Alas! it was a broken stair. A few steps down into the darkness, and the next step he took he found no footing, but fell down fifty or sixty feet, to be dashed to pieces amongst rocks, and then to have his mangled body buried in the lake.

CCCXXV. Christian Forbearance. Prov. xvi. 32.
"*He that is slow to anger is better than the mighty.*"

IN Mungo Park's relation of his travels in Africa, he gives

a striking example of the good effects of Christian forbearance, even among uncivilized men. He says after having passed through the greatest distresses, he arrived at the village of Song, where the people refused to receive him within the gate, though the country was infested with lions. Here Mungo Park with much difficulty collected grass for his horse, and lay down under a tree near the gate; but being aroused by the roar of a lion, he climbed the tree for safety. The inhabitants, who having believed him to be a Moor, would not admit him, notwithstanding the danger that threatened him, till midnight, when, convinced of their error, they opened the gate, declaring that no Moor ever waited long at the gate of any city without cursing all the inhabitants.

CCCXXVI. A Good Wife is from the Lord.
PROV. xix. 4. "*A prudent wife is from the Lord.*"

SOLOMON says, a prudent or good wife is from the Lord, and not a few have experienced the truth of his assertion. One reason why so many fail to get good wives is, that they do not ask the Lord for them. They follow their own impulses, or the suggestions of interest, and do not ask counsel of God and commit their way unto Him. In the most important of all earthly matters they take counsel of their feelings, and lean to their own understandings.

Thomas Shepherd, the first pastor of Cambridge, and one of the most godly and useful of the New England fathers, acted in accordance with Solomon's doctrine. " Now, about this time, I had a great desire to change my estate by marriage; and I had been praying three years before, that the Lord would carry me to such a place where I might have a meet yoke-fellow."

He was at length invited to take up his abode with Sir Richard Dailey, where his labours were blessed to the conversion of most of the members of the family, one of whom in due time became his yoke-fellow. " And when He had fitted a wife for me," says Mr. S., " He then gave me her, who was a most sweet, humble woman, full of Christ, and a very discerning Christian, a wife who was most incomparably loving to me, and every way amiable

and holy, and endued with a very sweet spirit of prayer.
And thus the Lord answered my desires."

Men may smile at the guileless simplicity with which
he tells his story, but they would do well to imitate his
example.

CCCXXVII. Slothful Habits. PROV. xix. 15. *"Slothfulness casteth into a deep sleep, and an idle soul shall suffer hunger."*

THE following is an anecdote of a venerated servant of
God—Charles Simeon : When I was an undergraduate, I
remember hearing a friend of his relate this anecdote of
him : " We were sitting," he said, " in his room at college,
three or four of us round his table. Dinner finished, we
entered into conversation. Charles Simeon led with that
wonderful power of conversation which so distinguished him.
Turning round to one of us, he said, ' Will you have a nut
to crack ? ' Thinking, for the moment, he referred to the
fruit lying on the table, some indefinite reply was made,
when he remarked with a smile, ' Oh, you do not understand ; I want you to crack a spiritual nut. The nut is a
very small one; it is a single word ; you will find it in the
third chapter of Philippians. I will read the passage to you,
and will you point out the emphatic word in the verse,
' Let us therefore, as many as be perfect, be *thus* minded :
and if in anything ye be otherwise minded, God shall reveal even this unto you.' They all agreed that ' *thus* ' was
the nut, the emphatic word, when he replied, ' Well, which
of you can crack it ? ' One said one thing, and another
said another. At last he replied, ' It seems to me to have
a threefold kernel; let me try and crack the nut, and give
you the kernel. As I read the whole chapter, I find
three prominent thoughts running through it, and they
are all summed up in that little word '*thus.*' Here are the
three—' *No lofty thoughts, no worldly ambition, no slothful
habits.* That is the kernel,' he says. Then he struck out
into a strain of conversation upon the subject, becoming
more and more energetic as he enlarged upon it, until he
came at last to the words, ' no slothful habits,' when he
sprang to his feet with the energy that characterised the
good old man, and ran round the room, as he said, ' Why,

the Apostle talks about running, not creeping, or trifling. Some of us go creeping to heaven, and the wonder is that we ever get there. St. Paul speaks of himself as pressing towards the mark. When a man is running a race he strains his every nerve to win it. Some of us fancy we are to be carried into the kingdom of glory, but if we would win the crown, we must throw all our energies into the race. It is not enough to accept this doctrine, and the theory, but let us remember that God has given us natural powers, in order that we may employ them; and only as we employ them, can we expect to win the prize.'"

CCCXXVIII. A Loan to the Lord. Prov. xix. 17.

"He that hath pity upon the poor lendeth unto the Lord, and that which he hath given will He pay him again."

A POOR man with an empty purse came one day to Michael Feneberg, the godly pastor of Seeg, in Bavaria, and begged three crowns, that he might finish his journey. It was all the money Feneberg had, but as he besought him so earnestly in the name of Jesus, in the name of Jesus he gave it. Immediately after he found himself in great outward need, and seeing no way of relief, he prayed, saying: "Lord, I lent Thee three crowns; Thou hast not yet returned them, and Thou knowest how I need them. Lord, I pray Thee, give them back." The same day a messenger brought a money-letter, which Gossner, his assistant, reached over to Feneberg, saying: "Here, father, is what you expended." The letter contained two hundred thalers, or about one hundred and fifty dollars, which the poor traveller had begged from a rich man for the Vicar; and the childlike old man, in joyful amazement, cried out: " Ah, dear Lord, one dare ask nothing of Thee, for straightway Thou makest one feel so much ashamed."

CCCXXIX. Can you Trust the Security? Prov. xix. 17.

"He that hath pity on the poor lendeth unto the Lord; and that which he hath given will He pay him again."

IT is said that Dean Swift was once called to preach on behalf of a public charity, and having taken the above as his text, he closed the book, and said, "Now, if you can trust the security, *down with your dust*. The collection will be made."

CCCXXX. Children's Help. PROV. xx. 11. *"Even a child is known by his doings, whether his work be pure, and whether it be right."*

THERE was a terrible storm one cold winter's night, a few years ago, and a ship was wrecked just opposite a fishing village in the north. The crew got into a boat and rowed for the shore. They were not a dozen yards from the beach, when their boat grounded on a sand-bar, and stuck fast. The fishermen ran down to help them, and the sailors flung them a rope, and told them to pull with all their might. The fishermen did so; but, though they were very fine fellows, they could not manage it. Then their wives said, "Let us take hold, and pull too." But though the *women* strained every nerve, the boat did not move! At last the *children* asked to join in; and those who could, got hold of the rope, and the rest got hold of their fathers' smocks and their mothers' gowns, and then came the "long pull! and the strong pull! and the pull ALL TOGETHER!" and the thing was done! the boat shot over the sand-bar, and the poor shipwrecked sailors were saved!

The *children's weight made all the difference in the pull!*

CCCXXXI. George Fox and his False Accusers. PROV. xx. 22. *"Say not thou, I will recompense evil; but wait on the Lord, and He shall save thee."*

AFTER being imprisoned for twenty weeks, the faithful servant of Christ, George Fox, was released in 1660. He thus speaks of his false accuser in his journal: "Thus I was set at liberty by the king's command, the Lord's power having wonderfully wrought for the clearing of my innocency, and Porter, who committed me, not daring to appear to make good the charge he had falsely suggested against me. Terror took hold of Justice Porter, for he was afraid I would take the advantage of the law against him for my wrong imprisonment, and thereby undo him, his wife and children. And, indeed, I was put on to make him and the rest examples; but I said I should leave them to the Lord: if the Lord did forgive them, I should not trouble myself with them."

CCCXXXII. Sabbath School Instruction. Prov. xxii. 6. "*Train up a child in the way he should go: and when he is old, he will not depart from it.*"

"SABBATH-SCHOOL instruction, although good as far as it goes, does not supply adequate moral education for the juvenile hordes which infest the streets of our large cities. The interval between Sabbath and Sabbath is too wide. It is like spreading a net with meshes seven inches wide instead of one, before a shoal of herrings. By the great gap of the week the little Arabs easily slip through, in spite of the stout string which you extend across their path on the Sabbath evening. Ply the work by all means, and ply it hopefully. Labour for the Lord in that department will not be lost. Saving truth is thereby deposited in many minds, which the Spirit of God will make fruitful in a future day. Ply the work of Sabbath schools, but let not the existence and abundance of these efforts deceive us into the belief that the work is adequately done. The Sabbath school cannot train up a child. The six days' training at home, if it be evil, will, in the battle of life, carry it over the one day's teaching in the school, however good it may be."

CCCXXXIII. Knowing the Scriptures from a Child. Prov. xxii. 6. "*Train up a child in the way he should go.*"

JOHN RUSKIN, in his "Præterita," describes his daily Bible lessons which his mother taught him. He says: "I have next with deep gratitude to chronicle what I owed to my mother for the resolutely consistent lessons which so exercised me in the Scriptures as to make every word of them familiar to my ear in habitual music; yet in that familiarity reverenced, as transcending all thought, and ordaining all conduct. This she effected, not by her own sayings or personal authority, but simply by compelling me to read the book thoroughly for myself. As soon as

I was able to read with fluency, she began a course of Bible work with me, which never ceased till I went to Oxford. She read alternate verses with me, watching, at first, every intonation of my voice, and correcting the false ones, till she made me understand the verse, if within my reach, rightly and energetically. It might be beyond me altogether; that she did not care about; but she made sure that, as soon as I got hold of it at all, I should get hold of it by the right end. If a name was hard, the better the exercise in pronunciation; if a chapter was tiresome, the better lesson in patience; if loathsome, the better lesson in faith that there was some use in its being so outspoken. After our chapters (from two to three a day, according to their length, the first thing after breakfast, and no interruption from servants allowed—none from visitors, who either joined in the reading, or had to stay upstairs—and none from any visitings or excursions, except real travelling), I had to learn a few verses by heart, or repeat, to make sure I had not lost, something of what was already known; and with the chapters thus gradually possessed from the first word to the last, I had to learn the whole body of the fine old Scottish paraphrases, which are good, melodious, and forceful verse, and to which, together with the Bible itself, I owe the first cultivation of my ear in sound."

CCCXXXIV. The Robber's Bible. PROV. xxii. 6.

"Train up a child in the way he should go: and when he is old, he will not depart from it."

THERE was a strange auction in one of the deep, inaccessible dells of the Black Forest, about a century ago. It was in the dead of night. The place was lighted by torches, which cast a ghastly glare through the darkness of the abyss. Savage-looking men, armed to the teeth, were sitting in a circle, while one stood in the midst, holding up articles for sale. It was a gang of brigands, who that evening had robbed a stage-coach. According to their custom, they were engaged in selling the stolen articles among themselves. After a good many pieces of dress and travelling-bags had been disposed of, and while the glass and the bottle were going from hand to hand, and each member of the company vied with his neighbour in making unseemly jokes and setting the assembly in a roar, a New Testament was held up last of all. The man who acted as auctioneer introduced this "article" with some blasphemous remarks, which made the cavern resound with laughter. One of the company suggested jokingly that he should read a chapter for their edification. This was unanimously applauded, and the auctioneer, turning up a page at random, began reading in a voice of mock-devotion. While the company were greatly amused at this sacrilegious scoffing, it was not observed that one of them, a middle-aged man, who was one of the oldest members of the gang, and used to be foremost both in their crimes and in their debauchery, became silent, and clasping his hands on his knees, was absorbed in deep thought. The passage which the auctioneer read was the same which that man's father had read thirty years ago at family worship on the morning of the day when he, to escape the hands of the police, fled from the parental dwelling, never to return again. At the sound of the words, which he remembered so well, the happy family circle of which he had been a member, rose to his fancy. In his imagination he saw them all seated round the breakfast-table, which was crowned with the blessings of a new day. He saw his venerable old father sitting with the open Bible reading the chapter that was to prepare them for prayer. He saw his kind, tender-hearted mother sitting by his father's side, attentively listening to the Word of God. He saw himself, with his brothers and sisters, joining in the devotional exercise, which entreated for them the guidance, protection, and blessing of God during the day. He saw it all as clearly before his mind as if it had happened that morning. Since leaving home, he had never opened a Bible, never offered up a prayer, never heard a single word that reminded him of God and eternity. But now, at this moment, it was as if his soul awoke out of a long sleep of thirty years—as if the snow of a long, long winter melted away on a sudden at the sound of that well-known Bible word; and all the words which his good father had spoken to him from his childhood, and all the lessons, admonitions, and prayers of his pious mother—which then were scornfully given to the winds—now came flying back to his memory, as the winter crop bursts forth through the snow when the vernal sun unshackles the fields, and causes the hidden life to rise from its long dreary grave. Perfectly absorbed in those hallowed recollections, he forgot all that was round him, heard nothing of all the scoffing, laughing, and blaspheming that was passing in his presence, until, on a sudden, he was awaked out of his reverie by a rude tap on the shoulder, which was accompanied by the question, "Now, old dreamer, what will you give for that book ? You need it more than any one of us, for you are undoubtedly the biggest sinner under the firmament." "So I am," he answered, struck to the very bottom of his heart by the truth which he recognised in that rough joke. "Give me the book. I will pay its full price." The next day the brigands dispersed through the neighbourhood to turn their bargains into money. The man who bought the bible went also on his errand ; but he directed his steps to no receiving-house. He repaired to a lonely place, where he spent the whole day and night in the agonies of unspeakable remorse, and but for the consoling words which his Bible held out to him, he would certainly have made away with himself. But God had mercy upon that repenting sinner, and sent a message of peace and reconciliation to his heart. The next day, on entering a village where he resolved to speak to a minister, he heard that the gang was overtaken the night before by a detachment of soldiers, and taken to prison. His resolution was confirmed now all the more. He told the minister the whole of his life's story, and requested him to direct him to the police office, where he gave himself up to the hands of justice. This proof of the sincerity of his repentance saved his life. His comrades were all put to death, but he obtained a reprieve from the Grand Duke, to whom his story was reported. After an imprisonment of some years, he was set free on account of his exemplary conduct. A Christian nobleman took him into his service, and he proved a blessing to his master's household, till he died in peace, praising Jesus Christ who came into the world to save sinners, of whom he confessed himself to be the chief.

CCCXXXV. Rebuking a King. Prov. xxii. 11. *"For the grace of his lips the king shall be his friend."*

THE timidity which hesitates to rebuke profanity was once shamed by a king who had been himself rebuked for profanity. Riding along the highway in disguise, and seeing a soldier at an inn, he stopped and asked him to drink ale with him. On an oath which the king uttered while they were drinking, the soldier remarked, "I am sorry to hear young gentlemen swear."

His majesty took no notice of it, but swore again.

The soldier immediately said, "I'll pay part of the ale, if you please, and go; for I so hate swearing that, if you were the king himself, I should tell you of it."

"Should you indeed?" asked the king.

"I should," was the emphatic reply of his subject.

Not long after, the king gave him an opportunity to be "as good as his word." Having invited some lords to dine with him, he sent for the soldier, and bade him to stand near him, in order to serve him if he was needed. Presently the king, not now in disguise, uttered an oath; And deferentially the soldier immediately said, "Should not my lord and king fear an oath?"

Looking at the heroic soldier, and then at his company of obsequious noblemen, the king severely remarked: "There, my lords, is an honest man. He can respectfully remind me of the great sin of swearing; but you can sit here and let me stain my soul by swearing, and not so much as tell me of it!"

CCCXXXVI. A Drunkard's Child. Prov. xxiii. 21. *"The drunkard and the glutton shall come to poverty."*

A SUNDAY-SCHOOL teacher handed to her scholars little slips of paper on which was printed the question, "What have I to be thankful for?" Among the replies that were given on the following Sunday was the following pathetic sentence, written by a little girl who had learned by bitter processes the painful truths it told: "I am thankful there are no public-houses in heaven."

CCCXXXVII. One who Delighted to Honour his Parents. PROV. xxiii. 24, 25. *"He that begetteth a wise child shall have joy of him. Thy father and thy mother shall be glad, and she that bare thee shall rejoice."*

A PLEASING incident is told of the late Henry Fawcett, Postmaster-General. He was very much attached to his old home, and he had been in the habit of writing a weekly letter to his parents. He happened one day to ask his sister what gave them most pleasure? She replied, "Your letters." From that time, though overwhelmed with official and parliamentary work, he wrote twice, instead of once a week. These letters are homely and affectionate, and everywhere imply that constant desire to give pleasure, which is more significant than the strongest professions of love.

CCCXXXVIII. Calvin's Motto. PROV. xxiii. 26. *"My son, give me thy heart."*

CALVIN'S seal had engraven on it a hand holding a burning heart, with the motto, "I give Thee all; I keep back nothing for myself!"

CCCXXXIX. For Teachers and Parents. PROV. xxiv. 10. *"If thou faint in the day of adversity, thy strength is small."*

THE Rev. Dr. Tyng, speaking of Sunday-school teachers who "get tired" and leave their classes, says: "Everybody gets tired except the devil; he is a bishop that is never out of his diocese." There is as much truth as blunt force in the remark. It is worth keeping in mind on entering the Christian campaign.

CCCXL. The Helping Hand. PROV. xxiv. 11. *"If thou forbear to deliver them that are drawn unto death, and those that are ready to be slain."*

THESE words which follow speak more loudly to us because they come from Bishop Simpson, one who was himself an illustration of what he commends:

"I shall never forget the feelings I had once when climbing one of the pyramids of Egypt. When half-way up, my strength failing, I feared I should never be able to reach the summit or get back again. I well remember the help given, by Arab hands, drawing me on farther; and the step I could not quite make myself, because too great for my wearied frame, the little help given me—sometimes more and sometimes less—enabled me to go up, step by step, step by step, until at last I reached the top, and breathed the pure air, and had a grand outlook from that lofty height.

"And so, in life's journey, we are climbing. We are feeble. Every one of us, now and then, needs a little help; and, if we have risen a step higher than some other, let us reach down for our brother's hand, and help him to stand beside us. And thus, joined hand in hand, we shall go on conquering, step by step, until the glorious eminence shall be gained. Oh, how many need help in this world—poor afflicted ones; poor sorrowing ones; poor tempted ones, who have been overcome, who have been struggling, not quite able to get up the step; trying, falling; trying, falling; trying, desponding; hoping, almost despairing! Oh, give such a one help, a little kindly aid, and the step may be taken, and another step may then be taken; and, instead of dying in wretchedness at the base, he may, by a brother's hand, be raised to safety, and finally to glory.

CCCXLI. An Evangelist. PROV. xxv. 11. *"A word fitly spoken is like apples of gold in pictures of silver."*

DR. TALMAGE says, "How few Christian people there are who understand how to fasten the truths of God and religion to the souls of men. Truman Osborne, one of the evangelists who went through this country some years ago, had a wonderful art in the right direction. He came to my father's house one day, and while we were all seated in the room, he said: 'Mr. Talmage, are all your children Christians?' Father said: 'Yes, all but De Witt.' Then Truman Osborne looked down into the fire-place, and began to tell a story of a storm that came on the mountains, and all the sheep were in the fold: but there was one lamb outside that perished in the storm. Had he looked me in the eye, I should have been angered when he told that story; but he looked into the fire-place, and it was so pathetically and beautifully done that I never found any peace until I was sure I was inside the fold, where the other sheep are."

CCCXLII. Balaam's Ass. PROV. xxvi. 5. *"Answer a fool according to his folly."*

"Do you really believe that an ass ever spoke to Balaam?" queried a man who prided himself on his intellect. Coleridge, to whom the question was put, reflected: "My friend, I have no doubt whatever that the story is true. I have been spoken to in the same way myself." The man of the inquiring mind retired for meditation.

He was answered according to his folly, which is often as good a form of reply as such quibblers deserve. Much of the beauty of the answer lay in the courtesy which said so little but meant so much. A hard word becomes all the harder by being softly spoken. To have called the man an ass would have shown great weakness, and betrayed warm temper, but Coleridge worded his remark well, and left the hearer to find out the sting for himself. Here is a lesson of practical common-sense which those who deal with sceptics would do well to learn.

CCCXLIII. Seeking the Society of Christians.
PROV. xxvii. 9. *"Ointment and perfume rejoice the heart; so doth the sweetness of a man's friend by hearty counsel."*

"Ane stick 'll never burn! Put more wood on the fire, laddie; ane stick 'll never burn!" my old Scotch grandfather used to say to his boys. Sometimes, when the fire in the heart burns low, and love to the Saviour grows faint, it would glow warm and bright again if it could only touch another stick. We are weak and imperfect. A hundred things—health, digestion, anxieties, little frets and cares—hinder our soul's progress. The spirit cannot soar, for the flesh constantly keeps it down. There is a true life begun in us, but it flickers like a candle in the wind.

What we need, next to earnest prayer to God and communion with Christ, is communion with each other. "Where two or three are gathered together," the heart burns; love kindles to a fervent heat. Friends, let us frequent the society of those who are fellow-pilgrims with us to Canaan's happy land. "Ane stick'll never burn" as a great, generous pile will be sure to.

CCCXLIV. Trust Not in Vain. Prov. xxviii. 25. *"He that putteth his trust in the Lord shall be made fat."*

DURING the commercial panic of 1837, there lived in the city of W——ton an earnest Christian worker. He had a large family, but was not rich in this world's goods. The denomination of which he was a member had for several years been struggling to complete their house of worship. He being an example unto the brethren, had made large contributions, and ere he was aware had given several thousand dollars to finish the church. Clouds of business depression were now gathering thick, and the storm of ruin was ready to break forth. About this time he bought and shipped a valuable cargo to a wealthy gentleman in New York. Several weeks after he was surprised by the cashier of the bank hastily entering his place of business, saying in an excited manner: "Sir! that New York man has failed, and the draft for the cargo has been returned, protested. Things are growing darker all the time; no one can tell what the end may be." The cashier was astonished to see how self-possessed he remained. He forgot that it had been written of the upright man, "He shall not be afraid of evil tidings: his heart is fixed, trusting in the Lord." But it was a great blow to him. What could be done? The draft was for thousands of dollars. The bank could grant no favours, and was bound to have the money. Collections were out of the question. Real estate would not bring one-fourth of its value. Ruin stared him in the face. There was no escape. It took a firm eye and a brave heart to stand in his home among his little ones and see the grim spectres of poverty and want overshadowing them.

Thirty days of grace were granted, but they were days of torture and almost despair. His refuge was in prayer. The last day came. The family were assembled as usual at the Throne of Grace. He poured out his soul unto God. As Hezekiah of old spread out the letter of the wicked

King of Babylon before the Lord, and prayed over it, so did he state his case to the Almighty. He arose comforted. Resignation had come. Yes, I can be poor. Yes, I can walk where God leads me. Yes, I can go to the bank to-day and make myself a pauper, sign away house, home, and all. God is still mine, my family are still mine—the promises in God's word are not changed; heaven shall be mine. I trust God for the future.

He dressed carefully, so as to go through his sad duties decently, and sat down to wait until the bank opened. While sitting there, three letters were brought in. He opened the first. Could his eyes deceive him? It contained a draft for $1,000, sent by a brother in New England. The next letter was from a New York bank, authorizing him to draw on it for any amount sufficient to tide him over his difficulties. The third letter was from the man to whom the cargo had been sent, telling him to draw again for the full amount, and the draft would be honoured. The tears of thanksgiving streamed down his cheeks. "Now do I know that there is a God in Israel: I was brought low, and He helped me."

When he reached the bank, the directors were in session discussing his case. They arose as he entered. The president, taking his hand, said: "Sir, we feel very sorry for you in your great misfortune. You have our deepest sympathy. We only wish we could help you."

"Gentlemen," he replied, "I am very much obliged to you for your kindness and sympathy. But I am all right," and forthwith cast the drafts on the table. Then there were hearty hand-shakings and congratulations. That which, according to human eyesight, came so near being his ruin, gave him thenceforth unbounded credit, and laid the foundation of a large fortune.

He was strong, active, cheerful at the age of eighty-four, increased in goods, full of years, still trusting in God, waiting, like Abraham, to be gathered unto his people. "Trust in the Lord, and do good; and He shall bring it to pass."

CCCXLV. A Wise Decision. Prov. xxx. 8, 9. *"Give me neither poverty nor riches; feed me with food convenient for me: Lest I be full and deny Thee, and say, Who is the Lord? or lest I be poor, and steal, and take the name of my God in vain."*

We have a quaint love-letter of Joseph Alleine's, written in 1655 to Mistress Theodosia, his future wife. It is full of beautiful godliness and manliness. In it he speaks of accepting a charge at Taunton, where the encouragements in point of maintenance were small. These are some of the principles upon which he went:—

"First, I lay this for a foundation, that a man's life consisteth not in the abundance of the things that he possesseth. It was accounted a wise prayer that Agur put up of old, that he might only be fed with food convenient for him. And certain it is, that where men have least of the world, they esteem it least, and live more by faith and in dependence upon God, casting their care and burden upon Him. The Holy Ghost seems to make it a privilege to be brought to a necessity of living by faith, as I think I have formerly hinted thee, out of Deuteronomy xi. 10, 11, where Canaan is preferred before Egypt, in regard to its dependence upon God for the former and latter rain, which in Egypt they could live without, and have supplies from the river. And certainly could we that are unexperienced, but feel the thorns of those cares and troubles that there are in gathering and keeping much, and the danger when riches increase of setting our hearts upon them, we should prize the happiness of a middle condition much before it.

"Secondly, I take this for an undoubted truth, that a dram of grace is better than a talent of wealth. 'Tis a strange thing to see how Christians generally do judge so carnally of things, looking to the things that are seen and temporal, and not the things that will stick by us to eternity. What is it worth a year? Is the maintenance certain and sure, and what changes are there like to be? These are the questions we commonly ask first. Yet—What good am I like to do? What good am I like to get? These should be the main interrogatories."

CCCXLVI. Ingratitude to Parents. Prov. xxx. 17.
"The eye that mocketh at his father, . . . the ravens of the valley shall pick it out."

This is a terrible denunciation against ingratitude to parents, and even in the present day is sometimes virtually fulfilled.

Some years ago, an Irish gentleman who was an extensive contractor on our public works, was reduced to poverty by the profligacy and dishonesty of an ungrateful son. The old man lost his wife; and to fill up the cup of his sorrow, he lost his sight. Thus poor, friendless, blind, forsaken, he found an asylum in the Franklin County Almshouse, Pennsylvania.

Whilst there, his wicked and ungrateful son travelled that way. He was informed of his father's situation and desire to see him; but he refused to see the kind father he had ruined. Notice the result. That very day this son was overtaken by a storm, and took a severe cold that resulted in the destruction of his eyes. He lay in Gettysburg in a critical state, until his funds were exhausted, and those who had him in charge took him to the Franklin County Alms-house. His father having died the day before, he was put in the same room and occupied the same bed, and in a short time followed his neglected and heart-broken father to the judgment-seat of Christ.

CCCXLVII. Value of a Christian Mother. Prov. xxxi. 1. *His mother taught him.*

The Bishop of Carlisle thus bears testimony to the value of a real Christian mother, at a meeting of mothers and daughters. Dr. Harry Goodwin said:—

"I am one of those who lost their mothers at a very early age. I was very little over six years old when my dear mother was suddenly taken from me. I mention my age that I may put before you the effect which my mother's teaching had upon me, and the tender age at which it ceased, and I think we may draw from it some useful lessons. Now, then, when I look back to the teaching of my mother, what do I think of it? I say deliberately, and without any amount of exaggeration, that though I have since that time been at school, been under tutors, been at college, and had all the experience of life, I do not believe that all the lessons that I have received since that time put together amount in value and in importance to the lessons which I learned from my mother before I was seven years old. What did she teach me? She did not put me through the fifth or the sixth standard—we had not any standards in those days—but she taught me a great many things which were better than standards.

"I will tell you one of the first lessons she taught me. She taught me always to speak the truth: and the lesson she gave me concerning truth has never been lost upon me. She always brought me up in the feeling that what was to be spoken was to be the whole truth, and nothing but the truth; that there was to be no evasion, that everything was to be stated simply and honestly, exactly as it occurred; and I will tell you how she enforced that lesson—she always spoke truth to me. I never caught her in any kind of deceit; I always knew that what she said to me she meant. I was always sure that if she told me she was going to do a thing, she would do it, and no amount of coaxing or persuasion would lead her to change her mind. Absolute truth, absolute in the smallest matters—that was her practice, and that was the lesson that she impressed upon me.

"Then she taught me to say my prayers. I have as vivid a recollection now, at a distance of sixty years, as I had at the time, of the manner in which she made me kneel down at her knees, and with her hand upon my head, taught me the simple prayers which are suitable for childhood. I remember how, when I rose up from my knees, she would talk to me about some simple matter suitable to my childish days. Those early lessons of prayer have never been lost to me; and I remember afterwards, when I was at school, and when I was submitted to all the temptations and the difficulties to which boys at school are submitted; when I was sleeping in a room with boys about me who did not pray, and who laughed at those who did, I remember well how the thought of my dear mother was like a guardian angel over me, and how she kept me from the evil which these boys would fain have pressed upon me. Then, again, she enforced upon me full and complete obedience. It was never enforced with a threat; there was no unkindness, on arbitrariness in the command; but I was never allowed to ask any reasons. I felt perfectly certain of the wisdom which dictated the command, and I was always taught to obey, and I learned to obey. Then, lastly, I was taught by her, and by practice more than words, to keep my temper. She taught me to do that by keeping her own."

CCCXLVIII. A Devoted Wife. PROV. xxxi. 11, 12.

"The heart of her husband doth safely trust in her, so that he shall have no need of spoil. She will do him good and not evil all the days of her life."

THE late Robert Moffat had a most noble and devoted wife in Mary Moffat, who laboured with him in Southern Africa unweariedly. She watched over her husband's health and comfort most anxiously for more than fifty years, and she used to say that it was a great satisfaction to her to provide for the temporal wants of a servant of Christ in the mission-field, and she felt, what was true, that he never would have been the missionary he was but for her care of him. The Home Secretary of the London Missionary Society says: "I shall never forget what took place in my official room at the Mission House soon after their return from Africa. While talking over their past labours, Mrs. Moffat, looking fondly at her husband first, turned to me and said, 'Robert can never say that *I* hindered him in his work!'

"'No, indeed,' replied Dr. Moffat; 'but I can tell you she has often sent me away from house and home for months together for evangelizing work, and in my absence has managed the station as well or better than I could have done it myself.'"

Even on the very shore of the dark river she would not rest until assured that his wants were being attended to.

Her husband's first exclamation on finding her really gone was, "For forty-three years I have had her to pray for me."

CCCXLIX. One of the Virtuous Women. PROV. xxxi. 20.

"She stretcheth out her hand to the poor: yea, she reacheth forth her hands to the needy."

HANNAH MORE did a great deal at the close of last

century for the elevation and instruction of the poor rural population round her home at Bath. She was the means of starting a number of schools in the country districts, where the people were very ignorant and wicked; and she wrote incessantly simple religious tracts and other literature, which she distributed far and near.

But in all she was very humble, speaking of herself thus: "God is sometimes pleased to work by the most unworthy instruments. I suppose to take away every shadow of doubt that it is His own doing. It always gives me the idea of a great author writing with a very bad pen."

CCCL. Labour and Sorrow. ECCLES. i. 2. *"Vanity of vanities, saith the Preacher."*

GOETHE, the greatest of German poets, whose long life was one success, said: "They have called me a child of fortune, nor have I any wish to complain of the course of my life. Yet it has been nothing but labour and sorrow; and I may truly say, that in seventy-five years I have not had four weeks of true comfort. It was the constant rolling of a stone that was always to be lifted anew."

CCCLI. An Eloquent Preacher. ECCLES. i. 2. *"Vanity of vanities, saith the Preacher, vanity of vanities; all is vanity."*

ONE night, young Bossuet, who possessed in such an eminent degree the power of eloquent speech, had gone to the brilliant *salon* of Rambouillet. There were gathered in that famous drawing-room some of the most illustrious of the French nobility, ladies and gentlemen representing the wit, the learning, and the cleverness of Paris. In the course of the evening, the Marquis de Fenquières referred to this young man as one about to enter upon an ecclesiastical career, and who, from what he had heard, seemed destined to be a great preacher. Suddenly some one suggested that he might interest the company by preaching a sermon. It would be a new diversion, and all the more delightful if the sermon were preached impromptu. Texts were written shaken up in a bag, and one of the illustrious ladies was to draw one out, and hand it to the preacher. The room was arranged, the text was drawn, and one of the ladies handed it to the youthful abbé. He was to have a quarter of an hour in which to think over the subject, but as the slip was handed to him he waived that privilege. How strangely the words struck on the assembly as the grave young preacher read, "*Vanity of vanities! all is vanity!*" At first some were inclined to laugh, but ere long the feelings of the assembly were swayed in another direction. The fervour, the boldness, the brilliance of that extemporaneous utterance astonished all ears and affected all hearts. The sermon was long, and, as will be guessed from the occasion, there is no report of it; but at its close the Duc d'Enghien pressed forward to grasp the preacher's hand, and to inquire who he was, and whence he came. He came from Dijon, and, unknown till that night, Bossuet forthwith took his place as "a bright particular star" in the religious firmament of France.

CCCLII. Worldly Honour. ECCLES. i. 2. "*Vanity of vanities, saith the Preacher.*"

ONE cannot read the posthumous memoirs of Chateaubriand, without being struck with the illusive nature of worldly honours and pleasures. Contemporary applause was not wanting to cheer the craving spirit of this scholar and statesman. The author of the "Genius of Christianity" and the ambassador of France at the Court of London could not complain that honour was denied him. He says, "I know not in history a reputation that would tempt me: and were it necessary to stoop to pick up from my feet and for my own advantage the greatest glory the world could offer, I would not give myself the trouble."

CCCLIII. The Courtier and the Christian. ECCLES. i. 14 "*Behold, all is vanity and vexation of spirit.*"

"I HAVE recently read Solomon with a kind of sympathetic feeling. I have been as wicked and as vain, though not as wise, as he (is that so?); but I feel the truth of his reflection, 'All is vanity and vexation of spirit.'" So said, at the last, the most brilliant wit, the most accomplished gentleman, the most cultivated speaker and the most classic scholar of the English nobility in the eighteenth century—Philip Dormer Stanhope, Earl of Chesterfield.

"By the grace of God I am what I am; nothing in myself, all in Christ." So said, at the last, a genial old man, whose bones rest in Westminster Abbey, whose services humanity will never forget, who could walk from Gore House to the Parliament Houses, repeating to himself the ninety-first psalm, and then by a persuasive eloquence, chastened by pure taste and enriched by classic allusion, hold the members of the House of Commons entranced while he depicted the horrors of the slave trade—William Wilberforce.

CCCLIV. A Hasty Temper. Eccles. vii. 9. *"Be not hasty in thy spirit to be angry: for anger resteth in the bosom of fools."*

La Fontaine, chaplain of the Prussian Army, once preached a very earnest and eloquent sermon on the sin and folly of yielding to a hasty temper. The next day he was accosted by a major of the regiment with the words:

"Well, sir! I think you made use of the prerogatives of your office to give me some very sharp hits yesterday."

"I certainly thought of you while I was preparing the sermon," was the answer; "but I had no intention of being personal or sharp."

"Well, it is of no use," said the major; "I have a hasty temper, and I cannot help it, and I cannot control it; it is impossible."

And, still adhering to this opinion, after some further conversation he went his way.

The next Sabbath, La Fontaine preached upon self-deception, and the vain excuses which men are wont to make.

"Why," said he, "a man will declare that it is impossible to control his temper, when he very well knows that were the provocation to happen in the presence of his sovereign, he not only could, but would, control himself entirely. And yet he dares to say that the continual presence of the King of kings and Lord of lords impose upon him neither restraint nor fear!"

CCCLV. How to Die Manfully. ECCLES. viii. 12.

"Though a sinner do evil an hundred times, and his days be prolonged, yet surely I know that it shall be well with them that fear God, which fear before Him."

DR. JOHN GODMAN was an eminent anatomist and naturalist, who, dying at the early age of thirty-one, had already made himself distinguished through the country.

For the greater part of his life he was avowedly an infidel of the French school, rejecting the Bible, and blind to the wonderful proofs, furnished by his profession, of the existence, power, and wisdom of God. But while lecturing, only three years before his death, to his medical class, he was called to the sick-bed, and, as it proved, the dying-bed of one of his students who was a Christian. Visiting this young man repeatedly, and witnessing his joyous anticipations of heaven, and his triumph over death, he saw what, as a sceptic, he was unable to comprehend. His philosophy could not explain it. He turned to the Bible, and there the secret was unfolded. There he found that Christ was the Conqueror of death, and that to the believer in Him its sting is taken away.

Now Dr. Godman turned to the *study* of the Scriptures, and soon found joy and peace in believing; so that, when he finished his course, commending his little family to the Father of the fatherless and the widow's God and portion, with uplifted eyes and a beaming countenance he resigned his spirit to the Redeemer, and sweetly fell asleep in Jesus.

Before this, however, in the last sickness of his friend Dr. Judson,—who, though a brother of the devoted missionary, was an open infidel,—Dr. Godman addressed to him a letter, which was the means of his conversion. "Philosophy," he says in that letter still extant, "is a fool, and pride, a madman. Many persons die with what is called manly firmness; they put on as smooth a face as they can, to compose on the spectators, and die firmly But this is all deception. The true state of their minds at the very time, in nine cases out of ten, is worse than the most horrible imaginings of hell itself. But the man who dies as a man ought to die, is the humble-minded believing Christian. He does not die manfully (in the world's sense of that term), but he rests lovingly and reverently on Jesus.

Dr. Judson also, pointed by this letter to the only Saviour, died in the faith; and through the testimony of *his* death, one other at least was pointed to the cross of Christ, and led to rest all his hopes upon it.

CCCLVI. Entering the Vineyard at the eleventh Hour. ECCLES. ix. 4. "*For to him that is joined to all the living there is hope.*"

AN old man of eighty-one had heard in his early youth the celebrated Mr. Flavel preach. Instead of pronouncing the blessing at the close, Mr. Flavel had said, "I cannot bless you! How can I bless those who do not love the Lord Jesus? If any man love not the Lord Jesus Christ, let him be accursed!" The solemn sentence came into the old man's remembrance in America, and at the eleventh hour he entered the vineyard.

CCCLVII. Do it Well. ECCLES. ix. 10. "*Whatsoever thy hand findeth to do, do it with thy might.*"

WHAT? Everything honest that you attempt to do at all!

A noble saying is recorded of a member of our British House of Commons, who by his own industry and perseverance had won his way to that high position. A proud scion of the aristocracy one day taunted him with his humble origin, saying, "I remember when you blacked my father's boots." "Well, sir," was the noble response, "*did I not do it well?*"

CCCLVIII. Perseverance. ECCLES. ix. 10. "*Whatsoever thy hand findeth to do, do it with thy might; for there is no work, nor device, nor knowledge, nor wisdom, in the grave, whither thou goest.*"

CYRUS FIELD, in giving his account of the Atlantic

telegraph, says, "It has been a long and hard struggle—nearly thirteen years of anxious watching and ceaseless toil. Often has my heart been ready to sink. Many times, when wandering in the forests of Newfoundland in the pelting rain, or on the deck of ships on dark, stormy nights, alone, far from home, I have almost accused myself of madness and folly to sacrifice the peace of my family, and all the hopes of life, for what might prove, after all, but a dream. I have seen my companions one after another fall by my side, and feared I, too, might not live to see the end. And yet one hope has led me on; and I have prayed that I might not taste of death till this work was accomplished. *That prayer is answered;* and now, beyond all acknowledgments to men is the feeling of gratitude to Almighty God."

CCCLIX. Courage in Helping the Wrong Doer.
ECCLES. ix. 10. "*Whatsoever thy hand findeth to do, do it with thy might.*"

DAVID KING, then a student going to Edinburgh University, had taken his passage from Montrose to Leith in a small coasting vessel. "He had gone down to the quay to embark, but the appearance of the passengers, and the filth and bad smells everywhere so disgusted him, that he was hesitating whether he should sail after all, when a man of respectable appearance accosted him, and pointing to a repulsive-looking character who was getting on board at that moment, said; 'That is a criminal flying from justice; and if, as I believe, you are studying for the ministry, you may have an opportunity of doing some good during the voyage.' The man indicated seemed a thorough scoundrel, who could be rough and scornful if interfered with; and the idea of being in the same dirty cabin with him, perhaps for days, was so utterly repugnant to the nervous and sensitive lad, that he left the vessel and went home. When he told his parents the circumstances, his father, after a little consideration, said: 'Well, I will not urge you; but in passing through life you will have need of moral courage, and it might be for your future good to show some nerve now.' These words sent him back to the vessel, and he went on board with a failing heart.

Scarcely were they out at sea when the man began to swear violently, took whisky out of his box, and, having drunk plentifully himself, handed it about to the sailors. The passengers became alarmed, the captain was appealed to, and under his authority the baggage of the offender was searched, all the spirits taken away, and severe measures threatened, if he caused further trouble. By this means the disturbance was ended, and the fears of the passengers calmed. But though all was quiet, the young student could find no repose; and urged by his conscience, which upbraided him with a neglect of duty, he rose at dead of night and sought the wretched runaway. On the deck of the little vessel he found him, and there, out at sea in darkness and solitude, the man was in a changed mood, and he received his visitor with a degree of courtesy. This was an opportunity not to be lost, and King began a serious conversation with him. After some earnest talk, he asked if any one had ever expostulated with him in such a manner before. 'No,' he answered; 'but I am not so ignorant as you might think. I have read a good many tracts, and most of them tell of sudden conversions, so that I have had an idea I might be converted suddenly some day myself.' 'And what if this be the day?' said the youth. '"Now is the accepted time, now is the day of salvation." If nobody has spoken with you in this manner before, perhaps nobody may again.' During the remainder of the passage the man was quiet, thoughtful, obliging, and at parting he testified deep gratitude to young King for his remonstrances, and expressed the hope of being thenceforth a changed character."

CCCLX. The Worm at the Root. Eccles. ix. 18.
" One sinner destroyeth much good."

A GENTLEMAN had two beautiful young mountain ash trees in his garden, which he tended very carefully from season to season. As might have been expected, the twin trees repaid his labour in their rapid growth and beauty of form. After a while, from some mysterious cause, one of the trees stopped growing. The other continued to spread out its branches and leaves, and seemed to wax taller and handsomer every day; but this one resisted all the combined the young man sang, the elder stopped dealing the cards, stared at the singer a moment, and, throwing the cards on the floor, exclaimed, 'Harry, where did you learn that tune?'

"'What tune?'

"'Why, that one you've been singing.'

"The young man said he did not know what he had been singing, when the elder repeated the words, with tears in his eyes, and the young man said he had learned them in a Sunday-school in America.

"'Come,' said the elder, getting up; 'come, Harry; here's what I won from you; go and use it for some good purpose. As for me, as God sees me, I have played my last game, and drank my last bottle. I have misled you, Harry, and I am sorry. Give me your hand, my boy, and say that for old America's sake, if for no other, you will quit this infernal business.'"

CCCLXIII. Family Worship. ECCLES. xi. 6. *"In the morning sow thy seed, and in the evening withhold not thine hand."*

THE following is one of the most interesting circumstances in the life of the late John Ryland, Baptist minister at Northampton :—

Being on a journey, he was overtaken by a violent storm, and compelled to take shelter in the first inn he came to. The people of the house treated him with great kindness. When the hour of rest approached, the stranger appeared uneasy, and looked up every time the door opened, as if expecting something essential to his comfort. His host informed him that his chamber was prepared whenever he chose to retire.

"But," said he, "you have not had your family together."

"I don't know what you mean," said the landlord.

"To read and pray with them," replied the guest.

The landlord confessed that he never thought of doing such a thing.

"Then, sir," said Mr. Ryland, "I must beg you to order my horse immediately: I had rather brave the storm than venture to sleep in a house where there is no prayer. Who can tell what may befal us before morning?"

The landlord remonstrated with him, and said he had no objection to call his family together, but he should not know what to do when they came. Mr. Ryland then proposed to conduct family worship, to which all consented.

When he rose from his knees, almost every individual present was bathed in tears, and the inquiry was awakened in every heart, "What must I do to be saved?" This day was indeed the beginning of days to that family, and they became the means of diffusing a knowledge of the Gospel in a neighbourhood which had been before proverbially dark and destitute.

CCCLXIV. Resistance to Melancholy. ECCLES. xi. 7. *"Truly the light is sweet, and a pleasant thing it is for the eyes to behold the sun."*

DANTE condemns to the Stygian marsh those who had been sad under the blessed sunlight. "Sad were we in the sweet air that is gladdened by the sun, bearing sluggish smoke in our hearts; now lie we sadly here in the black ooze."

CCCLXV. Reverencing Conscience. ECCLES. xi. 9. *"But know thou that for all these things God will bring thee into judgment."*

AN ancient Persian fabulist tells the story of a king, who, having hanged his general because he had lost a battle, resolved in his rage to kill the widow and children of the unfortunate officer also. The whole country was in distress because of this cruel and unjust resolution, and numerous petitions were sent in. But all was in vain. The despot grew the more implacable the more his sense of humanity was appealed to. One day the king's chief counsellor threw himself at the feet of his master, and asked for justice. He was accompanied by his daughter, a woman of unparalleled beauty. "Ruler of the world," he said, "your physician, seeing that my daughter surpasses his daughter in beauty, as the sun surpasses the moon in glory, has in a fit of jealousy deformed my child by throwing a caustic fluid over her face." Having said these words, he unveiled his daughter's head. An ugly black spot was exposed, which monstrously disfigured the otherwise beautiful countenance of the poor girl.

The king, roused to anger by the sight, immediately sent for his physician.

"Why have you done this to the woman?" he asked.

The physician gave no reply.

"By the sun and all his hosts," cried the king, "with thy head shalt thou pay for this offence!"

He beckoned to the captain of the guard, who at once stepped forward to execute the verdict. But the physician produced a sponge from his bosom, and, dipping it into a basin of water, with one stroke thoroughly washed away the black spot.

"What is this?" asked the king, in a voice of glad surprise.

"Ruler of the world," the counsellor answered, "you have sentenced my friend the physician to death because he only disfigured a girl's face by a stain which could be washed off easily, but what sentence will the eternal Judge have to pass upon you, if you cast such a stain upon your conscience as you purpose—a stain which all the water of the ocean cannot wash away?"

The king, deeply struck by this question, abandoned his cruel intention, and sent the widow and children of the deceased general home, enriched with tokens of his princely munificence.

This fable, in spirit like many other passages in the writings of the heathen authors, confirms the truth of the observation, that reverence for a pure conscience is so deeply implanted in our nature, that even sin, with all its destructive effect upon man's moral sense, has not been able altogether to destroy it.

CCCLXVI. Conspicuous for exceeding Sin.

ECCLES. xi. 9. "*Rejoice, O young man, in thy youth; and let thy heart cheer thee in the days of thy youth, and walk in the ways of thine heart, and in the sight of thine eyes: but know thou, that for all these things God will bring thee into judgment.*"

ABOUT a century ago, there flourished in the city of

Glasgow a club of young men, which, from the extreme profligacy of its members, and the licentiousness of their orgies, was commonly called the Hell Club. Besides their other meetings, it was their custom to hold one great annual gathering, at which each tried to surpass the other in extravagance of riot; and on these occasions one young man—who, gifted with brilliant talents and a handsome person, had at one time raised hopes which he had subsequently destroyed—was ever conspicuous for his exceeding sin.

On retiring to rest after one of these annual festivals, he had the following dream:—He fancied that he was mounted upon a favourite black horse, and was riding homeward in the dusk, when a stranger, whom the gloom prevented him from seeing distinctly, seized his horse's rein, saying, "You must go with me."

"And who are you?" exclaimed the young man with an oath, as he struggled to free himself.

"That you will see presently," returned the other, in a tone which thrilled such an unaccountable terror through even his reckless breast that, plunging his spurs into his horse, he attempted to fly, but in vain; however fast the animal flew, the stranger was still at his side, till at length, in his desperate efforts to escape, the rider was thrown, but instead of being dashed to the ground, he found himself falling—falling—falling still, as if sinking into the bowels of the earth.

"Where am I? Where are you taking me to?" he gasped out.

"To hell," replied the stranger, while interminable echoes repeated the fearful sound, "To hell! to hell! to hell!"

On coming to a standstill, he found himself at the entrance of a splendid building. Instead, however, of the expected cries and groans and lamentations, nothing was heard but sounds of music and rejoicing. On entering, he soon perceived that he was amongst old acquaintances, whom he knew to be dead, and all of them he observed were following the pursuits which had most engrossed them on earth. Approaching one of these—a lady whom he had known as an inveterate gambler—he asked her to cease awhile from play, and to introduce him to the pleasures of a place which seemed so very unlike what he expected.

But, with a cry of agony, she answered that there was no rest in hell; that they must for ever toil on in those very pleasures and pursuits to which they had abandoned themselves while on earth. In the midst of the terror which this inspired, his conductor returned, and on his earnest entreaty restored him again to earth, leaving him, however, with the words, "Remember! in a year and a day we meet again!"

At this crisis of his dream the sleeper awoke, feverish and ill; and, either from the effects of the dream, or from his previous excess, he was for several days seriously unwell. During this period he had time for grave reflection, which ended in a resolution to abandon the club and his licentious companions altogether.

After getting well, however, his companions, to whom he told the reason of his leaving them, soon contrived to make him ashamed of his good resolutions. He resumed his former course of life, and when the next annual meeting came round, he was, as usual, the most reckless of all the guests.

On rising to make the customary speech, the president observed, "This being leap-year, it is *a year and a day* since our last anniversary." The words struck on the young man's ear like a knell; but ashamed to expose himself to the jeers of his companions, he sat out the night, drowning fearful thoughts in wine and revelry. Then, in the gloom of a winter's morning, he mounted his horse to ride home.

Some hours afterwards the horse was found quietly grazing by the roadside, whilst a few yards off lay the corpse of his master.

CCCLXVII. A Soldier's Bible. ECCLES. xi. 9.

"Rejoice, O young man, in thy youth, and let thy heart cheer thee in the days of thy youth; and walk in the ways of thy heart, and in the sight of thine eyes: but know thou, that for all these things God will bring thee into judgment."

IT was customary in Cromwell's time for his soldiers to carry each a Bible in his pocket; among others, a profligate young man, who was ordered out to attack some fortress. During the engagement a bullet had perforated his Bible, and gone so far as to rest opposite the above text. These words, so appropriate to his case, powerfully affected his mind, and proved, by the blessing of God, the means of his conversion. He used to observe, that the Bible had been the happy means of saving both his soul and his body.

CCCLXVIII. The Day of Affliction. ECCLES. xii. 3.
"In the day when the keepers of the house shall tremble, and the strong men shall bow themselves."

IT is told of the saintly Joseph Alleine, that in his last illness he suddenly lost the use of all his limbs. Looking at his dead hands, he said, "The Lord gave, and the Lord hath taken away, and blessed be the name of the Lord." Some of his old friends having gathered round him, he said to them, "I have lived a sweet life by the promises, and I hope, through grace, can die by a promise. It is the promises of God, which are everlasting, that will stand by us. Nothing but God in them will stead us in a day of affliction."

CCCLXIX. The Grave. ECCLES. xii. 5. *"Man goeth to his long home."*

A WELSH pastor reaching his house after following his wife to the grave, said, "I have seen my grave to-day, but having seen Calvary long ago, I am not afraid of it."

CCCLXX. Nearly Home. ECCLES. xii. 5. *"Man goeth to his long home."*

"ALMOST well, and *nearly at home*," said the dying Baxter, when asked how he was by a friend. A martyr, when approaching the stake, being questioned as to how he felt, answered, "Never better; for now I know that I am almost at home." Then looking over the meadows between him and the place where he was to be immediately burnt, he said, "Only two more stiles to get over, and I am at my Father's house." "Dying," said the Rev. S. Medley, "is sweet work, sweet work; home! home!" Another on his death-bed said, "I am going home as fast as I can, and I bless God that *I have a good home to go to.*"

CCCLXXI. Retribution. Eccles. xii. 14. *"For God shall bring every work into judgment with every secret thing, whether it be good, or whether it be evil."*

THE doctrine of *retribution* is held by the Moslems in its most rigid form—more rigid, indeed, than in the Christian system; for there is no atonement for sin. The judgment is inexorable; it is absolute and eternal. Before their eyes ever stands the Day of Judgment—the Dies Iræ—when all men shall appear before God to receive their doom.

But in that last day, when unbelievers shall be destroyed, the followers of the Prophet shall be saved. They can go to the tribunal of their Maker without trembling. One day riding outside the walls of Constantinople, we approached a cemetery just as a funeral procession drew near, bearing the form of the dead. We stopped to witness the scene. The mourners gathered around the place where the body was laid, and then the ulema approached the grave, and began *an address to the dead*, telling her (it was a woman) not to be afraid when the angel came to call her to judgment, but to appear before the bar of the Almighty, and answer without fear, for that no follower of the Prophet should perish.

CCCLXXII. A Malarial Atmosphere. Song of Sol. i. 6. *"Mine own vineyard have I not kept."*

MALARIAS are dangerous because they do not address themselves to any sense. We can put up lightning-rods to ward off thunder-bolts, but no man can put up rods that will protect him from a poisonous atmosphere. The sweetest and most beauteous days in New Orleans are those in which death strikes most terribly in times of pestilence. It cannot be detected by sight or by touch, and that is what makes it so dreadful. Now we are walking in a malarial atmosphere continually—not one that attacks the body, but one that infects the soul. There are in the atmosphere of the world silent corrupting forces of which men are quite unconscious—pride, vanity, the love of money, greed, rivalries, and various other noxious elements, and nothing but the inward spiritual vigilance will make man a match for these things.

CCCLXXIII. Beware of the Ivy Green. Song of Sol. ii. 15. *"Take us the foxes, the little foxes that spoil the vines."*

IN the gardens of Hampton Court you will see many trees entirely vanquished and well nigh strangled by huge coils of ivy, which are wound about them like the snakes around the unhappy Laocöon; there is no untwisting the folds, they are too giantlike, and fast fixed, and every hour the rootlets of the climber are sucking the life out of the unhappy tree. Yet there was a day when the ivy was a tiny aspirant, only asking a little aid in climbing; had it been denied then the tree had never become its victim, but by degrees the humble weakling grew in strength and arrogance, and at last it assumed the mastery, and the tall tree became the prey of the creeping, insinuating destroyer. The moral is too obvious. Sorrowfully do we remember many noble characters which have been ruined little and little by insinuating habits. Drink has been the ivy in many cases. Reader, see to it, lest some slowly advancing sin overpower you: men who are murdered by slow poisoning die just as surely as those who take arsenic.

CCCLXXIV. Early and Late with God. Song of Sol. iii. 2. *"I will seek him whom my soul loveth."*

ALLEINE once wrote to a dear friend, "Though I am apt to be unsettled and quickly set off the hinges, yet, methinks, I am like a bird out of the nest, I am never quiet till I am in my old way of communion with God; like the needle in the compass, that is restless till it be turned towards the pole. I can say, through grace, with the Church, 'With my soul have I desired thee in the night, and with my spirit within me have I sought thee early.' My heart is early and late with God; 'tis the business and delight of my life to seek him."

CCCLXXV. The Legend of St. Marguerite. Song of Sol. iv. 16. *"Blow upon my garden, that the spices thereof may flow out. Let my beloved come into his garden, and eat his pleasant fruits."*

THE peasantry of the Litoral tell a singular legend to the first founder of the Abbey. They say that when St.

Honorat arrived on the island shore he was accompanied by his sister, St. Marguerite, who had a number of nuns as her companions. The mind of her brother, however, was not satisfied at seeing the island thus occupied by the female portion of the community; and yet he did not know what to do. The two islands at that distant period formed but one. However, he thought much upon it, and at last he proposed to his sister that she and her companions should betake themselves to the farthest shore, near where the fortress of St. Marguerite now stands, and that he and his monks would retain the abbey. Still he did not feel happy about it; and at last, after a restless night, during which loud peals of thunder reverberated among the mountains, and lightning flashes played along the snow-girt peaks of the Alps, and the tall pines were torn up by the roots, and the fierce waves moaned around the abbey shore, when St. Honorat went forth at dawn, he saw to his amazement that a deep, broad channel now intervened between the islands—the island having been rent in twain.

For a time St. Honorat was content. He used to pay a visit occasionally to his sister; and as he dearly loved strawberries, he chiefly then, when this fruit was in season, went to his sister's isle, where, in the sunny shelter of this, the warmest spot of the Litoral, the fruit used to grow abundantly. At last his over-scrupulous mind began to question whether it was even right for him to visit the island at all. Many a restless night the saint passed, his mind oscillating between affection for his sister and the overstrained dictates of a morbid mind.

When St. Marguerite, who had no such manner of scruples, perceived that her brother came not as often as before, she reasoned with him, and at last he agreed still to continue his visits as long as the strawberries should bear fruit, but for the rest of the year he determined never to visit St. Marguerite. And now his sister dispatched messengers to all the countries round, and charged them to bring back the earliest and the latest flowering strawberry plants that they could find. In fact, she managed it so well that one quarter of the island became an immense strawberry bed. . . .

Many an anxious hour was spent by St. Marguerite on her own island, as she superintended the work of strawberry planting in the sunniest spots of the myrtle-shaded shore. St. Honorat had now been a long time without paying her a visit. And as she paced along the margin of the blue waters, and gazed towards the white crests of the maritime Alps that towered far inland, and marked the grey gnarled olive trees, that like a woodland sea extended beneath the nearer heights of Pezou, Grand Pine, and the crest on which Mougins lifts his walls, many a time she grieved that her brother should have listened to the too rigid suggestions of an ascetic mind, when she had rejoiced in listening to the holy counsels and loving admonitions which flowed from his lips.

The winter passed away—the spring came on—the mistral came blowing fiercely from his caverns in the Esterelles; and at last a messenger announced to Honorat that the season for strawberries had arrived. Gladly he passed over to see Marguerite, and to pick the fruit. The next day he came again; a week passed, and still he came; a month was over, and still more strawberries. Three months passed, and lo! daily a fresh supply of rich fruit was witnessed. Half a year passed, and yet the strawberries came on without cessation, and at last December saw some coming freshly in; and when Honorat witnessed spring again bringing its ripe fruit, he was constrained to tell Marguerite that such a wondrous plenty of strawberries was a plain manifestation that he was wrong in coming to the decision of only visiting her rarely, and that henceforth he would come to see her, without let or hindrance, from day to day.

We may preserve fellowship with our Lord Jesus by cultivating those sweet graces which he loves. If we would bring forth the flowers of holiness all the year round, we might see His face every day. Are we as earnest to use means to detain him, as Marguerite to win her brother's company? It is to be feared not. Let us henceforth be more anxious to obtain daily, hourly fellowship with our Lord.

CCCLXXVI. Seeing no Beauty in Christ. SONG OF SOL. v. 9. "*What is thy beloved more than another beloved?*"

CORREGGIO has a picture of St. Catherine of Sienna's

mystical marriage. This mediæval saint had a vision, in which she saw the Saviour approach and place on her hand a ring, in which blazed a diamond of unearthly purity and beauty, with which He espoused her to Himself. The jewel ever burned with a splendid radiance to her eye, though invisible to all others.

CCCLXXVII. Light. SONG OF SOL. vi. 10. *"Fair as the moon, clear as the sun."*

LIGHT has always been a favourite symbol of seats of learning. "Dominus illuminatio Mea" is blazoned on the arms of Oxford. Cambridge writes, "Hunc lucem et pocula sacra." In the Song of Solomon, the lover names the beloved "Fair as the moon, clear as the sun."

CCCLXXVIII. An Irish Bishop. ISA. i. 25. *"I will purely purge away thy dross, and take away all thy tin."*

"Yet Thou my shield and glory art,
  Th' uplifter of mine head.
I cry'd, and, from His holy hill,
  The Lord me answer made.

"I laid me down and slept, I wak'd;
  For God sustained me.
I will not fear though thousands ten
  Set round against me be."

THIS was the text from which Bishop Bedell preached to his fellow-prisoners in the time of the Irish rebellion in 1642, when he and the Protestants of the district were shut up in hold, and in danger of death at any moment. He was one of the best bishops who ever lived in Ireland, and had his example been more general the Reformation would have made much greater progress in the country. He learned the Irish language, had the Bible translated into it, was assiduous in Christian work, and was filled with the spirit of meekness and self-sacrifice. So much did he commend himself that, when he died in the midst of these troubles, the Irish did him uncommon honour at his burial, fired a volley at his interment, and cried *Requiescat in pace ultimus Anglorum*. He lived from 1570 to 1642. He had a deep feeling of sin, and as the word *Bedel* in Hebrew signifies *tin*, he took for his motto

Isa. i. 25, "I will purely purge thy dross and take away all thy (bedel) tin."

CCCLXXIX. The Last Hour. ISA. ii. 11. "*The lofty looks of man shall be humbled, and the haughtiness of men shall be bowed down, and the Lord alone shall be exalted in that day.*"

A MINISTER named Mr. Winstanley was the means of comforting and edifying the great Dr. Johnson on his death-bed. In a letter to a friend, Hannah More, alluding to this, says: "I cannot conclude without remarking what honour God has hereby put upon the doctrine of faith in a crucified Saviour. The man whose intellectual powers had awed all around him, was in his turn made to tremble when the period arrived at which all knowledge appears useless, and vanishes away, except the knowledge of the true God, and of Jesus Christ, whom He has sent. Effectually to attain this knowledge, this giant in literature must become a little child. The man looked up to as a prodigy of wisdom must become a fool that he might be wise."

What a comment is this upon that word: "The loftiness of man shall be bowed down, and the haughtiness of men shall be made low, and the Lord alone shall be exalted in that day"!

CCCLXXX. Living in the Lives of Others. ISA. vi. 8. "*Whom shall I send, and who will go for us? Then said I, Here am I; send me.*"

BEING sick with the pleurisy, John Woolman was brought so near to the gates of death that he forgot his own name. "Being then desirous to know who I was," he writes, "I saw a mass of matter, of a dull, gloomy colour, between the south and the east, and was informed that this mass was human beings in as great misery as they could be and live; and that I was mixed in with them, and henceforth might not consider myself as a distinct and separate being. In that state I heard a pure and melodious voice, more soft and harmonious than any voice I had heard with my ears before, and I believed that it was the voice of an angel who spoke to the other angels. The words were, *John Woolman is dead.* Yet, knowing that I was alive in the body, I greatly wondered what that heavenly voice could mean."

He tells us then, with the simplicity and power of Bunyan, how the mystery was opened to him; how that John Woolman was to live only henceforth in the lives of these others—most wretched ones.

The vision lifted his whole life. It was thereafter a perpetual unconscious self-sacrifice. Every action in it, it is true, shows the effect of his lack of education and of the ignorance that surrounded him. The water of life flowed through a narrow pipe. But it was a pure rill.

CCCLXXXI. The Conscience. ISA. viii. 20. "*To the law and to the testimony.*'

THE late Dr. Guthrie thus speaks in one of his sermons:—
"According to an Eastern tale, a great magician presented his prince with a ring. The gift was of inestimable value, not for the diamonds and rubies and pearls that gemmed it, but for a rare and mystic property in the metal. It sat easily enough in ordinary circumstances; but so soon as its wearer formed a bad thought or wish, designed or committed a bad action, the ring became a monitor, Suddenly contracting, it pressed painfully on his finger, warning him of sin. Such a ring is not the peculiar property of kings—all, the poorest of us, those that wear none other, possess and wear it—for the ring of the fable is just that conscience, which is the voice of God within us; which is His law written, not on Sinai's granite tables, but on the fleshy tablets of the heart; and which, enthroned in every bosom, commends us when we do right, and condemns us when we do wrong. But conscience, as an expression of the law or will and mind of God, is not now to be depended on. True to its office in Eden, it was shattered and overturned by the Fall; and now lies, as I have seen a sun-dial in the neglected garden of an old, desolate, ruined castle, thrown from its pedestal, prostrate on the ground, and covered by tall, rank weeds.

So far as doctrines and duties are concerned, not conscience, but the Book of Revelation, is our one only sure and safe directory. "Search the Scriptures," says our Lord, "for in them ye think ye have eternal life, and they are they which testify of Me." "To the law and to the testimony," says another, "if they speak not according to these, there is no truth in them."

CCCLXXXII. Is God here? ISA. xi. 6. *"And a little child shall lead them."*

A YOUNG man had been extremely profane, and thought little of the matter. After his marriage to a high-minded, lovely wife, the habit appeared to him in a different light, and he made spasmodic efforts to conquer it. But not until some years had passed did he become victor, when the glowing evil was set before him, by a little incident, in its real and shocking sinfulness.

One Sunday morning, standing before the mirror shaving, the razor slipped, inflicting a slight wound. True to his fixed habit, he ejaculated the single word "God!" and was not a little amazed and chagrined to see reflected in the mirror the pretty picture of his little three-year-old daughter, as laying her dolly hastily down she sprang from her seat on the floor, exclaiming as she looked eagerly and expectantly about the room, "Is Dod here?"

Pale and ashamed, and at a loss for a better answer, he simply said "Why?"

"'Cause I thought He was when I heard you speak to Him."

Then noticing the sober look on his face and the tears of shame in his eyes as he gazed down into the innocent, radiant face, she patted him lovingly on the hand, exclaiming assuringly, "Call Him again, papa, and I dess He'll surely come."

Oh, how every syllable of the child's trusting words cut to his heart! The still, small voice was heard at last. Catching the wondering child up in his arms, he knelt down, and for the first time in his life implored of God forgiveness for past offences and guidance for all his future life, thanking Him in fervent spirit that he had not "surely come" before in answer to some of his awful blasphemies. Surely "a little child shall lead them."

CCCLXXXIII. Exalting God. ISA. xxv. 1. *"O Lord, Thou art my God: I will exalt Thee."*

"DR. BELLAMY made God big," said an old negro to Dr. Backus, his successor.

He is no true Christian who does not exalt Christ. A minister, whose congregation had long deplored the cold and dry style of his preaching, found one Sunday morning, on entering the pulpit, a slip of paper on the cushion with the words in John xii. 21 written on it: "*Sir, we would see Jesus.*" His conscience supplied the application of the text, and after much thought and self-examination he resolved, with God's help, to preach Christ more clearly; and next Sunday he took for his text John xx. 20: "*Then were the disciples glad when they saw the Lord.*"

CCCLXXXIV. The Divine Fatherland. ISA. xxv. 8. *"He will swallow up death in victory: and the Lord God will wipe away tears from off all faces."*

AN American minister thus speaks in one of his sermons: "When the regiments of the British army are on foreign stations the bands are forbidden to play 'Sweet Home,' lest the beautiful tune, with its touching associations, should make the men saddened and disheartened. But no such effect is produced in the Christian soul by singing to him of heaven. On the contrary, it gives him joy, and contentment, and strength, and consolation. For this purpose I have spoken of it now to you. Is it a comfort? That will depend on whether or not you are a child of God. Hark! amid the darkness the clock strikes out, with booming sound, the long midnight hour, and as it is heard by the watchman on his weary beat, he rejoices that he is so much nearer the time of his release at the day dawn. But as it falls on the ears of the condemned criminal in his cheerless cell, it sends a shiver through his frame, for he is an hour nearer his execution on the morn. How is it with you and the ringing out of the old year, in this regard? Does it fill you with gladness or with dread? Oh, if with dread, let me urge you at once to break away from sin, and enter into the family of God, so that your terror may be turned into joy. They tell that in the armies of the first Napoleon, when the '*Ranz des vaches*' was played by the regimental bands, some Swiss soldiers, under the influence of the old home tune, were sure to desert before the morning. Child of God, I have tried to move your heart by awaking within you the associations of your divine fatherland. I have sung to you the Christian home-song; and if you have enlisted into any army of sin, or shame, or cruelty, or wrong, may the effect upon you be, to cause you to desert at once and hasten back to your Father's embrace."

CCCLXXXV. Our Last Hour. Isa. xxvi. 3. "*Thou wilt keep him in perfect peace whose mind is stayed on Thee.*"

In a lecture on "The Trinity: a Practical Truth" Joseph Cook speaks thus of the late Charles Kingsley:—' In 1875, Charles Kingsley, having bidden adieu to Westminster Abbey and Windsor Castle, lay dying; and, with the breath of eternity on his cheeks, the central thought of this modern man was that 'only in faith and love to the Incarnate God our Saviour can the cleverest, as well as the simplest, find the peace of God which passeth all understanding.' 'In this faith,' says his wife, 'he had lived; and as he had lived, so he died—humble, confident, unbewildered.' In the night he was heard murmuring: 'No more fighting; no more fighting.' Then followed intense, earnest prayers, which were his habit when alone. His warfare was accomplished; he had fought the good fight; and on one of his last nights on earth his daughter heard him exclaim: 'How beautiful God is!' The last morning, at five o'clock, just after his eldest daughter and his physician, who had sat up all night, had left him, and he thought himself alone, he was heard, in a clear voice, repeating the words of the Burial Service: 'Thou knowest, O Lord, the secrets of our hearts; shut not Thy merciful ears to our prayer; but spare us, O Lord most holy, O God most mighty, O holy, merciful Saviour, Thou most worthy Judge Eternal, suffer us not, at our last hour, from any pains of death, to fall from Thee.' He turned on his side after this, and never spoke again."

CCCLXXXVI. I will Remember Thee. ISA. xxvi. 8. *"The desire of our soul is to Thy name, and to the remembrance of Thee."*

DR. JESSUP, the Syrian missionary, says that when his father, long a Vice-President of the American Board of Missions, had been twice paralyzed, his memory gone, and even his own house no longer recognised, he was at home when he got into his church, or remembered the Missionary Board, and wrote a letter to its representatives, full of the spirit of missions. He could conduct family prayers as well as ever, and was perfectly sound in mind and memory as to the Redeemer's kingdom. It was like the disintegrated quartz falling away from the pure gold.

CCCLXXXVII. Strong Drink. ISA. xxviii. 7. *"But they also have erred through wine, and through strong drink are out of the way."*

A TREE in South America, called the Judas Tree, has beautiful scarlet blossoms, but it has a deadly opiate. The insects are charmed with it. But under and all around this tree there are millions of dead carcases lying.

CCCLXXXVIII. Erring through Strong Drink. ISA. xxviii. 7. *"The priest and the prophet have erred through strong drink."*

MR. J. W. KIRTON, author of "Buy your own Cherries," etc., tells a painful story of a clergyman of the Church of England—a man of such power that he filled every seat and aisle with a congregation, and wherever he preached cleared out the chapels and churches for miles round. Souls were converted, and a blessed influence rested on the town. By-and-by a whisper got abroad that he was fond of drink, and ultimately it proved to be too true. He was seen staggering in the streets; the bishop instituted inquiries, and the case turned out so bad that the clergyman's gown was taken from him, and he was deprived of his living. All restraint seemed then removed. He wandered about the town, sold his library, and spent the money in drink amongst the worst characters in the town where he had preached the gospel for years. His plate followed, then his furniture, and ultimately he marched to the workhouse and asked for admission. He was received, and week after week he went with the other paupers into the very church where he used to preach. His friends took compassion upon him, took him out of the workhouse, put him into a cottage, and started him as a schoolmaster; but he eventually "broke out" again, spent all he had in drink, had another attack of *delirium tremens*, and was taken, a hopeless maniac, to the county lunatic asylum.

CCCLXXXIX. God's Searching. ISA. xxviii. 10.

"For precept must be upon precept, precept upon precept; line upon line, line upon line; here a little, and there a little."

PERPORA, the great Italian music master, kept one of his pupils learning the same lesson for three years. The pupil began to murmur, but the master was firm. Four, five, six years passed, and yet he was still at the same, until at last, when he began to fear he might, after all, be just at the beginning, the great teacher set him free with the words, "Go, my son, for thou hast nothing more to learn," and he found himself the first singer of Italy. So God keeps teaching us the same lesson over and over again—our utter nothingness, our complete helplessness, and our perfect sinfulness.

CCCXC. Jargon without Knowledge. ISA. xxix. 13.

"This people draw near Me with their mouth, and with their lips do honour Me, but have removed their heart far from Me."

MR. SPURGEON says: "I heard two persons on the Wengern Alp talking by the hour together of the names of ferns; not a word about their characteristics, uses, or habits, but a medley of crack-jaw titles, and nothing more. They evidently felt that they were ventilating their botany, and kept each other in countenance by alternate volleys of nonsense. They were about as sensible as those doctrinalists who for ever talk over the technicalities of religion, but know nothing by experience of its spirit and power. Are we not all too apt to amuse ourselves after the same fashion? He who knows mere Linnæan names, but has never seen a flower, is as reliable in botany, as he is in theology who can descant upon supra-lapsarianism, but has never known the love of Christ in his heart.

> True religion's more than doctrine,
> Something must be known and felt."

CCCXCI. Sanctify My Name. ISA. xxix. 23. "*They shall sanctify My Name, and sanctify the Holy One of Jacob, and shall fear the God of Israel.*"

MR. BAXTER says: "Some holy Nonconformists I have known that would rarely mention God, but with their hats put off, or bowing down their heads, and it hath often affected me more than a sermon."

CCCXCII. The Fear of Hell peoples Heaven. ISA. xxx. 33. "*For Tophet is ordained of old.*"

THERE is a legend that the devil once put on a monk's hood, and went into the pulpit and preached hell and its terrors. As he knew his subject so well, he sent all his congregation into transports of terror, ready to say they believed anything, or to confess or promise anything, so that only they might escape such horror and despair. And when he returned from his mission, his friends bitterly reproached him, and said, "What have you done? Don't you know that men say, 'The fear of hell peoples heaven'? You have ruined and undone your own kingdom." But he replied, "Never fear: I know what I am doing. The heaven which the fear of hell peoples is one of my own devising (for its roots are in selfishness), and the more men seek that, the better for me! Since thus shall they never know that love of God, which is the one thing that utterly defeats and thwarts me."

CCCXCIII. The Covert from the Tempest. ISA. xxxii. 2. "*And a man shall be as an hiding-place from the wind, and a covert from the tempest.*"

YOU remember, perhaps, the incident—on the St. Bernard mountain—of the freezing traveller who was just settling down into the snow-drifts, despairing and half dead. The whirling snow-flurries were fast weaving the white shroud around his dying form. Just as he is about sinking into the numb insensibility, he hears the distant cry of another traveller who, like himself, is perishing in the storm. He rouses up. He makes a sturdy effort to reach his companion in suffering—finds him—chafes him—lifts him on his feet, and supports his trembling steps onward towards the welcome light of the Hospice that now glimmers through the driving snow. The effort warms his own freezing frame into life again, and in trying to save another, he saves himself. Join hands with some friend who is yet out of Christ, and together struggle on towards the blessed "covert from the tempest."

CCCXCIV. Beyond the River. Isa. xxxiii. 17.
"Thine eyes shall see the King in His beauty: they shall behold the land that is very far off."

Our Father is leading us home: and the more rough and rugged the road near its close, the more we relish the greensward beyond the grave. Could we look upwards with a steadier and more ardent eye, we should scarce feel the fluctuations of this changeable scene. When a man feels dizzy, in riding through a torrent, by looking down on the stream, the best way to restore his head to calmness is to fix his eye on the stationary objects on the other side of the river.

CCCXCV. Begin at the Beginning. Isa. xxxiii. 22.
"For the Lord is our Judge, the Lord is our Lawgiver, the Lord is our King; He will save us."

Dr. Duncan, of the New College, Edinburgh, in conversation once with a lady, addressed these remarkable words to her:—"It's a *grand* thing to begin at the beginning,—to begin with the Lord as our Maker, and to learn who and what He is, Jehovah, I Am; and then to learn of Him as the Lawgiver; and then to meet Him as a Judge, and to be reconciled to His holy law,—to hear Him pronounce the curse that we deserve, and to say Amen to it; and then to lie at His feet, confessing that hell is our due, and, lying there, to take at His own hand, Christ, instead of hell,—

Christ free, instead of hell deserved. That's just salvation, and no way but that will do for you or me. Try to get it fresh on your conscience every day, that hell is your desert, and that you take Christ instead."

CCCXCVI. Loyalty. Isa. xxxiii. 22. *"For the Lord is our Judge, the Lord is our Lawgiver, the Lord is our King. He will save us."*

THREE centuries ago the Spaniards were besieging the little town of St. Quentin, on the frontiers of France. Its ramparts were in ruins, fever and famine were decimating its defenders, treason was gliding among its terrified population. One day the Spaniards shot over the walls a shower of arrows, to which were attached little slips of parchment, promising the inhabitants that if they would surrender, their lives and property should be spared. Now, the governor of the town was the great leader of the Huguenots, Gaspard de Coligni. As his sole answer he took a piece of parchment, tied it to a javelin, wrote on it the two words *Regem habemus*—"We have a king"— and hurled it back into the camp of the enemy. There was his sole answer to all their threats and all their seductions. Now that was true loyalty—loyalty in imminent peril, loyalty ready to sacrifice all. But who was that king for whom, amidst sword and flame, amid fever and famine, Coligni was defending those breached and battered walls? It was the weak and miserable Henry II. of France, whose son, Charles IX., was afterwards guilty of the murder of Coligni and the infamies of St. Bartholomew.

Have you a king? Is Christ your King? Ah, if He be, He is not a feeble, corrupt, false, treacherous man like Coligni's master, but a King who loves you, who died for you, who pleads with you even now on the right hand of the Majesty on High. Are you loyal to Him as Coligni was to the wretched Henry II.? Are you loyal at all— much more, would you be loyal to Christ, even unto death? If so, what will you do for Him? That is the test.

CCCXCVII. Story of a Jerusalem Child. Isa. xl. 11.
"He shall gather the lambs with His arm."

Miss Fletcher tells the story of the death of a dear little child called Naglie, who died in Jerusalem not long before her own death: "I heard the touching account of her death from her mother, a young Christian, who had learned to love Jesus in Miss Arnott's School at Jaffa. Naglie was only two years and a half old when she died, but she was a strange child. She and her brother loved each other like two doves. Often she said, 'I do not want to stay here; I want to go to my dear Jesus.' On Sunday she went to church, but did not seem well. She came home and lay in her little bed, with eyes fixed, but they were looking at Jesus. Once or twice she said, 'I want to lie in my cold bed,' meaning the grave. She asked her father to sing to her. Then she said, 'It is Jesus, father, my dear Jesus, who has come to take me.' She looked up; she saw what we saw not, and smiling, said, "There, He is at the foot of my bed; He calls me to come.' Then all was over. She was but six hours ill. Naglie ever loved the pictures best at school which showed the dear Jesus. One day when her mother put flowers in her hair, she said, 'Mother, Jesus had thorns on His head, and not flowers.'"

CCCXCVIII. "The Lambs in His Arms." Isa. xl. 11.
"He shall gather the lambs with His arm, and carry them in His bosom."

In a Chinese Christian family at Amoy, a little boy, the youngest of three children, on asking his father to allow him to be baptized, was told that he was too young; that he might fall back if he made a profession when he was only a little boy. To this he made the touching reply, "Jesus has promised to carry the lambs in His arms. I am only a little boy; it will be easier for Jesus to carry me." This logic of the heart was too much for the father. He took him with him, and the dear child was ere long baptized. The whole family, of which this child is the youngest member—the father, mother, and three sons—are all members of the Mission Church at Amoy.

CCCXCIX. God's Infinity. ISA. xl. 26. "*Lift up your eyes on high, and behold who hath created these things, that bringeth out their host by numbers: He calleth them all by names by the greatness of His might.*"

JEAN PAUL RICHTER says, "God called up from dreams a man into the vestibule of heaven, saying, 'Come thou hither, and see the glory of My house.' And to the servants that stood around His throne He said, 'Take him and undress him from his robes of flesh; cleanse his vision, and put a new breath into his nostrils; arm him with wings for flight, only touch not with any change his human heart—the heart that weeps and trembles.' It was done, and with a mighty angel for his guide, the man stood ready for his infinite voyage: and from the terraces of heaven, without sound or farewell, they wheeled away into endless space. Then came eternities of twilight that revealed but were not revealed. To the right hand and to the left, toward mighty constellations, depth was swallowed up in height insurmountable, height was swallowed up in depth unfathomable. Suddenly, as thus they rode from infinite to infinite; suddenly, as they tilted over abyssmal worlds, a mighty cry arose—that systems more mysterious, worlds more billowy, other heights and other depths were nearing at hand. Then the man sighed, stopped, shuddered and wept. His overladen heart uttered itself in tears; and he said, 'Angel, I will go no farther. For the spirit of man aches under this infinity. Insufferable is the glory of God's house. Let me lie down in the grave, that I may find rest from the persecutions of the infinite; for end I see there is none.' And from all the listening stars that shone around issued one choral chant, 'Even so it is: Angel, thou knowest that it is: end there is none that ever yet we heard of.' The Angel demanded: 'And is this the sorrow that kills you?' But his voice answered that he might answer himself. Then the Angel threw up his glorious hands to the heaven of heavens, saying, 'End is there none to the universe of God. Lo! also there is no beginning.'"

Mere infinity frightens the spirit: it is only from the teachings of revelation and Christ as the manifested wisdom, power, and love of God, that the infinity of the Divine Being becomes a friend and not a fear to man.

CCCCII. A Bruised Reed. ISA. xlii. 3. *"A bruised reed shall he not break."*

IN one of his sermons, Mr. William Birch says, "I remember some years ago, while riding over one of the deserts of northern Africa, meeting with a company of Arab travellers, and dining with them in the primitive way of sitting on the sand. After dinner one of the men brought out his pipes to play. These pipes were two reeds, something like the tin whistles on which boys sometimes play, but made of cane. The man put the end of the reeds in his mouth and played Arab tunes with them, the music thus produced being soft and tremulous. When he had finished playing, he placed the reeds on the ground, and a horse happening to tread on one, it was injured. I at once thought of the passage of Scripture, referring to Christ, which says—'A bruised reed shall He not break,' and I wondered for a moment what this Arab would do. He took up the reed, and though it was bruised he did not throw it away, but sat down on the ground, and for probably half an hour tried gently and patiently to straighten and repair it, so that he might be able to use it again for his cheering tunes, as it was the only instrument of music in that little caravan."

CCCCIII. The Praying Light-Keeper. ISA. xlii. 10. *"Sing unto the Lord a new song, and His praise from the end of the earth, ye that go down to the sea."*

WE were fog-bound in Penobscot Bay, and made harbour at Eagle Island. Just as the sun was setting we went on shore, and, walking toward the lighthouse, were attracted by the voice of some one in prayer. It was an impressive scene. Before us stretched out the broad Atlantic; the gathering shades of evening deepened the solitude. In the light above us was the keeper, where he had just lighted his lamp. His face was turned toward the sea; his long hair and beard were whitened with the snows of many winters. His arms were outstretched and his voice alone broke the silence, as he besought the Almighty, in the hollow of whose hands the seas are held, to protect the sailor, and to forgive his sins.

"Them prayers will go higher than the light," said our skipper, and all of us felt that we had come into the near presence of God, on that lonely island far at sea.

Who can measure the Divine Providence that shines out from the lighthouse on Eagle Island, because of that praying lighthouse-keeper?

CCCCIV. A Death Song. ISA. xliii. 2. "*When thou passest through the waters I will be with thee.*"

A COASTING vessel once struck on the rocks in a gale in the British Channel. The captain and crew took to the boats and were lost. They might have been saved had they remained on board, for a huge wave carried the vessel up among the rocks, where the ebbing tide left her high and dry. In the captain's cabin a hymn-book was found lying on the table; it was open at a particular page, and the pencil still lay in it which had marked the favourite lines of the sailor when just entering the jaws of death. While the hurricane was howling outside, the captain had drawn his pencil beside these glorious words of cheer:—

> "Jesu, lover of my soul,
> Let me to Thy bosom fly,
> While the billows *near me* roll,
> While the tempest still is high:
> Hide me, O my Saviour, hide,
> Till the storm of life is past!
> Safe into the haven guide,
> O receive my soul at last!"

Blessed death-song!

CCCCV. To Die is Gain. ISA. xliii. 2. "*When thou passest through the waters, I will be with thee.*"

THE testimony of John Rogers, of Bridport, was one of the many beautiful death-beds of which we have heard. The night before he died he said, "I am going home." Putting out his arm, and beckoning and smiling, he said, "Coming, coming." Early next morning he asked for his favourite testament, and, placing it close to his heart, he said, "I am dying, resting on Jesus: nothing remains but the death-struggle. Christ is my all in all." The passage was repeated to him, "Yea, though I walk through the valley of the shadow of death, I will fear no evil: for Thou art with me." He said, "And He will be with me to the end." Then he gently fell asleep.

CCCCVI. Fear Not. ISA. xliii. 2. "*When thou passest through the waters, I will be with thee; and through the rivers, they shall not overflow thee.*"

AMONG the few remains of Sir John Franklin that were found far up in the Polar regions, there was a leaf of the "Student's Manual," by Dr. John Todd, the only relic of a book. From the way in which the leaf was turned down, the following portion of a dialogue was prominent: "Are you not afraid to die?" "No." "No! Why does the uncertainty of another state give you no concern?" "Because God has said to me: 'Fear not. When thou passest through the waters, I will be with thee; and through the rivers, they shall not overflow thee.'" This leaf is preserved in the Museum of Greenwich Hospital, among the relics of Sir John Franklin.

CCCCVII. Sinning against Light. ISA. xliii. 8. "*Bring forth the blind people that have eyes.*"

CARLYLE quotes out of the Koran a story of the dwellers by the Dead Sea, to whom Moses was sent. They sniffed and sneered at Moses; saw no comeliness in Moses; and so he withdrew. But Nature and her rigorous veracities did not withdraw. When next we find the dwellers by the Dead Sea, they, according to the Koran, are all changed into apes. "By not using their souls, they lost them." "And now," continues Carlyle, "their only employment is to sit there and look out into the smokiest, dreariest, most undecipherable sort of universe. Only once in seven days they do remember that they once had souls. Hast thou never, O traveller! fallen in with parties of this tribe? Methinks they have grown somewhat numerous in our day."

The old Greek proverb was that the avenging deities are shod with wool; but the wool grows on the eyelids that refuse the light. "Whom the gods would destroy, they first make mad;" but the insanity arises from judicial blindness.

Jeremy Taylor says that whoever sins against light kisses the lips of a blazing cannon.

CCCCVIII. Times of Blessing. ISA. xliv. 3. *"For I will pour water upon him that is thirsty, and floods upon the dry ground."*

DURING Mr. Sherman's ministry in Reading, his flock was visited by remarkable "times of refreshing," which can never be forgotten. He says himself: "One Whit-Sunday morning, I was preaching from Isa. xliv. 3–5, 'For I will pour water upon him that is thirsty, and floods upon the dry ground,' and as if to illustrate it, the Spirit of the Lord came like a flood over the parched souls of the congregation, and all became sensible that there was something more than human argument convincing the judgment. The congregation was melted to tears, and one poor back-slider, on whom my hopes had long rested, unable to restrain himself, when I cried out, 'Who will "subscribe with his hand to the Lord" to-day?' cried out, 'I will.' The congregation caught the infection, and hands seemed involuntarily stretched out, as if ready to sign their names. It pleased God to move eighty-one souls, most of them young, to devote themselves to His service that day."

CCCCIX. Sin Blotted Out. ISA. xliv. 22. *"I have blotted out, as a thick cloud, thy transgressions."*

AN illustration which effectively shows the "blotting out" of sin, is that of Charlotte Elizabeth's Happy Mute, "who dreamed that he died and stood before the judgment-seat, and the books were opened." And when he saw beneath his name a long, dark catalogue of sins, he was ready to sink with terror. But Jesus cast on him a gracious look, and saying with unspeakable tenderness, "John!" lifted the pierced hand from which oozed drops of blood, and *passed it over* the black record. John's sins were all "blotted out," and there was only now the mark of the blood.

CCCX. Need of a Saviour. Isa. xlv. 21, 22. *"A just God and a Saviour; there is none beside Me. Look unto Me, and be ye saved, all the ends of the earth."*

IN a letter to Mr. Aubrey De Vere, Sir W. R. Hamilton says: "Without any appreciable or expressible change in my religious views, I feel that there has been for some time back a decided improvement in my religious habits, tastes, and feelings: the sum and substance of which seems to be, that I feel more than before my *need* of a Saviour, of *The* Saviour."

CCCXI. Not till they are Rooted. Isa. xlviii. 10. *"Behold, I have refined thee, but not with silver; I have chosen thee in the furnace of affliction."*

I WENT into the kitchen the other day with a bit of black velvet in my hand and a whole pall of black in my heart.

All the morning I had been brooding, brooding over my loneliness, shutting out all the light, and looking only at the darkness. A year before, I had lost my precious baby; and though God had blessed me in a thousand ways, had surrounded me with love and comfort, the withdrawal of this special joy had blighted everything.

All the year I had tried with varying success to lift myself to such a state of trust that I could joyfully think of my darling as far more tenderly cared for than he could be with me—far more safe than in this world of temptation. There had been many hours, many of them, when I attained at least calmness; but on the morning on which I speak, the whole sky was black, with not even a star to call my look upward.

I stood at the ironing-table, renewing my velvet, when one of the girls began taking in some sickly-looking plants that she was trying to cultivate in pots.

"I take them in every day," she said, "when the sun gets up."

"An' sure, isn't the sun good for them?" said the other girl.

"Not till they get rooted," was the reply, in a tone of surprise at the ignorance displayed by the question.

"Not till they get rooted," said I over and over to myself, as I went upstairs. That sentence answers all my questions. God is too good and wise to give us sunshine in too great measure till we get rooted—He knows that we should soon wither and die. So He sets us where the light is shaded to our need; He gives our root the moisture of tears, and when we grow strong through reaching after the Divine, little by little He gives us more sun.

"Not till they get rooted."

Well, I knew that before my baby died I had given the world far too much of my heart. I had been swayed hither and thither by those who were not my rightful guides. I had been content with low standards and frivolous pursuits. I had been far from a healthy, genuine growth. Evidently the sun had withered, instead of strengthening me. I was not rooted.

To be rooted is the first essential of a healthy growth. Till the root has firm hold of the soil, till it is able to choose and absorb that which it needs from all surrounding elements, the life cannot increase—there can be neither flower nor fruit. The soul cannot safely bear much sunshine till it is rooted in God. Till then it must have shadow, or be wasted and sickly. Let me then lift up my thought constantly to the Divine realm, the summer land of the soul, for help and guidance. Let me make God my own, and then all that He possesses will be mine also. Let me through obedience enter into love, so shall I find all that I have lost.

CCCCXII. The Furnace of Affliction. ISA. xlviii. 10. *"I have chosen thee in the furnace of affliction."*

THE late Professor George Wilson thus quaintly expresses the various effects of affliction in a letter to his friend, Daniel Macmillan: "The furnace of affliction puffs away some men in black smoke, and hardens others into useless slags, and melts a few into clear glass. May it refine us into gold seven times purified, ready to be fashioned into vessels for the Master's use." And like the effect of affliction is that of the habitual prospect of death. In a letter to the same friend, in 1848, he says, "I have been reading lately, with great sadness, the Memorials of Charles Lamb, and the Life of Keats. There is something in the noble brotherly love of Charles to brighten, and hallow, and relieve the former; but Keats's death-bed is the blackness of midnight, unmitigated by one ray of light. God keep you and me from such a death-bed! We may have physical agonies as great to endure. It is the common lot. I feel that our heavenly Father can better choose for us than we can for ourselves, of what we should die; but I pray our blessed Lord and Master to be with us in our last fight with the last enemy, and to give us the victory. If He does, what shall pain be but like other bitter medicines, the preparative for the unbroken health of an endless life?"

CCCCXIII. "Time Enough." Isa. xlviii. 18. "*O that thou hadst hearkened to My commandments.*"

A YOUNG man, about eighteen, was anxious about his soul. He had strong convictions of sin, and of the danger of his lost condition. The word of God had reached his conscience, and he was persuaded that he must repent and seek the Lord, or he could not be saved. The Spirit of God was striving with him, but he would not yield; there was "time enough,"—it was not a convenient season. He was taking a new situation where there were many ungodly men, and he dare not confess Christ, so he purposed to wait awhile, and say nothing about religion until the way was easier. From that time he fell back; he gave it all up; he became as careless and unconcerned as ever; he forsook the house of God, and went right back to the world.

But the Lord was merciful to him, and did not leave him without fresh calls. About the age of five-and-thirty he had again many serious impressions. He began to inquire and to pray, and seemed on the very threshold of the kingdom. He truly wished to become a Christian and follow Christ the rest of his life, but the old temptation came back in a new form. He had reached the prime of life, but he was again led to delay further. He was now taking a business for himself, and he was assured that it could not be carried on without Sunday trading; the customers would be supplied on that day, or go elsewhere.

Unhappily he yielded to the snare. He made up his

mind to turn to God, but not now. A few months or years could not make much difference, he thought; so he again put off the matter. He could not decide yet—it was too great a sacrifice to give up all for Christ. Alas, again he quenched and grieved the Spirit, and became hardened in his unbelief and sin! Business prospered with him, and he was content to live without God. Many years passed by, and he thought nothing of the great eternity to which he was fast hastening.

By-and-by old age crept on him, and his latter end was rapidly approaching. At the age of seventy-two he was brought low and compelled to look death in the face; but now the hope of peace and salvation seemed very far off. There was nothing but a certain fearful looking for of judgment and fiery indignation. A faithful minister of Christ visited him from time to time, but the word of promise and pardon seemed to find no entrance. To the very last the servant of the Lord was by his side, hoping against hope, telling him that Christ was able to save to the uttermost, and reminding him of the dying thief, and urging him to accept mercy; but there was no response. There seemed a barrier in the way: darkness and despair shut out the view of the merciful and long-suffering Saviour. At last he raised himself in the bed, and three times raising up his hands he exclaimed, "I'm lost! I'm lost! I'm lost!" So saying, he fell back on his pillow and expired. Such an end tells its own tale. Such was the issue of all the man's purposes and resolutions; such was the result of delay in deciding for Christ.

CCCCXIV. The Infidel and the Missionary.

ISA. xlviii. 22. *"There is no peace, saith the Lord, unto the wicked."*

A MISSIONARY party shipped for Suez in a vessel whose captain was a notorious infidel, blasphemer, and drunkard. "If you can convert that captain," those who knew him said, "we will believe." The captain himself rubbed his hands in glee at the prospect of putting down the missonaries. All approaches to him were met by blasphemy and infidel argument. "Had he read the Bible?" "Yes, knew it through and through, and it was all bosh!" After a fruitless interview of two hours, Mr. Studd remarked as a close to the conversation : " Well, all I have to say is, I have a peace which the world cannot give." The man seemed struck by the remark, grew serious, and said : " We are all seeking that, but we never find it." " You can have it by simple trust in the Lord Jesus Christ," was the reply. The captain then opened his heart, and revealed its secret of unrest. After separating from the young missionary, he went down and shut himself in his cabin. The next that was seen of him was his writing a letter home, asking forgiveness for having left his family rudely and without a word. He gave his heart to Christ, and became completely changed, and all the crew marvelled greatly.

CCCCXV. What shall we give to Jesus? Isa. lix. 16. *"His arm brought salvation."*

A LITTLE girl named Mary Ann Day, a native of Ulceby, in Lincolnshire, fell from the *Magna Charta* steamer into New Holland harbour. A brave man named John Ellerthorpe, " sprang in after her and brought her ashore, though at a great risk of his own life. The noise of the paddle wheels, the screams of the child's mother, and the confusion and shouts of the passengers, made it a very exciting scene, but it was soon over, and the little girl having got some dry clothes on, her mother brought her to John, and said to her, ' Now, what will you give this gentleman for saving your life ? ' when she held out her little chin, and with a full heart said, '*A kiss.*' John Ellerthorpe, in telling the tale, said, ' I felt myself well paid for the trouble, and had a greater sense of delight and higher satisfaction when that grateful child kissed me, than I did when my fellow-townsmen presented me with one hundred and thirty guineas.' "

Believing reader, you and I were originally passengers on board the ship *Innocence*, and, falling overboard through sin, were in danger of being drowned in the deep of Divine wrath ; but at the moment when all refuge failed, and no eye pitied, and no arm was outstretched to save, " God laid help upon one that was mighty," and the Lord of life and glory Himself became our deliverer.

> "With pitying eyes the Prince of peace
> Beheld our helpless grief;
> He saw, and oh! amazing love,
> He sprang to our relief."

"Emptying Himself" of His former glory, and with the cry "Lo, I come to do Thy will, O God," He plunged into the dark and dreadful waters of death, determining to rescue the unworthy object of His wonderful compassion, not at the mere risk of losing His life, but in the certain knowledge that it must be sacrificed. Then was He heard to say, "Deep calleth unto deep at the noise of Thy waterspouts: all Thy waves and Thy billows are gone over Me."

But in dying He overcame death. In sacrificing Himself He saved us—and to the deep and infinite joy of His Father and ours, and amid the acclamations of angels, "He drew us out of many (great) waters." "He delivered us because He delighted in us."

> "Oh, for this love let rocks and hills
> Their lasting silence break,
> And all harmonious human tongues
> The Saviour's praises speak."

But what shall we give to Him who "saved us" at such a cost?

The little girl gave her deliverer a kiss—doubtless, it was the best way in which she could express her thankfulness; what shall we give "Jesus who delivered us from the wrath to come?" Have we "no kiss" that He will accept and count precious—no kiss of *gratitude?*

CCCCXVI. The Liberty of the Captives of Sin.

ISA. xlix. 24. *"Shall the prey be taken from the mighty, or the lawful captive delivered?"*

JOHN ELIAS was one of Wales' greatest preachers. On one occasion the text was Isaiah xlix. 24 : "Shall the prey be taken from the mighty, or the lawful captive delivered?"

"Satan," exclaimed he in a very peculiar manner, "what do you say, 'Shall the prey be taken from the mighty?'" "No, *never, never;* I will increase the darkness of their minds, the hardness of their hearts, the lusts of their souls, the strength of their chains; and my holds shall be made stronger. The captives shall *never* be delivered. I utterly despise the puny efforts of ministers."

"Gabriel, messenger of the Most High God," exclaimed the preacher in a different tone, looking upwards, "'Shall the prey be taken from the mighty?' what dost thou say?" "Ah! I apprehend not: I have been hovering these two days over this vast assembly hearing the word of God, expecting to see some chains broken, some prisoners liberated; but now the opportunity is near over, and the multitudes are on the point of separating. Ah! there is no sign of one being converted, and I shall not have to convey the glad tidings of one sinner repenting of his sins to the heavenly world."

Then turning to the preachers he asked, "What think you, ministers of the living God, 'Shall the prey be taken from the mighty?'" "'Alas, who hath believed our report, and to whom is the arm of the Lord revealed?' 'We have laboured in vain, and spent our strength for nought.' The Lord seemeth to hide His face from us; His arm is not stretched out. Oh! we fear there is but little hope of the captives being liberated."

"Zion, 'Shall the prey be taken from the mighty?' What do you say?" "'Ah, the Lord hath forsaken me, and my Lord hath forgotten me.' I am left alone, and am childless; so that my enemies say, 'This is Zion, whom no man seeketh after.' Oh, I am afraid none shall be delivered."

"Praying Christians, what do you think, 'Shall the prey be taken from the mighty?' 'Lord God, *Thou* knowest: high is Thy hand, and strong is Thy right hand.' O that Thou wouldst put forth Thy strength and overcome! Let the sighing of the prisoners come before Thee: according to the greatness of Thy power preserve Thou those that are appointed to die. Though I am nearly weary in crying, yet I have a slender hope that the year of jubilee is at hand."

Then looking up seriously, as if about to speak to the Almighty, he asked, "And what is the mind of the Lord respecting these captives? 'Thus saith the Lord, even the captives of the mighty shall be taken away, and the prey of the terrible shall be delivered.' O delightful!

CCCCXVII. A Chain of Precious Books. Isa. l. 4.

"The Lord God hath given me the tongue of the learned, that I should know how to speak a word in season to him that is weary."

YEARS ago an old Puritan doctor, Sibbes, wrote a book called the "Bruised Reed," which fell just at the right time into the hands of Richard Baxter, and brought him under the influence of the enlightening power of the Spirit of God; and then Baxter's ministry was like the sun in his strength, and he wrote a book called "The Call to the Unconverted," which continued to speak long after Baxter himself had ceased to speak with human tongue. That "Call to the Unconverted" went preaching on until it got into the hands of Philip Doddridge (prepared by his pious mother's teaching from the Dutch tiles of a mantel-piece with very quaint Scriptural stories), and it was the means of enlightening him to a broader knowledge, and a richer faith, and a deeper experience of the things of God.

And then Doddridge wrote a book called "The Rise and Progress of Religion in the Soul," which, just at a critical period in his history, fell into the hands of William Wilberforce, who wrote a book called "Practical Christianity," which, far down in the sunny Isle of Wight, fired the heart of a clergyman, who has attained, perhaps, in connection with the Tract Society, the broadest and widest reputation of all—for who has not heard of Legh Richmond? He wrote the simple annal of a Methodist girl, and published it under the title of "The Dairyman's Daughter;" and I should like to know into how many languages that has been translated, and been made of God a power for the spread of truth.

The same book on "Practical Christianity" went right down into a secluded parish in Scotland, and it found there a young clergyman who was preaching a Gospel that he did not know, and it instructed him in the way of God more perfectly, and he came forth a champion valiant for the truth upon the earth until all Scotland rang with the eloquence of Thomas Chalmers. Look at it. Not a flaw in the chain. Richard Sibbes, Richard Baxter, Philip Doddridge, William Wilberforce, Legh Richmond, Thomas Chalmers.

CCCCXVIII. Blocking up the Broad Way.
Isa. lii. 7. *"How beautiful upon the mountains are the feet of him that bringeth good tidings, that publisheth peace."*

ONE of the most eminent of Methodist lay preachers was William Dawson. His personal piety was deep and unaffected, and his gifts of address were marvellous.

Set free from secular labour towards the close of his life, to give one-half of each year to the advocacy of the mission cause, Dawson had from the first showed an extraordinary power of moving men's sympathy for the cause of missions, and of unbuttoning their pockets. He would roll up the slip of paper on which a notice or a resolution had been written, and using it as a telescope, describe what he saw. And just before sitting down, he would once more apply his telescope to his eye, and say, "I see a good collection." And a good collection there would be.

Little did deputies sent from some place where he was less known, conceive the power of the man they found hedging and ditching with his own hands, and who accompanied them as soon as he had time to change his working clothes for a suit of decent black. On one occasion he described the aim of missions to be, "to block up the broad way, to cover it with verdure, to prevent even the keen eye of the recording angel from seeing so much as the print of a human foot upon it."

Dawson died, after a lifetime of as constant labour as probably any man ever lived, in the town of Leeds, in 1841; and a great multitude followed his mortal remains to the grave.

CCCCXIX. Newton and Jay.
Isa. lii. 10. *"All the ends of the earth shall see the salvation of our God."*

A FEW years since, Mr. Jay was invited to preach before the Baptist Missionary Society in London, with several of the founders of which he was well acquainted. The sermon was a fine illustration of piety and of fraternal love. He beautifully sketched the origin of the missionary spirit, and the difficulties it had to encounter. He stated that he himself, then a comparative youth, had some doubts as to whether the time was come for the evangelization of the earth, and at length he determined to call and converse on the subject with the venerable John Newton. The aged apostolic clergyman received his younger brother with ardent affection, and requested him to detail the peculiar difficulties which oppressed his mind. Mr. Jay did this at considerable length, especially insisting on the manifold obstacles which idolatry and human depravity, in all their various forms, presented to the extension of the gospel. When he had ceased, the venerable clergyman slowly laid down his pipe, gathered up his form to an erect posture, and looking his junior brother full in the face, said, in a most emphatic tone, " My brother, I have never doubted the power of God to convert the heathen world since he converted *me!* " "Never from that period," said the preacher, " have I had a doubt on the subject. Facts, too, have proved the fulfilment of Divine prophecies, and have gone so far to accomplish the Divine oath."

CCCCXX. Three Links. ISA. liii. 1. " *Who hath believed our report ?* "

WILLIAM CARTER in a sermon to the outcasts of London, said : " Hear what Jesus declares : ' Verily, verily, I say unto you, he that heareth My word, and believeth on Him that sent me, hath everlasting life, and shall not come into condemnation, but is passed from death unto life.' Here, my friends, there are three links in the blessed chain of truth —hearing, believing, and having. The devil always tries to cut these links off, and give three links of his own forging, viz. doing, praying, feeling."

This item was copied into a religious weekly newspaper in this country, and was there read by a gentleman, when after three weeks of waiting for the *feeling* of a change in his heart, he had given up all hope, and concluded that there was no salvation for him. God's way of salvation at once seemed plain, and the gentleman was soon a happy Christian.

CCCCXXI. Belief in the Atonement. Isa. liii. 6.
" The Lord hath laid on Him the iniquity of us all."

DORA GREENWELL beautifully says, "Belief in that one great doctrine of the Atonement is to me like the blue flower of the German legends; long sought and hidden, but when found, admitting into every guarded treasure, which, without the possession of it, would have been closed up."

CCCCXXII. Attempting Great Things for God.
Isa. liv. 2, 3. *"Enlarge the place of thy tent, and let them stretch forth the curtains of thy habitations: spare not, lengthen thy cords, and strengthen thy stakes."*

ON the 30th of May, 1792, William Carey, the future missionary, was appointed to preach at an Association in Nottingham. His sermon on this occasion has become historical. The building in which it was preached is still in existence, though diverted to quite a different purpose. The text on which the discourse was founded was Isaiah liv. 2, 3: "Enlarge the place of thy tent, and let them stretch forth the curtains of thine habitations: spare not, lengthen thy cords, and strengthen thy stakes; for thou shalt break forth on the right hand and on the left; and thy seed shall inherit the Gentiles, and make the desolate cities to be inhabited." The preacher observed that the Church is here addressed as a desolate widow, dwelling in a small tent by herself; that the command to enlarge her tent implied that there should be an enlargement of her family; that to account for so unexpected and marvellous a change, she was told, "Thy Maker is thy Husband," and that at a future day He would be called "the God of the whole earth." He then proceeded to establish and illustrate the two great principles involved in the text, and that have since become "household words" throughout the Christian world in reference to the missionary enterprise— I. *Expect great things from God;* II. *Attempt great things for God.* In this sermon the thought and feeling of years were concentrated. The effect which it produced was electrical. Dr. Ryland, who was present, said, "If all the people had lifted up their voices and wept, as the children of Israel did at Bochim, I should not have wondered at the effect: it would only have seemed proportionate to the cause; so clearly did he prove the criminality of our supineness in the cause of God."

CCCCXXIII. Comforted of God. ISA. liv. 5. "*Thy Maker is thine Husband.*"

AN eminent physician, who, in visiting the sick, sought to administer to the soul as well as to the body, one day called upon a poor widow, whom, on a previous visit, he had found in great darkness of mind. She was now in a happy frame, and, on asking her what had been the means of her comfort, she said it had been these words in Isaiah liv. 5 —" Thy Maker is thine Husband; the Lord of Hosts is His Name." On asking her what she had felt in these words to cheer her, her answer was: " I've been thinking that if that be true, I should be beginning to live up to His income."

CCCCXXIV. A Bitter Cup. ISA. liv. 11. "*O thou afflicted, tossed with tempest and not comforted, behold, I will lay thy stones with fair colours, and lay thy foundations with sapphires.*"

IT is delightful to sit down beside a child of God who has in his hand a bitter cup of trial. Jesus has turned the bitterness into such a blessing that he "tastes the love" of Jesus in every drop.

I love to hear old Richard Baxter exclaim, after a life of constant suffering, "O my God! I thank Thee for a bodily discipline of eight-and-fifty years."

I love to sit down by Harlan Page and hear him say, "A bed of pain is a precious place, when we have the presence of Christ. God does not send one unnecessary affliction. Lord! I thank Thee for suffering. I deserve it. I deserve death eternal. Let me not complain nor dictate. I commit myself to Thee, O Saviour, and to Thy infinite love. I stop my mouth, and lie low beside Thee!" So God built up that blood-built soul faster than disease was pulling down the frail tenement in which it dwelt. And through the rents heaven's glory shone in with rapturous radiance!

CCCCXXV.   Children in Prison.   ISA. liv. 13.
"Thy children shall be taught of the Lord."

An interesting circumstance occurred lately in Finland. Some children from seven to nine years of age were so brought under the sensible influence of the Spirit of God, convincing them of their sins, that, on their going to or from school, they retired into the woods, and there put up their prayers to the Lord, with many tears. By degrees their number increased. The parents of some of them found them thus engaged, and with rebukes and stripes dispersed them; but the parents of others, who had noticed the increased sobriety and good behaviour of their children, encouraged them to meet together in their houses, and not to go out into the woods. The children did so; and some of these parents, observing their religious tenderness, and hearing their solemn prayers to the Lord, the Redeemer, and Saviour of sinners, felt themselves strong convictions of sin. They joined their children in their devotions, and a great reform took place in that part of the country. This excited the angry feelings of the priest, who was a bad man and a drunkard. He went to the magistrate to enter his complaints against both children and parents. The prosecution issued in their all being sent to prison.

They had seen some months in confinement, when the Prince Alexander Galitzin heard that *children* were in prison on account of religion. He thought it so strange an occurrence that he sent confidential persons to inquire into it. They found so much religious sensibility and tenderness in the children, that they were greatly surprised, especially at the simplicity with which they related how they had been brought under trouble because of their sinful hearts, and how they had felt that they must pray to the Lord Jesus Christ, who alone could forgive them and enable them to live in a state of acceptance before God. Being inquired of if their parents or others had not put them on doing this, they said that so far from that, they were afraid that their parents or any one else should know how it was with them, that they retired privately in the woods to pray and cry with tears unto the Lord. The parents also stated that the children had been the instruments of bringing them to a sense of their sinful lives, and to seek the Lord that He might give them a new heart, and pour forth His Spirit upon them. Moreover, it was found that the conduct of these people and children had been such during their imprisonment as to comport with their Christian profession. The prince ordered their release, and had the priest and the magistrates severely reprimanded and removed from their offices. The emperor having heard of all this, and of the great sufferings to which these families were reduced in consequence of their long imprisonment, which took place just before harvest, ordered that all their losses should be liberally made up to them, making ample provision, also, for their present support.

CCCCXXVI. Hearing, not Reading. Isa. lv. 3.

"*Incline your ear, and come unto Me; hear, and your soul shall live.*"

A POOR man being on his death-bed, asked that the fifty-fifth chapter of Isaiah should be read to him. Though weak, and faint, and full of pain, yet when he heard the words, "Incline your ear, and come unto Me; hear, and your soul shall live," he gathered up his strength to say, "What a mercy, sir, that it is not '*Read*, and your soul shall live;' for if it had been, I could not have been saved, for you know I am no scholar! But blessed be God, it is '*Hear*, and your soul shall live;' I have heard, and believed, and trust I shall be saved."

CCCCXXVII. Trust the Promises. Isa. lv. 3.

"*The sure mercies of David.*"

LAST winter a man crossed the Mississippi on the ice, and, fearing it was too thin, began to crawl on his hands and knees in great terror; but when he gained the opposite shore, all worn out, another man drove past him gaily, sitting upon a sled loaded with pig-iron. That is just the way most Christians go up to the heavenly Canaan, trembling at every step lest the promises shall break under their feet, when really they are secure enough for us to hold our heads and sing with confidence as we march to the better land.

CCCCXXVIII. Joy and Peace in Dying. Isa. lv.
12. *"For ye shall go out with joy, and be led forth with peace."*

Lady Lush's deathbed was characterized by the joyfulness of a Christian about to enter the glorious presence of the Lord. Dr. Landels, in his memorial sermon, said : "Amidst all her bodily sufferings, her inward peace never failed. The Lord was with her all through, and never withdrew from her for a moment the light of His countenance. 'The Lord is with you, dear,' whispered the voice of affection. 'Yes, He is never absent,' was the calm, glad response. And again, 'Is it peace, dear?' to which she replied, 'Peace does not express it—it is joy.'"

CCCCXXIX. The Close of Life. Isa. lvii. 15.
"Eternity."

Albert Barnes, in his sermon on "Life at Threescore," illustrates the magnitude of eternal things as he approaches the end of life, compared with those which ordinarily occupy the attention of mankind, by the following figure:—

"The earth, as it moves in its orbit from year to year, maintains its distance of ninety-five millions of miles from the sun; and the sun, except when seen through a hazy atmosphere, at its rising or its setting, seems at all times to be of the same magnitude—to human view an object always small, as compared with our own world. But suppose the earth should leave its orbit, and make its way in a direct line towards the sun. How soon would the sun seem to enlarge its dimensions! How vast and bright would it become! How soon would it fill the whole field of vision, and all on the earth dwindle to nothing! So human life now appears to me. In earlier years, eternity appeared distant and small in importance. But at the period of life which I have now reached, it seems to me as if the earth had left the orbit of its annual movement, and were making a rapid and direct flight to the sun. The objects of eternity, towards which I am moving, rapidly enlarge themselves. They have become overpoweringly bright and grand. They fill the whole field of vision, and the earth, with all which is the common object of human ambition and pursuit, is vanishing away!"

CCCCXXX. A Great God and a Little God.
Isa. lvii. 15. "*For thus saith the high and lofty One that inhabiteth eternity, whose name is Holy; I dwell in the high and holy place, with him also that is of a contrite and humble spirit.*"

COLLINS, the freethinker, met a plain country man going to church. He asked him where he was going. "To church, sir." "What to do there?" "To worship God." "Pray, whether is your God, a great or a little God?" "He is both, sir." "How can He be both?" "He is so great, sir, that the heaven of heavens cannot contain Him, and so little that He can dwell in my heart." Collins declared that this simple answer from the country man had more effect upon his mind than all the volumes which learned doctors had written against him.

CCCCXXXI. An Arctic Explorer and Sabbath Keeping.
Isa. lviii. 13. "*If thou turn away thy foot from the Sabbath, from doing thy pleasure on My holy day; and call the Sabbath a delight, the holy of the Lord, honourable; and shalt honour Him, not doing thine own ways, nor finding thine own pleasure, nor speaking thine own words.*"

DR. SCORESBY, of Arctic fame, was a devoted Christian, and not ashamed of the gospel of Christ amid the pursuits and honours of science.

It was in the year 1820 that he introduced on board of his ship the regulation as to no fishing on the Sabbath, to the successful working of which he long after published an emphatic testimony. He always kept up the habit of reading prayers and sermons on board ship, and one of his own prayers, offered in name of the whole ship's company, on setting out on a voyage, has been preserved in his biography, and is singularly rich, and humble, and full of unction. We may notice that, during his stay in Edinburgh, on one occasion, he made the acquaintance of Sir Walter Scott, and, being invited to meet a party at his house on the Sabbath Day, wrote in reply—"I fear I cannot have the honour of waiting upon you on Sunday at dinner, agreeably to the arrangement you were so kind and polite as to propose. For some years, indeed, I have declined visiting on that day of the week; though I readily and honestly acknowledge that in this instance the privation is greater than on any occasion that ever before occurred."

CCCCXXXII. Keeping the Sabbath Holy. ISA. lviii. 13. *"If thou turn away thy foot from the Sabbath, from doing thy pleasure on My holy day; and call the Sabbath a delight, the holy of the Lord, honourable; and shalt honour Him, not doing thine own ways, nor finding thine own pleasure."*

MR. POWELL was an eminent Welsh minister who was born in 1617. He was a vain and thoughtless youth, and a ringleader among his associates in folly and wickedness, but the Spirit of God graciously arrested him in his sinful career. As he was, on one Lord's Day, standing and looking at a number of people breaking the Sabbath by divers games, one of the Puritans passed by and addressed him: "Doth it become you, sir, that are a scholar, to break the Lord's Day thus?" To which he replied, like the scoffers in Malachi: "Wherein do I break it? You see me only stand by; I do not play at all." "But you find your own pleasure herein by looking on, and this God forbids in His holy Word."

So he opened his Bible, and read those words in Isaiah lviii. 13, particularly noting that expression, "Not finding thine own pleasure on My holy day." He resolved there and then never to transgress in that way again, and God enabled him to stand to his resolution.

CCCCXXXIII. God's Power to Save. ISA. lix. 1. *"Behold, the Lord's hand is not shortened, that it cannot save; neither His ear heavy, that it cannot hear."*

DR. KRAPF was a missionary to the Wanica people, and was often much cast down by their blindness and ignorance. On one occasion, being very despondent about their condition, he went out and looked up to the starry heavens, and he found all his misgivings scattered by that text flashing into mind: "Who is gone into heaven, and is on the right hand of God; angels and authorities and powers being subject to Him." He meditated much on these glorious words, and thought, "Need I despair of these poor Wanicas? Can I doubt His power? for was not my own heart as hard and blind as theirs, and can He not convert them too?"

CCCCXXXIV. Light in the World. ISA. lx. 1.
"Arise, shine; for thy light is come."

THERE is a little church on a lonely hillside where they have neither gas nor lamps, and yet on darkest nights they hold Divine service. Each worshipper, coming a great distance from village or moorland home, brings with him a taper and lights it from the one supplied and carried by the minister of the little church. The building is thronged, and the scene is said to be "most brilliant!" Let each one of our lives be but a little taper—lighted from the Life of Christ, and carrying His flame—and we shall help to fill this great temple of human need and human sin with the light of the knowledge of the glory of God.

CCCCXXXV. Christ's Kingdom is Growing.
ISA. lx. 2. *"For, behold, the darkness shall cover the earth, and gross darkness the people: but the Lord shall arise upon thee, and His glory shall be seen upon thee."*

AT a Church Missionary meeting the Bishop of Moosonee, furnishing proofs of the growing civilization of the Indians, said:—

"I am here to speak of the conversion of men to God through the work of the missionaries, and I can tell you of men who evidence by their lives that they have been born again of the Holy Spirit of God. While speaking some time ago to an Indian, I said to him, 'My friend, I should be glad if you would give me a picture of the Indians as they were before they received Christianity.' I took down the man's words in reply from his own lips, and they were these:—'Before we were Christians we were very, very wicked; we knew nothing save the devil and the devil's works. We lied, we stealed, we conjured; we thought we could prophesy. The Indians robbed men of other tribes; the Indians robbed each other. Their lives were very ; very wicked.' They were indeed wicked. Let me mention a case in point :—

"A few years before I went to the country there was a post belonging to the Hudson Bay Company, fifty miles distant from Moose. A gentleman lived there with his wife and children, and some servants, and he thought they were living in perfect security. The Indians came to the place regularly to trade, and he appeared never to have suspected that they would rise against him and take his wife. He had charge of a large store, where there were things that gladdened the Indian's heart; there was plenty of tea, plenty of sugar, plenty of guns, plenty of ammunition. The Indians determined that they would attack that place, and rob the store of all that it contained. And one day they rose against the master and his family, and his servants, and killed every one of them, with the exception of the youngest servant, who fled to Moose factory, which he reached with great difficulty, having been pursued for many miles on his way. The murderers were afterwards pursued and captured. One of them was asked, 'How could you dare to act in such a way towards people who had always shown you the greatest kindness?' He said, 'We were instigated to it by our conjurers; they told us to do it.' The conjurers were asked how they dared to give such advice to the people, and they said, 'Our Moneto' (that is, spirit) 'told us to do it. He told us to attack the store, and not respect the lives of those who had charge of it—the lives of the father, the mother, the children, or the servants.' These Indians had no feelings of hostility towards the people at that post, but they paid attention to their sorcerers and conjurers, and they thought, perhaps, that they were doing their duty. How is it with the missionaries and their families now? They live in those regions in the greatest imaginable security. The most precious treasure which I have in this world is my wife and children, and I should not feel the slightest anxiety in entrusting them to the charge of these Indians. I should be sure they would be well and kindly treated, and that they would be protected day and night. That is, I think, saying a good deal."

CCCCXXXVI. Gone into the World of Light.
Isa. lx. 19. *"The Lord shall be unto thee an everlasting light."*

NEVER since the great minstrel of the border was borne from Abbotsford to Dryburgh Abbey has the valley of the Tweed been so moved as when the sage of Allerly, Sir David Brewster, was carried to his tomb in the old abbey of Melrose, amidst sorrowing crowds of friends and neighbours, and representatives from the seats of learning and science. There he rests till the resurrection morn, and the stone that marks the spot where he lies bears the simple and appropriate words—"THE LORD IS MY LIGHT."

CCCCXXXVII. An Inscription of a Tombstone.
Isa. lx. 20. *"Thy sun shall no more go down: for the Lord shall be thine everlasting light, and the days of thy mourning shall be ended."*

OF all the inscriptions in the necropolis of Glasgow, none strikes a visitor so much as the texts of Scripture inscribed on the monument of Dr. Beattie, who died in his fortieth year. One gives the mortal side: "Thy sun shall go down while it is yet day;" the other turns the medal, and we read the inscription, full of immortality: "Thy sun shall no more go down: for the Lord God shall be thine everlasting light, and the days of thy mourning shall be ended."

CCCCXXXVIII. Captives. Isa. lxi. 1. *"To proclaim liberty to the captives, and the opening of the prison to them that are bound."*

A BAND of Algerian pirates had taken many prisoners, who were chained to the oars to row their masters. Suddenly ships of war were seen in the distance, and the captives knew there was hope. But their masters came on deck. "Pull for your lives," cried they. The whip was laid on, and the poor captives were forced to pull, and thus, by their own efforts, to fly from their rescuers. So Satan is a hard taskmaster, and when

Jesus comes to the soul, and it is about to yield, Satan places all sorts of snares for it.

CCCCXXXIX. Dancing for Joy. ISA. lxi. 10. "*I will greatly rejoice in the Lord, my soul shall be joyful in my God.*"

A REMINISCENCE of the late Professor (Rabbi) Duncan is incidentally given by Dr. Bonar. "One day he said to me, and said it sorrowfully, in one of our many walks, 'I was as nearly an atheist as I believe it possible for a man to be,'—implying that, from his own experience, he was inclined to conclude that there never was such a being as an out-and-out atheist. His dread of his own doubtings was seen strikingly in what he said to a friend, regarding the breaking of the light: 'When first I saw *there could be a* GOD, *I danced for joy.*' It was when walking out alone that this light broke. It was on 'the Brig o' Dee' that he 'danced for joy.'"

CCCCXL. Christ Covering the Sinner. ISA. lxi. 10. "*He hath covered me with the robe of righteousness.*"

AN American citizen had been condemned in a Spanish court, and was to die; but the consul interposed, and declared that the Spanish authorities had no power to put him to death. Being determined to save him, he was wrapped round in the flags—the stars and stripes. "Now fire, if you dare," he said. "If you do, you defy the great nation represented by these flags." There stood the man, and before him the soldiers; and yet he was invulnerable, as though in a coat of mail. So is the sinner, wrapped round by the blood-red robe of Christ.

CCCCXLI. God's Constant and Personal Supervision of His People. ISA. lxiii. 13. "*That led them as an horse in the wilderness, that they should not stumble.*"

THE following is an incident of travel in which light is thrown upon a beautiful expression of Isaiah, "That led them as an horse in the wilderness, that they should not stumble," of which the commentators give many distracting representations. Two English gentlemen were conveying their horses across the wilderness to be used in Palestine. The journey lasted for more than six weeks, and during all that time these horses were only occasionally mounted; they were led by hand almost every step of the way, being watched over with particular care by special attendants, that they might take no harm from the somewhat rude ordeal to which their owners thought it well to expose them. And when I saw those two horses led thus carefully through the rocky desert, and marked how carefully the guides picked out the easiest tracks for them, and paid continual attention to their food, and to their health, and to the state of their hoofs, which were sorely tried by the hard and burning soil on which they trod, I could neither help recalling this passage in Isaiah, nor recognising in the picture an illustration of the prophet's idea.

Each master would take the bridle of his steed upon his arm, and would walk beside him, encouraging him with kindly words. Especially when the track led over one of the frightful passes of the Sinaitic region, where a sort of staircase of slippery rock leads up or down on the edge of a yawning ravine, the master would be sure to give his personal aid in guiding his terrified favourite safely over so perilous a place. I can fancy I see the picturesque group at this moment; the skilful Arab groom and the affectionate English master busied in restraining the snorting, rearing creature whose reluctance taxed all their patience and gentle force. One time they would cover his eyes, that he might not see all the danger that lay in front of him; at another time they would urge him forward with mingled caresses and blows; sometimes they would stoop down to plant his feet in the securest spots, and when safe ground was reached at length, they would lavish a thousand endearments upon him, as though he had verily done something worthy of reward and praise, instead of owing all his success to the wisdom and care of his anxious guides.

CCCCXLII. What must Heaven be? ISA. lxv. 17.

"For, behold, I create new heavens and a new earth."

HAJI HAGOP was an Armenian convert to Christianity, and in the increasing infirmities of old age he longed to depart and be with Christ. Taking a book from beneath his cushion, he said to a missionary, "Next to my Bible, this is precious to my soul; I am now reading it through for the third time." It was a worn copy of Baxter's "Saints' Rest" in Armenian. When told that the "Saint" wrote the book when sick and with heaven full in view, he was greatly interested, and said, "I shall meet him there, and will tell him how it has comforted me in my pilgrimage." He then gave the visitor an account of what some one had told him of the wonders of American cities—of the broad, clean streets, the churches, the khans (hotels) like palaces, etc. He added, "It was wonderful, and as I listened, I thought after this manner: 'What must *heaven* be?' If he should tell all this to a poor Koord, who had never seen or heard of anything better than his hole in the ground, what idea would he get? Just none at all: you might as well describe the light to a blind man. And then I said to myself, 'So little can *I* understand of heaven; but thanks be to God, through the blood of His dear Son, I shall one day see and know it all for myself.'"

CCCCXLIII. The Corruption of Sin. JER. vi. 14.

"They have healed also the hurt of the daughter of My people slightly."

LIKE snow-drift when it has levelled the churchyard mounds, and glistening in the winter sun, lies so pure and fair and beautiful above the dead who fester and rot below, a very plausible profession, wearing the look of innocence, may conceal from human eyes the foulest heart-corruption.

CCCCXLIV. Entreating Sinners to come to Jesus. JER. ix. 1.

"Oh that my head were waters, and mine eyes a fountain of tears, that I might weep day and night for the slain of the daughter of my people!"

ONE of Mr. Sherman's members writes thus of his ministry: "This I can testify, that his sermons sent us home to our closets, and made us careful to harrow in the good seed of the Word before the birds of the air had time to rob us of it." There is an anecdote told of a careless Sabbath-breaker who stumbled into his chapel one Sunday evening, when he was engaged in prayer. He took his stand in the aisle, and seeing the tears rolling down the minister's cheeks and falling on the book as he was pleading for the conversion of sinners, he was aroused, and said to himself: "This man is evidently in earnest; there must be something in the condition of sinners that I do not understand." He remained, was instructed and converted, and became a useful and steady member of the congregation.

CCCCXLV. The Handwriting of God. JER. x. 12. *"He hath made the earth by His power, He hath established the world by His wisdom, and hath stretched out the heavens by His discretion."*

THOMAS CARLYLE, having on one occasion spoken of the First Epistle to the Corinthians as being part of a Bible about the Divine authority of which many wise and good men have been doubtful, went on to say, "at any rate, we are sure that in the rocks and seas and stars we have the authentic handwriting of the Most High."

CCCCXLVI. Christ not Needed. JER. xii. 5. *"How wilt thou do in the swelling of Jordan?"*

A PROMINENT business man thus expressed himself to a Christian minister: "I am interested in Church matters, and always glad to see ministers when they call. But I have thought the subject over long and carefully, and have come to the deliberate decision that I have no need of Jesus." A single week had not passed before that man was taken sick. His disease was accompanied with such inflammation of the throat as forbade his speaking at all. This enforced silence continued until the hour of death, when he was enabled to utter simply this one despairing whisper: *"Who shall carry me over the river?"*

CCCCXLVII. The Weeping Intercessor. JER. xiii. 17. *"But if ye will not hear it, my soul shall weep in secret places for your pride."*

THERE is a distinct connection between importunate agonizing and true success, even as between the travail and the birth, the sowing in tears and the reaping in joy. "How is it that your seed comes up so soon?" said one gardener to another. "Because I steep it," was the reply. We must steep all our teachings in tears, "when none but God is nigh," and their growth will surprise and delight us. Could any one wonder at Brainerd's success, when his diary contains such notes as this?—"Lord's Day, April 25th.—This morning spent about two hours in sacred duties, and was enabled more than ordinarily to agonize for immortal souls; though it was early in the morning, and the sun scarcely shone at all, yet my body was quite wet with sweat." The secret of Luther's power lay in the same direction. Theodorus said of him: "I overheard him in prayer, but with what life and spirit did he pray! It was with so much reverence, as if he were speaking to God, yet with so much confidence, as if he were speaking to his friend."

CCCCXLVIII. A Barren Tree. JER. xv. 15. "*Take me not away in Thy longsuffering.*"

THOMAS SCOTT, the commentator, tells the following incident: "A poor man, most dangerously ill, of whose religious state I entertained some hopes, seemed to me in the agonies of death. I sat by his bed for a long time, expecting to see him expire; but at length he awoke as from a sleep, and noticed me. I said, 'You are extremely ill.' He replied, 'Yes, but I shall not die this time.' I asked the ground of this strange confidence, saying that I was persuaded he would not recover. To this he answered, 'I have just dreamed that you, with a very venerable-looking person, came to me. He asked you what you thought of me. "What kind of tree is it? Is there any fruit?" You said, "No; but there are blossoms!" "Well then, I will spare it a little longer!"' This dream so exactly met my ideas as to the man's state of mind, and the event so answered his confidence by recovery, that I could not but think there was something peculiar in it. I have since learned that after many backslidings the man became a decidedly religious character—and his case furnishes a most striking instance of the longsuffering and tender mercy of our God!"

CCCCXLIX. A Subject neither Studied nor Understood. JER. xv. 16, 17. *"Thy word was unto me the joy and rejoicing of mine heart: for I am called by Thy name, O Lord God of hosts. I sat not in the assembly of the mockers."*

SIR ISAAC NEWTON set out in life an unbeliever; but on a careful examination of the evidences of Christianity, he found reason to change his opinion. When the celebrated Dr. Edmund Halley was talking infidelity before him, Sir Isaac Newton addressed him thus: "I am always glad to hear you when you speak about astronomy, or other parts of the mathematics, because that is a subject you have studied and well understand; but you should not talk of Christianity, for you have not studied it. I have, and am certain you know nothing of the matter." This was a just reproof, and well suited to present-day infidels.

CCCCL. Nero. JER. xvii. 9. *"The heart is deceitful above all things, and desperately wicked: who can know it?"*

THE beginning of Nero's reign was marked by acts of the greatest kindness and condescension,—by affability, complaisance, and popularity. The object of his administration seemed to be the good of his people; and when he was desired to sign his name to a list of malefactors that were to be executed, he exclaimed, "*I wish to Heaven I could not write!*" He was an enemy to flattery; and when the senate had liberally commended the wisdom of his government, Nero desired them to keep their praises till he deserved them. Yet this was the wretch who assassinated his mother, who set fire to Rome, and destroyed multitudes of men, women, and children, and threw the odium of that dreadful action upon the Christians. The cruelties he exercised towards them were beyond description, while he seemed to be the only one who enjoyed the tragical spectacle.

CCCCLI. Columba and His Ministry. JER. xxiii. 4. *"I will set up shepherds over them which shall feed them."*

ON Iona, Columba built his monastery and cell, rudely

constructed and thatched with reeds. Round his dwelling rose the wattle huts inhabited by his followers ; and here the little band, headed by their chief, devoted the time to evangelizing pursuits.

Occasionally assisting in the agricultural occupations of the brethren, in studying Holy Scripture and transcribing passages of the sacred text for the use of the community, Columba passed the first days of sojourn at Iona ; but in no long time wounded, dark souls, crying for the light,—craving peace beyond all else,—began to flock to the island sanctuary, and numerous wayfarers gathered about the missionary's dwelling.

Adamnan, Columba's ecclesiastical biographer, thus records a dialogue that took place between the evangelist and one of the wanderers who had found his way to Iona.

Being informed one day that a stranger from Ireland had arrived, Columba hastened to the *hospitium* to welcome him and inquire into his history. The new-comer informed him that it was his desire, in exile, and bound by monastic vows, to repent of his misdeeds. To test his sincerity, Columba drew a dismal picture of the austerities and obligations of the island-life.

"I am prepared," was the reply, "to undergo the humblest and most galling conditions that can be imposed."

He then made his confession, and on bended knee vowed that he would endure whatsoever penance he was commanded.

"It is well," said Columba. "Now rise and begone. Thou must first labour and repent in the neighbouring isle of Tiree for seven years, after which I will see thee again."

"But," said the penitent, "how can I expiate a perjury of which I have not yet spoken ? Before I left my country, I slew a man. I was placed in fetters and about to suffer death as the penalty of my offence, when a wealthy kinsman paid the ransom demanded for my life. Out of gratitude I swore to serve him all my days ; but after a short time of servitude I deserted him, and here I am notwithstanding my vow."

Upon hearing this confession, Columba decided that, until the seven years of probation had expired, the penitent should not be admitted to communion. At the end of the term, Columba admitted the penitent into the Church, and sent him back to Ireland (bearing an ivory-handled sword as his ransom) to his kinsman and former master.

The kinsman, however, refused to take the ransom, deeming himself unworthy; but without fee or reward he pardoned and released the returned exile. The freed man remained in Ireland until the death of his parents, and ultimately returned to Iona as to home, bringing with him the ivory-handled sword, which had severed the chains of slavery.

This incident points to the influence wielded by Columba over men's souls, and also demonstrates the precautions he used to prevent the unworthy sharing in Church membership, or gaining premature admission into the brotherhood.

And vigilance was needed, by reason of the number of applicants; for as Columba and his disciples meditated in the quiet of their cells, or cheerily carried on the work of ploughing, sowing, and reaping, the shouts of new-comers daily reached their ears from the shore of Mull. Then the boats were launched to ferry the unbidden but welcome guests across the strait; and having obtained the aid they had journeyed weary miles to seek, the pilgrims returned home with glowing hearts to make known the glad tidings learned at the island-mission, while others remained to be in due time admitted into the community, or to be sent forth to strive and suffer as evangelists.

CCCCLII. A Seasonable Rebuke. JER. xxvi. 3. "*If so be they will hearken, and turn every man from his evil way.*"

IT is related, in the "Life of Mrs. Savage," an excellent sister of Matthew Henry, that when some respectable pious gentlemen were one Sabbath evening assembled together, they unhappily engaged in conversation unsuitable to the day. Betty Parsons, a good old woman, overhearing them, said: "Sirs, you are making work for repentance." This short and seasonable rebuke restrained them, and turned their conversation into a different and better channel.

CCCCLIII. Concentration of Heart. JER. xxix. 13.

"And ye shall seek Me, and find Me, when ye shall search for Me with all your heart."

A BROKEN heart is a great blessing, when it is broken by contrition for sin; but a *divided heart* is often a fatal disease.

One secret of success in life is concentration; and many of our young men find it out too late. The founder of the Vanderbilt family bent his whole powers upon money-making, and left the richest family on the Continent. Sir Isaac Newton's famous explanation of his splendid success was, "I intend my whole mind upon it." Prof. Joseph Henry, of Washington, our great Christian scientist, used to say: "I have no faith in universal geniuses: my rule is to train all my guns on one point until I make a breach." In these days of hot competition there is no room on the street for any man who puts only a fraction of himself into his business.

CCCCLIV. Pliny's Myrtle and Christ's Cross. JER. xxx. 17.

"For I will restore health unto thee, and I will heal thee of thy wounds, saith the Lord."

THE heathen naturalist, Pliny, tells of a peculiarly fragrant myrtle-tree which grew in great abundance in his own time, and which he represents as possessing a strange and even miraculous virtue. A spray cut from it and carried in the hand could so continuously sustain the body that weariness was impossible, while it exercised such an exhilarating potency over the mind that no feeling approaching the sense of discouragement or despondency could ever be experienced. That fabled tree was a fitting emblem of the efficacy of grace in healing all the soul's diseases, and, in its ultimate result, delivering the body also from every malady which may now afflict or oppress it, raising it up on the resurrection-day in the likeness and loveliness of the glorious body of the Son of God.

CCCCLV. Restoration of Israel. JER. xxxii. 37.

"Behold, I will gather them out of all countries, whither I have driven them in Mine anger, and in My fury, and in great wrath; and I will bring them again unto this place."

IN the year 1808 a gentleman was riding with Mr. Lewis

Way through a fine park in Devonshire. "Do you know," said the gentleman to Mr. Way, "that these oaks have rather a strange condition attached to them? A lady, who formerly owned this park, stipulated in her will that these trees should not be cut down until Jerusalem should again be in possession of Israel; and they are growing still." Mr. Way's interest was roused by this story, and the idea of the Jews' restoration took hold of his mind; and, shortly afterwards, he was the means of forming the London Society of the Jews.

CCCCLVI. Process of Wine-Making. JER. xlviii. 11. *"Moab hath not been emptied from vessel to vessel."*

IN a foreign land we were once witness to the process of wine-making. A series of tuns were ranged in order, and into one of these the expressed liquid was poured, when the process of fermentation was to begin. It began in the first of the series of tuns, and, after some time, the liquid was drawn off to another, and another, leaving a sediment in each; and the process was prolonged till the desired degree of purity was secured. At each successive stage, the refinement becomes more and more obvious to an experienced eye, while the wine becomes better and more costly; and that is the Scriptural emblem for the promoting of holiness in the soul.

CCCCLVII. A Storm at Sea. JER. xlix. 23. *"There is sorrow on the sea; it cannot be quiet."*

ON one occasion, Dr. Macfarlane dined with Mr. Spurgeon at the house of Mr. Boustead, and, during the course of the evening, Mr. Spurgeon mentioned a very striking coincidence. His brother was married to a daughter of Field-Marshal Sir J. B——, whose son was captain of the great turret-ship *Captain*, which went down in the storm of the evening of September 7th, 1870. Lady B—— told Mr. Spurgeon that she had been deeply impressed with her reading on that night in his "Evening by Evening," from these words in Jeremiah xlix. 23: "There is sorrow on the sea; it cannot be quiet." The meditation begins thus: " Little know we what sorrow may be upon the sea at this moment. We are safe in our quiet chamber, but far away on the salt sea, the hurricane may be cruelly seeking for the lives of men."

CCCCLVIII. The "Ninety and Nine." JER. l. 6.
"My people hath been lost sheep."

A WRITER describes a scene which he once saw that brought our Lord's parable of the "ninety and nine" before his eyes :—

"On the Aletsch Glacier I saw a strange, a beautiful sight—the parable of the 'ninety and nine' reacted to the letter. One day we were making our way with ice-axe and alpenstock down the glacier, when we observed a flock of sheep following their shepherds over the intricate windings between crevasses, and so passing from the pastures on one side of the glacier to the pastures on the other. The flock had numbered two hundred, all told. But on the way one sheep had got lost. One of the shepherds, in his German patois, appealed to us if we had seen it. Fortunately, one of the party had a field-glass. With its aid we discovered the lost sheep far up amid a tangle of brushwood on the rocky mountain-side. It was beautiful to see how the shepherd, without a word, left his hundred and ninety-nine sheep out on the glacier waste (knowing they would stand there perfectly still and safe), and went clambering back after the lost sheep until he found it. And he actually put it on his shoulder and 'returned rejoicing.'"

CCCCLIX. God Unwilling to Afflict. LAM. iii. 33.
"For He doth not afflict willingly nor grieve the children of men."

SIR WILLIAM ROWAN HAMILTON, in writing to a friend about the common feeling that when prosperity is great, chastisement must be due, says : " The ancients had much of this feeling, and partly from it they drew their idea of the goddess Nemesis, a mysterious power of whom one function was to chastise the too prosperous among men. To appease this imagined jealousy or envy of some divinity, a king (I think Polzerates of Samos) is reported to have been advised, by one of the wise men of Greece, to inflict on himself some voluntary suffering. The king accordingly threw into the sea a ring of great cost, and one which he otherwise valued. The ring was the next day presented to him by his cook, who had found it in the stomach of a fish; on hearing which, the wise man withdrew himself from the king's society, thinking that one whose prosperity had been hitherto so uninterrupted must be destined for some signal and vindictive visitation of adversity. But this is not a Christian feeling. *Our* God indeed chasteneth those whom He loveth, but not because He grudges them prosperity. Let us commit ourselves to His hands without fear that He will visit us with affliction for its own sake, or because we are happy now."

CCCCLX. Insensibility to Daily Mercies.
LAM. iii. 22. "*The Lord's mercies.*"

As the Dead Sea drinks in the river Jordan, and is never the sweeter, and the ocean all other rivers, and is never the fresher, so we are apt to receive daily mercies from God, and still remain insensible of them, unthankful for them.

CCCCLXI. God Fulfilling His Threatenings.
LAM. v. 18. "*Because of the mountain of Zion, which is desolate, the foxes walk upon it.*"

IT is said that two rabbis, when coming near Jerusalem, saw a fox running up the hill of Zion. The oldest of the two men began to weep at the sight, but Rabbi Eliezar laughed. "Wherefore dost thou mourn?" he said. "I mourn because I see fulfilled before mine eyes that was written in Lamentations: 'Because of the mountain of Zion, which is desolate, the foxes fall upon it.'" "And that is the reason of my laughter," repeated Rabbi Eliezar, "for when I see with mine own eyes that God is fulfilling His threatenings to the letter, I have in it a sure pledge that not one of His promises shall fail, for He is more willing to be gracious than to chastise."

CCCCLXII. A Quaker Tailor. EZEK. i. 3. "*The word of the Lord came expressly unto Ezekiel the priest.*"

JOHN WOOLMAN was the son of a poor farmer near the village of Mount Holly in New Jersey. He was first apprenticed, as a child, to a baker, then to a tailor. A tailor he remained through life. He was not a scholar; he was a man neither of exceptional intellectual force nor of personal magnetism; he taught no new creed, said and did nothing to startle the world. Yet the little Quaker tailor was a power while living, and is still a power in the world, although he has been dead more than a century.

What was his secret? It was a simple matter enough. When he was a boy of seven, sitting alone by the roadside, one day, he read the words: "And I beheld a pure river of water of life, clear as crystal, proceeding out of the throne of God." They moved him as only children can be moved. The idea of this pure water of life flowing from God wholly possessed him as he grew older. It was Truth. In his journal, Truth always means God. While at his school, or at work in his shop, the thought persistently came to him—if he could make of himself a conduit through which this water of life should pass to men; stifle all his own wishes and traits, obliterate his own character if necessary, and stand ready and passive for God to use!

The only point wherein John Woolman differed from other men was that he succeeded in doing this. In great actions, and in the least, he waited to feel the "divine drawing" in his mind before he moved. It was the story of the Hebrew prophets over again.

CCCCLXIII. Christmas Evans on Preaching.

EZEK. iii. 17. "*Son of man, I have made thee a watchman unto the house of Israel: therefore hear the word at My mouth, and give them warning from Me.*"

CHRISTMAS EVANS makes the following remarks on preaching: "I want preachers to read all they can, and make use of ideas which fall like the manna of old; but let them take them home to grind, and boil, and bake in the mill of prayer and the heated pot of reflection; then place them like the twelve loaves of shewbread on the golden table of the ministry before the worshippers and holy priesthood. I want the entire word to be preached, because it is given of God; but with such connections as exist in the Solar System, or in the human body, which, if disconnected, the life and effect depart. The sun is 'the world's life and a globe of fire.' Were a husbandman who tilled and cultivated the earth for its products to hold a sackcloth towards the sun, he would be esteemed an ignorant owl in our sight. Were a surgeon to amputate a limb, a hand or leg from the body, so that the connection with the great artery of the heart be broken, and then endeavour to make the blood circulate through the severed limb, to quicken and to warm it, we should only say, 'Reunite the limb to the body that the blood may pervade it in its course, or else as soon as you like, bury it in the earth.' Many preachers, I understand, have more interest in preaching about the earth's being stricken and punished with drought last year than about Jesus being struck on the cross all red with His blood! Christ's sacrifice and the Holy Spirit's grace occupy the place of the central sun and of the heart's blood in the Christian system as those do in their own systems. I have observed that an unevangelical style like that described has latterly crept in amongst all denominations in Wales in preaching duties. What good has preaching the dead cross ever done? Are the churches more heavenly, industrious, and striving? or are they more unspiritual, insipid, and lethargic? Here is gun, here is leaden bullet, here is flint, here is touch-hole, here is finger, but where is the powder? The ball will never start without that. He is the mover of the whole, 'Christ the power of God, and the wisdom of God.' 1. Let us, then, preach the whole truth evangelically. 2. Faithfully, for souls are in danger. 3. Plainly and clearly, since heaps of our hearers know less than we imagine. 4. Affectionately, fervently, and winningly! for the flame of Calvary's love is intense, and should cause a glow in the pulpit, melting everything to its own consistency, and joining man to God by the cross, to be one spirit for ever and for ever."

CCCCLXIV. Black, Cold, Hard. EZEK. xi. 19.
"I will take the stony heart out of their flesh."

THEODORE MONOD made use of a beautiful illustration at the last Dublin convention. He said: "If a piece of iron could speak, what would it say? It would say, 'I am black, I am cold, I am hard.' Perfectly true. But put that piece of iron into a furnace and wait a while, and what would it say?—'The blackness is gone, and the coldness is gone, and the hardness is gone'—it has passed into a new experience. But if that piece of iron could speak, surely it would not glory in itself, because the fire and the iron are two distinct things that remain distinct to the last. If it could glory, it would glory in the fire, and that in itself —in the fire that kept it a bright, molten mass. So in myself. I am black, I am cold, and I am hard; but if the Lord takes possession of my soul, if I am filled with love, if His Spirit fills my being, the blackness will go, and the coldness will go, and the hardness will go, and yet the glory does not belong to me, but to the Lord who keeps me in a sense of His love."

CCCCLXV. The Evil Heart of Unbelief. EZEK. xi. 19. "*I will take the stony heart out of their flesh.*"

AN old friend of Sir W. Rowan Hamilton's wrote him after a long silence, and took occasion to express interest in his inner life, and specially in his spiritual state, and the following is an extract from his correspondence on the subject: "My struggles and alternations in the spiritual life have not been between belief and doubt, but between warmth and coldness. My *intellect* has never ceased to embrace Christianity with satisfactory and complete conviction: it is the evil heart of unbelief which has, too often, departed from the living God."

CCCCLXVI. "I was Born so." EZEK. xi. 19. "*I will put a new spirit within you; and I will take the stony heart out of their flesh, and will give them an heart of flesh.*"

BISHOP HALL says, that the last Cardinal ever seen in England, when a skilful astrologer pretended to tell him something of the future from a calculation of his nativity, said: "Such, perhaps, I was born; but since that time I have been born again, and my second nativity has crossed my first." And on this remark of the Cardinal, Bishop Hall observes, "The power of nature is a good plea for those that acknowledge nothing above nature; but for a Christian to excuse his intemperateness by his natural inclination, and to say, 'I was born so,' is an apology worse than the fault." Right, most worthy bishop, right for you, and well for good people of all degrees to bear in mind this sober bit of truth. "I was born so," is the standing and all-sufficient excuse which thousands of Christians make to themselves for those infirmities of character of which they are conscious, but which they do not care to correct. One finds secret pleasure in the indulgence of a passion that God cannot approve, and he persuades himself it is not so very wrong, because it is so natural to him. Again, he has faults which render him unhappy oftentimes, and very disagreeable to his neighbours, but he makes no effort to reform them, on the same plea: "I was born so, and cannot help it." He is morose in his temper; he knows it; but he says it is his way, it is natural to him, and it is useless to try and be otherwise. He has a quick way of speaking his mind, regardless of the feelings of others, and quite careless of times, places, and persons; and when the fault is hinted to him, he says, "Oh, that's my way." So it is, and a very bad way; and because it is your way, you ought to change it.

CCCCLXVII. The Forest-guarded Highway.
EZEK. xviii. 4. "*The soul that sinneth, it shall die.*"

A TRAVELLER relates that, when passing through an Austrian town, his attention was directed to a forest on a slope near the road, and he was told that death was the penalty of cutting down *one of those trees*. He was incredulous until he was further informed that they were the protection of the city, breaking the force of the descending avalanche, which, without this natural barrier, would sweep over the quiet home of thousands. When a Russian army was marching there, and began to cut away the defence for fuel, the inhabitants besought them to take their dwellings instead, which was done.

Such, he well thought, are the sanctions of God's *moral law*. On the integrity and support of that law depends the safety of the universe. "The soul that sinneth, it shall die," is a merciful proclamation. "He that offends in one point is guilty of all," is equally just and benevolent. In this view, to every sinner out of Christ, God must be "a consuming fire." To transgress once is to lay the axe at the root of the tree which represents the security and peace of every loyal soul in the wide dominions of the Almighty.

CCCCLXVIII. "Jesus Opposers." Ezek. xxii. 2.
"*The people of the land have used oppression.*"

THE story of the triumphs of the Gospel in Japan are most interesting, but there are still many "Jesus opposers."

For some time past there has been strong opposition to Christianity on the part of certain people calling themselves the "Yaso Taiji," or "Jesus opposers." They have been lecturing all over the country, and have drawn large crowds of people to hear what they had to say. Some of the speakers are renegade Greeks and Catholics, who said, "We have tried this religion, and have found it a deception and fraud. It is a subtle and wicked scheme to get possession of the country. As Christ taught His followers to love one another, so if any Christian nation makes war upon Japan, the Japanese Christians would not fight, but yield at once to their enemies."

Of course such persons have never been sincere Christians, and have doubtless professed to be in the hope of gain.

A Christian physician recently went to Yokosuka, and when his belief was made known, his companions said he must renounce his religion or become an outcast from their society. He was much troubled, and shut himself up for two days in order that he might give himself to the study of the Bible and prayer. He then said to his friends: "Let come what will, I shall not deny my Master," and he went about his duties with a firm trust in God. He has continued to live as a Christian, and to his great joy his companions do not oppose as he expected, but some of them are now attending religious services, and are apparently sincere inquirers. The influence of his exemplary character and joyful life has been to lead those who once opposed to seek for the same precious hope and experience.

CCCCLXIX. Hearing your Funeral Sermon.
Ezek. xxiv. 17. "*Forbear to cry, make no mourning for the dead.*"

THE eulogiums which one often hears and reads of living personages, calls up the experience of an eccentric characer, who had always insisted that every man ought to hear his own funeral sermon, since it concerned *him* more than anybody else! So when he was very ill, and sure in his own mind that he was "elected to die," he sent his wife to the old minister, who kindly complied with the novel request. When he had prepared the sermon, he came with all gravity to read it to the sick man. "I never was much given to being proud, or sot up," said the old man (who lived to tell the story), "but that sermon almost did the business for me—to think of the church crowded with people, and me lying there in my coffin, and the minister looking down from the pulpit and saying all that for an hour! Why, I almost backslode! I came mighty nigh falling from grace! I tell you, if there's anything that'll make a man proud and sot up, it's hearing his own funeral sermon."

CCCCLXX. A Mighty Noise. Ezek. xxvi. 13.
"And I will cause the noise of thy songs to cease."

"THE singing of an army, to beguile the weary march, do you not remember it, old soldiers, with hairs just turning grey? It is an ascertained fact of acoustics that the surface of a plain trembles with the sound and the air fairly rocks with such melodious concussion. When Xenophon's army first caught sight of the Euxine, after an exhaustive march of suffering, they cried out, '*Thalatta, thalatta!*' 'The sea, the sea!' and birds fell dead from the mighty shout. So fish are killed by the thunder of heavy ordnance. I remember, at the first 'Peace Jubilee' in Boston, that the singing of so vast a chorus, with accompaniments, wrought me to the pitch of wildness; my nerves turned tyrants, and I fled the building, lest I died."

CCCCLXXI. Groaning, but not Grumbling. Ezek. xxx. 24.
"He shall groan before him with the groanings of a deadly wounded man."

"A RELIGIOUS commander being shot in battle, when the wound was searched and the bullet cut out, some standing by pitying his pain, he replied, 'Though I groan, yet I bless God I do not grumble.' God allows His people to groan, though not to grumble."

CCCCLXXII. The Dumb Bell. EZEK. xxxiii. 22.

"*And my mouth was opened, and I was no more dumb.*"

MR. GATTY, in his book on "Bells," gives the following anecdote, on the credit of Cardinal Baronius: "When Charles II., King of France, A.D. 615, was at Sens, in Burgundy, he heard a bell in the church of St. Stephen, the sound of which pleased him so much that he ordered it to be transported to Paris. The Bishop of Sens, however, was greatly displeased at this, and the bell so sympathised with him that it turned dumb on the road and lost all its sound. When the king heard of this, he commanded that the bell should be carried back to its old quarters, when, strange to relate, as it approached the town, it recovered its original tone, and began to ring so as to be heard at Sens, whilst yet about four leagues distant from it."

The true preacher grows silent if forced to any other service than his Lord's. If he attempts to speak on any other topic than that which concerns his Lord and the Gospel, he misses his former force; he is not at home, he is glad to end his speech and sit down. Our bell is dumb if it does not ring out for Jesus. The world would soon dismiss us if it had hired us to be its orator, for our heart is elsewhere, and only upon the one dear, familiar theme can we be eloquent.

CCCCLXXIII. Charlotte Elliot's Hymn. EZEK. xxxiii. 32. "*A very lovely song.*"

SOME fifty years ago, that eminent minister, Cæsar Malan of Geneva, was a guest of the Elliots, a well-to-do family in the West End of London.

One evening, in conversation with the daughter, Charlotte, he wished to know if she was a Christian. The young lady resented his question, and told him that religion was a matter which she did not wish to discuss. Mr. Malan replied, with his usual sweetness of manner, that he would not pursue the subject then if it displeased her, but he would pray that she might "give her heart to Christ, and become a useful worker for Him."

Several days afterwards the young lady apologised for her abrupt treatment of the minister, and confessed that his question and his parting remark had troubled her.

"But I do not know how to find Christ," she said. "I want you to help me."

"Come to Him *just as you are*," said Mr. Malan.

He little thought that one day that simple reply would be repeated in song by the whole Christian world.

Further advice resulted in opening the young lady's mind to spiritual light, and her life of devout activity and faith began. She possessed literary gifts, and having assumed the charge of the *Yearly Remembrancer* on the death of its editor, she inserted several original poems (without her name) in making up her first number. One of the poems was:—

> "Just as I am, without one plea,
> But that Thy blood was shed for me,
> And that Thou bidd'st me come to Thee,
> O Lamb of God, I come!"

The words of Pastor Malan, realized in her own experience, were of course the writer's inspiration.

Beginning thus its public history in the columns of an unpretending religious magazine, the little anonymous hymn, with its sweet counsel to troubled minds, found its way into devout persons' scrap-books, then into religious circles and chapel assemblies, and finally into the hymnals of the "Church universal." Some time after its publication a philanthropic lady, struck by its beauty and spiritual value, had it printed on a leaflet, and sent for circulation through the cities and towns of the kingdom; and in connection with this an incident at an English watering-place seems to have first revealed its authorship to the world. Miss Elliot, being in feeble health, was staying at Torquay, in Devonshire, under the care of an eminent physician. One day the doctor, who was an earnest Christian man, placed one of those floating leaflets in his patient's hands, saying he felt sure she would like it. The surprise and pleasure were mutual when she recognised her own hymn, and he discovered that she was its author.

CCCCLXXIV. Among the Flock. EZEK. xxxiv. 12.
> "*As a shepherd seeketh out his flock in the day that he is among his sheep that are scattered.*"

THE late Irenæus Prime gives the following account of his father's visiting among his flock:—

"As soon as my father arrived at any house in his

current in the Apostolic Church, that to be 'near Christ' is to be 'near the fire,' it is also true that to be *in* the fire is to be with Christ; and if we are in the furnace with the Son of man, the fire will not consume, but purge and refine."

CCCCLXXXI. An Old Martyr for Christ. DAN. iii. 21. *"Then these men were bound in their coats, their hosen, and their hats, and their other garments, and were cast into the midst of the burning fiery furnace."*

RAWLINS WHITE, an old martyr, was very decrepid, and for years he had been bowed almost double, and could hardly walk; but he was condemned to death, and on his way to the stake, we are told, the bonds of his body seemed to break, and he roused himself up as straight and exuberant as an athlete, and walked to the fire singing victory over the flames. Ah, it was the joy of dying for Jesus that straightened his body, and roused his soul!

CCCCLXXXII. An Innovation. DAN. iii. 22. *"The King's commandment was urgent."*

JOHN WESLEY received many of his most remarkable traits from his mother. He had the same regard for order and authority, and yet the same readiness to follow up an opportunity in defiance of all precedent.

Mrs. Wesley, loving order and sticking by formal rule as she did, could act a very bold and independent part once she was certain that conscience spoke clear in her breast. When the rector was away on one of his more lengthened absences at Convocation, she had gathered her children and the servants together to read and converse with them on the Sunday afternoon. The neighbours soon heard of it, and many of them wished to join the circle at the rectory. The numbers increased, till at last not a few had to go away from want of space. The rector had been advised of the innovation by the curate, and wrote to his wife that her conduct was singular, and counselled greater prudence. But the wife was able to give a reason for her course:—

"I cannot conceive why any should reflect on you be-

CCCCLXXVIII. Able to Deliver. DAN. iii. 17.
"Our God whom we serve is able to deliver."

A BOAT was once seen driving on along the rapid that hurries to the Falls of Niagara. To the horror of some that watched it from the shore, they saw one aboard, and asleep. They ran, they shouted, they cried. The sleeper woke, and at one wild glance took in all his danger. Yet what won't a man do for his life! To seize the oars, to pull her head round to the shore, was the work of an instant. With death in the thunders of the cataract roaring loud and louder in his ear, how he pulled! It was cruel to waken him; there was no hope, unless God had sent down the eagle that was sailing overhead to bear him away upon her wings; the wild waters shot him like an arrow to the brink. As near hell as that, you may be saved—plucked from the very brink of ruin.

CCCCLXXIX. In the Furnace. DAN. iii. 25.
"He answered and said, Lo, I see four men loose, walking in the midst of the fire, and they have no hurt; and the form of the fourth is like the Son of God."

BLANDINA was one of the early Christian martyrs at Lyons, in the year 177 A.D. They roasted her on a red-hot iron chair, put her in a net, and exposed her to the horns of the wildest oxen; whirled her in instruments of torture till her senses were lost, and then plunged her into flames; and day after day did that, while she apparently experienced little pain, calling out at every interval when her strength came back: "I am a believer in the Father, the Son, and the Holy Ghost, one God, who is with me. There is no evil done among us. I am a Christian." And so she passed hence, but speaks to us as one yet living.

CCCCLXXX. "Near Christ, near the Fire."
DAN. iii. 25. *"Lo, I see four men loose, walking in the midst of the fire, and they have no hurt; and the form of the fourth is like the Son of God."*

A PREACHER has said, speaking on the subject of the good effects of trial, "If it be true, according to a fine saying this great change. She told him it was the grace of God which had made her a Christian and had changed her heart.

He said to himself, "I don't believe that God has anything to do with it, though she thinks He had. But it is a wonderful change that has taken place in her, and I should like to be as good as she is. I *will* be so." Then he formed a set of good resolutions. He tried to control his tongue and his temper, and kept a strict watch over himself. He was all the time doing and saying what he did not wish to do and say. And, as he failed time after time, he would turn and study his good cousin's example. He would read this *living Bible*, and said to himself, "How does it happen that she, who has not as much knowledge or as much strength of character as I have, can do what I can't do? She must have some help that I don't know of. It must be as she says, the help of God. I will seek that help." He went into his chamber and prayed to that God whose very existence he had denied. He prayed earnestly. God heard him, helped him, and he became a Christian.

CCCCLXXVII. Human Thought and Heavenly Light. DAN. ii. 22. "*He revealeth the deep and secret things: he knoweth what is in the darkness, and the light dwelleth with Him.*"

SHORTLY before his death, St. Thomas Aquinas fell into a state of profound and rapturous contemplation, and on coming to himself, he did not sit down to his desk, nor would he dictate anything, although he was still engaged on part of his famous "Summary."

Even his nearest friends, who knew him intimately, could not account for this. At last his secretary said, "My father, why hast thou cast on one side so great a work which thou didst begin for the glory of God and the illumination of the world?" All St. Thomas Aquinas replied was, "Non possum,"—"I cannot write any more." Being constantly implored to continue writing, the saint ever made the same reply, "I cannot, for everything that I have written appears to me as simply rubbish."

So in proportion to the clearness of vision must ever seem the noblest reaches of human thought, compared with the heavenly light.

aroused, by reading a tract, to deep anxiety about the salvation of his soul, travelled nearly two hundred miles to visit a missionary to inquire about the truth. On one occasion he was much interested in reading Bunyan's "Pilgrim's Progress." He said several times to the missionary, that it was better than the Bible. The missionary pointed to the scene before them and said, "Do you see that beautiful mango tree there?" "Yes," was the reply. "Don't you see its beautiful fruit, eat it, and enjoy its sweetness?" "Yes." "And where would that tree be if there was no root to it?" "Oh," said the man, "now I see what you mean! The Bible is the root, and all the other good books in the world are produced from it."

The lesson was a timely one, nor should we ever forget, while enjoying the sweetness of some work which the Christian press sends forth, that the Bible is the root from which it springs. Plant that blessed root in any soul, and by-and-by the sweet fruit of Christian literature will appear. Fail to plant the Bible, and we shall look in vain for all the sweet and refreshing fruits.

CCCCLXXVI. The Power of a Living Bible.

EZEK. xxxvi. 27. *"And I will put My Spirit within you, and cause you to walk in My statutes."*

NOWHERE is it more true than in the Christian life that actions speak louder than words. A young man had become an infidel, and would no longer read the printed Bible, but he could not help seeing the fruits of faith in the life of another.

In his father's house a young lady resided, who was a relative of the family. Her fretful temper made all around her uncomfortable. She was sent to a boarding-school, and was absent some time. While there she became a true and earnest Christian. On her return she was so changed that all who knew her wondered and rejoiced. She was patient and cheerful, kind, unselfish, and charitable. The lips that used to be always uttering cross and bitter words now spoke nothing but sweet, gentle, loving words. Her infidel cousin George was greatly surprised at this. He watched her closely for some time, till he was thoroughly satisfied that it was a real change that had taken place in his young cousin. Then he asked her what had caused

"The children were called in, and were examined, as I have hinted, in the catechism, in which they were regularly instructed by their parents. The doctrines therein contained were familiarly explained, and the young were most earnestly persuaded to give their hearts to the Saviour, while yet in the morning of their days. As the congregation was widely extended, Mr. Prime would give notice on the Sabbath, that during the week on a certain day, he would visit in such a neighbourhood, and at three o'clock in the afternoon he wished the families in that vicinity to assemble at a house named, for religious conversation and prayer. And those were good meetings, you may be sure; the farmer's house in which it was held would be filled with parents and children, the halls and the staircase crowded; a little stand, with a Bible and Psalm-book, would be set for the minister at some point from which his voice could easily be heard over all the house, and such prayers and such appeals would be then and there made as the Spirit of God delights to attend and bless. How many tears did the children shed in those meetings! not alarmed by terrible words of coming wrath, but melted with the pathos of gospel love, and moved by the strong appeals of that holy man. Impressions, I know, were made at those meetings that eternity will only brighten and deepen, as the memory of those solemn, yet happy hours, mingles with the joy of immortal bliss.

"The effects of this ministry were, as might be expected, immediate and permanent. The Word of the Lord had free course and was glorified. The young grew up to manhood with strong attachments to the faith of their fathers, the members of the Church were steadfast in their adherence to the truth as they had received it, and it was rare to see a man in the community who was not a professor of religion. The institutions of the Gospel commanded the respect and reverence of the whole people. Impiety was scarcely known in the town, so deep-settled and wide-spread was this regard for the truths of God's Word and the ordinances of His house."

CCCCLXXV. The Root. EZEK. xxxiv. 29. "*I will raise up for them a plant of renown.*"

A SON of one of the priests of Mysore, who had been

scattered and extended parish, all the ordinary cares of the family were suspended, and the whole time of every member given to him. On his first induction to this people, it was the custom of the good woman of the house to begin to fly about when the minister came, to fix up the best parlour, and get ready some warm biscuit for tea, or a pair of chickens for dinner, if he came before noon, and thus all her time was spent, like that of Martha, in much serving. Mr. Prime soon put an end to that mode of entertainment, by informing his people from the pulpit, that when he came to see them at their houses, it was not to be feasted, but to feed their souls, and the souls of their children; and, therefore, if they wished to please him, they would do as Mary did, sit still and listen. This hint, after sundry repetitions, had the desired effect, and he was able to enjoy the whole time of his visit in those great duties which he felt to be of unspeakable importance to the spiritual welfare of the family. The heads of the household were first conversed with freely on the progress which they were making in personal religion ; if they had doubts, and fears, or any other difficulties about which they needed direction, they were encouraged to make them known, and from the stores of his well-furnished mind, and the richer treasures of a deeply spiritual experience and great familiarity with the Word of God, he was able to impart just that counsel which their trials seemed to require. If they were backward in their performance of any of the acknowledged duties of Christian life, if the worship of God in the family was not faithfully attended to, if they were at variance with any of their neighbours, or slack in the discharge of their obligations to their fellow-men, he would in all kindness, but with skilful decision, as their soul's physician, give them those prescriptions without which it was impossible for their souls to thrive. Such fidelity and freedom on his part, so far from alienating their affections, did but endear him to them the more, as they saw his affectionate interest in their soul's concerns, and felt the power and truth of the admonitions which he gave. And then these admonitions were often blessed of God to the great comfort and edification of the people, who thus found in their own happy experience the ineffable value of a faithful pastor, whom they loved even when he came to wound.

cause your wife endeavours to draw people to church, and to restrain them from profaning the Lord's Day, by reading to them and other persuasions. For my part, I value no censure on this account. I have long since shook hands with the world, and I heartily wish I had never given them more occasion to speak against me. As to its looking particular, I grant it does. And so does almost everything that is serious, or that may any way advance the glory of God or the salvation of souls, if it be performed out of a pulpit, or in the way of common conversation; because in our corrupt age the utmost care and diligence has been used to banish all discourse of God, or spiritual concerns, out of society, as if religion were never to appear out of the closet, and we were to be ashamed of nothing so much as of confessing ourselves to be Christians.

"As for the proposal of letting some other person read, alas! you don't consider what a people these are. I don't think one man among them could read a sermon without spelling a good part of it. Nor has any of our family a voice strong enough to be heard by such a number of people.

"But there is one thing about which I am much dissatisfied; that is, their being present at family prayers. I don't speak of any concern I am under, merely because so many are present. For those who have the honour of speaking to the great and holy God need not be ashamed to speak before the whole world; but because of my sex I doubt if it is proper for me to present the prayers of the people to God. Last Sunday I would fain have dismissed them before prayers; but they begged so earnestly to stay, I durst not deny them."

After having stated all her reasons in justification of the course she had taken, she wound up with these characteristic words: "If you do, after all, think fit to dissolve this assembly, do not tell me you *desire* me to do it, for that will not satisfy my conscience; but send me *your positive command*, in such full and express terms as may absolve me from guilt and punishment for neglecting the opportunity of doing good, when you and I shall appear before the great and awful tribunal of our Lord Jesus Christ."

CCCCLXXXIII. Suggestions to the Sick. DAN. vi. 35. *"He doeth according to His will in the army of heaven, and among the inhabitants of the earth: and none can stay His hand, or say unto Him, What doest Thou?"*

ELLICE HOPKINS tells the following story in speaking of some practical suggestions to the sick. "We deal with the sick too exclusively religiously, or, as I would rather say, too narrowly, since God is the God of all consolation. We say to them, with sinking heart and tears in our eyes, 'It is God's will, and you must bear your burden'; but we forget the ropes and pulleys and levers which might, with a little contrivance on our part, help to lift it—all the helps to bearing it—which may be also in God's will. As an instance of what I mean, I may take the case of one my father loved almost as a son. As a young man, with splendid abilities and a brilliant career just opening before him, he was suddenly shot stone blind, not through any carelessness on the part of him who did it, but owing to his being, in the eagerness of a sportsman, a little out of the proper line. His life thus suddenly plunged into darkness, for days he remained completely prostrate. Doubtless those around him spoke to him of the love of God and submission to His will; but it seemed impossible to raise him up out of the darkness within and without that had fallen upon him. The first thing that roused him was a letter from my father. I had often wondered what it was in that letter that succeeded when all else failed, and many years after it came into my hands, having been carefully preserved in the family. It too spoke of submission to the will of God, but the main part of the letter was taken up in carefully pointing out all that great powers of mind, even with the drawback of blindness, could accomplish, the branches of science which required, for further development, the abstract thought to which blindness would be favourable; the lines of political life to which it would be no impediment. Submission to God's will was enforced, but the helps to realizing it as a loving will at the same time carefully suggested. He to whom that letter was addressed is now one of our leading men."

CCCCLXXXIV. Touching God in Prayer. DAN. vi. 10. *" He kneeled upon his knees three times a day, and prayed, and gave thanks before his God, as he did aforetime."*

THERE is an old story of mythology about a giant, named Antæus, who was born by the earth. In order to keep alive, this giant was obliged to touch the earth as often as once in five minutes, and every time he thus came in contact with the earth he became twice as strong as before. The Christian resembles Antæus. In order to be a living Christian, he must often approach his heavenly Father in prayer; and every time he thus approaches, he becomes stronger and more able to resist the wiles and assaults of the adversary.

CCCCLXXXV. Religion a Thing for Every Day. DAN. vi. 20. *" Thy God, whom thou servest continually."*

HENRY WARD BEECHER, speaking of taking religion into the week, says: "The tides come twice a day in New York harbour, but they only come once in seven days in God's harbour of the sanctuary. They rise on Sunday, but ebb on Monday, and are down and out all the week. Men write over their store door, 'Business is business,' and over the church door, 'Religion is religion'; and they say to religion, 'Never come in here,' and to business, 'Never go in there. Let us have no secular things in the pulpit. Here we want repose, and sedatives and healing balm; we have enough of knives and probes and lancets in the week. Here let us have poetry; we want to sing hymns and to hear about heaven.' God's law is not allowed to go into the week. If the merchant spies it in the store, he throws it over the counter. If it is found in the street, the multitudes pursue it, pelting it with stones, as if it were a wolf escaped from a menagerie, and shouting, 'Back with you! you have got out of Sunday.' There is no religion in all this. It is mere sentimentalism. Religion belongs to every day. High in an ancient belfry there is a clock, and once a week the old sexton winds it up; but it has neither dial-plate nor hands. The pendulum swings, and there it goes ticking, ticking, day in, day out, unnoticed and useless. What the old clock is in its dark chamber, keeping time to itself, but never showing it, that is the mere sentimentality of religion, high above life, in the region of airy thought, perched up in the top of Sunday, but without dial or point to let the people know what o'clock it is, of time or eternity!"

CCCCLXXXVI. The Light of Eternity. DAN. xii. 2. *"And many of them that sleep in the dust of the earth shall awake, some to everlasting life, and some to shame and everlasting contempt."*

MICHAEL ANGELO once went into the studio of a young artist who had just executed a statue to stand in the public square. Angelo saw its grave defects, and pointed them out to his young friend. The exultant artist did not appreciate the criticism of his work, and supposed the greater man to be moved with envy. So he told him, in the dim obscurity of his workshop he could not see the defects which were so apparent to the aged critic, and in passion sneered at the opinion given. "Well," said Angelo, not the least disturbed, "the light of the public square will test it."

"The light of the public square will test it." Ah, yes! The light of the public square is to test every human life. Eternal blaze shall pour upon it, and defects unseen by the poorer light of earth will grow to ghastly deformities. The light of the public square will test it!

CCCCLXXXVII. "Some to Everlasting Life." DAN. xii. 2. *"And many of them that sleep in the dust of the earth shall awake, some to everlasting life, and some to shame and everlasting contempt."*

THERE is an Eastern story of the "Amreeta water of Immortality," which, when drunk by the impure, ran through their veins in the liquid fire of unspeakable agony; but, when drunk by the pure, this water spread through their whole being the glow of eternal life and peace.

CCCCLXXXVIII. An Awakening. DAN. xii. 2.

"And many of them that sleep in the dust of the earth shall awake, some to everlasting life, and some to shame and everlasting contempt."

A YOUNG somnambulist got out of her garret window upon the roof and, in the sight of a silent and trembling crowd, walked up and down the giddy height, dreaming perhaps of a coming festival, for she kept smiling and murmuring her gay songs. They were powerless to help her, and held their breath in very horror as she sometimes approached the edge. Suddenly a little candle was lit in an opposite window and flashed upon her eyes. She woke, and there was a scream and a deadly fall. It had killed her!

CCCCLXXXIX. God's Care of His People.

Hos. ii. 18. *"And in that day I will make a covenant for them with the beasts of the field."*

JOHN HUGHES was a most holy, devoted man, and greatly beloved, and his name is held in honour wherever he was known. As superintendent minister of a circuit, he had to visit three congregations, administer the Lord's Supper in each, and return to preach in the evening at Wrexham. He left in good time in the morning. When not far on his journey he saw a large, fierce-looking dog following him. But neither stones nor scolding would make it go away. When he had gone into the pulpit he saw the dog lie down quietly by the side of it. So it did to the second and third chapels. On Mr. Hughes' return home he was waylaid by two men, who demanded his purse. Mr. Hughes felt he could not contend with the two powerful men, but on whistling the dog was at once at his side, and furiously attacked the would-be robbers. They took to their heels, and Mr. Hughes walked on unmolested till he reached town, when the dog left him, and he saw it no more. Mr. Hughes never spoke of this incident but in a spirit of astonishment and gratitude.

CCCCXC. A Personal God. Hos. v. 15. *"In their affliction they will seek Me early."*

A LEADER of thought in Germany, famous as a poet, famous as a man of letters, who had through his long literary career fought against the idea of a personal God, when poor in purse, paralytic in body, and in his last week of life, wrote thus to one of his old class-mates, and under its style of banter there is a pathetic minor tone of earnest feeling :—

"A religious reaction has set in upon me for some time. God knows whether the morphine or the poultices have anything to do with it. It *is* so. I believe in a personal God. To this we come when we are sick to death and broken down. Do not make a crime of it. If the German people accept the personal king of Prussia in their need, why should not I accept a personal God ? My friend, here is a great truth. When health is used up, money used up, and sound senses used up, Christianity begins."

CCCCXCI. Go on, Go on. Hos. vi. 3. *"Then shall we know, if we follow on to know the Lord."*

ARAGO says, in his Autobiography, that his master in mathematics was a word or two of advice which he found in the binding of one of his text-books. Puzzled and discouraged by the difficulties he met with in his early studies, he was almost ready to give over the pursuit. Some words which he found on the waste leaf used to stiffen the cover of his paper-bound text-book caught his eye and interested him. "Impelled," he says, "by an indefinable curiosity, I dampened the cover of the book and carefully unrolled the leaf to see what was on the other side. It proved to be a short letter from D'Alembert to a young person disheartened like myself by the difficulties of mathematical study, and who had written to him for counsel. 'Go on, sir, go on,' was the counsel which D'Alembert gave him. 'The difficulties you meet will resolve themselves as you advance. Proceed, and light will dawn and shine with increasing clearness on your path.'

"That maxim," says Arago, "was my greatest master in mathematics." Following out those simple words, "*Go on, sir, go on,*" made him the first astronomical mathematician of his age. What Christians it would make of us! what heroes of faith! what sages in holy wisdom should we become, just by acting out that maxim, *Go on, go on!*

CCCCXCII. Prayers Set Aside with Physic Bottles. Hos. vi. 4. "*Your goodness is as the morning cloud, and as the early dew it goeth away.*"

"A COUPLE of men, in a crazy craft, being caught in a squall, betook themselves, one to praying to the Virgin, and the other to poling toward the shore. Soon the latter touched bottom, and turning to his devout comrade, said: 'What's the use of praying when you can touch the bottom with the pole?' So say multitudes by their conduct, who would not, for the world, say anything so ludicrous by word. The only difference is, that they are not half so truthful in expressing themselves as bold unbelievers are, but their piety is of no higher type. Such persons act towards the Divine Helper as they do towards their physician—turn to him when they can find no possibility of helping themselves. Many have no use for ministers—unless it may be to ridicule them and their work—until they are smitten with disease; and when their cases become too desperate for the skill of the doctor, they send post-haste for the minister, and without reference to either time or convenience, he must come. As they have never had any use for him before, so much the more necessary that he should be at their call now, to pray them up on their feet again.

"We had occasion to rebuke one of this kind, whose stock of wit consisted in low sneers at ministers and their work. Not long after he became very sick. The doctors said he would die. He sent for us ('because,' he said, 'we had been faithful in our rebuke,') to administer to his spiritual wants, which could be summed up in one sentence—he did not want to burn. He made great promises; one that he would give five hundred dollars to our Church—though he did not say so, the inference was clear—if we either got him well or in heaven. Unaccountable to tell, he got well. Our prayers were not so refreshing with returning health. They were set aside with the physic bottles. Soon he avoided us. He never spoke of the five hundred dollars; he would neither pay nor pray, since he could 'touch the bottom with the pole.' At last we asked him for the money he had promised the Church. He became angry, and compromised on one hundred dollars.

"A father came to a Young Men's Christian Association in great distress, with a request that prayer should be offered for his son, who was lying dangerously ill. It was a surprise to learn that the father did not profess to be a Christian, and great hopes were entertained that he would be. He came to church several evenings, and his son recovered. But he has never been heard of since. 'What is the use of praying when you can touch the bottom with the pole?'

CCCCXCIII. A Choice of Three Sins. Hos. xiii. 2.
"And now they sin more and more."

THERE is a story which tells of a man who had the choice of three sins he would commit—drunkenness, adultery, or murder. He chose drunkenness as being apparently the least; but when intoxicated he committed both the other sins, and so became guilty of all three. One sin leads to another, and is like the letting in of water.

CCCCXCIV. Death a Bed to the Weary. Hos. xiii. 14. *"I will ransom them from the power of the grave."*

THE martyr Renwick had a weakly constitution at the best, and his incessant labours, aggravated as they were by exposure and sleepless anxiety, ere long wore him out, so that even his undaunted spirit was sometimes wrapped in gloomy clouds. His letters, as time went on, expressed an increasing sense of weariness, but continued to be brightened by beams of heavenly faith and hope.

In 1687 he writes to Sir Robert Hamilton:—"My business was never so weighty, so multiplied, and so ill to be guided, to my apprehension, as it has been this year, and my body was never so frail. Excessive travel, night wanderings, unseasonable sleep and diet, and frequent preaching in all seasons of weather, especially in the night, have so debilitated me that I am often incapable for any work. I find myself greatly weakened inwardly, so that I sometimes fall into fits of swooning and fainting. I take seldom any meat or drink, but it fights with my stomach; and for strong drink I can take almost none of it. When I use means for my recovery, I find it some ways effectual; but my desire to the work, and the necessity and importunity of people, prompt me to do more than my natural strength will well allow, and to undertake such toilsome business as casts my body presently down again. I mention not this through any anxiety, quarrelling, or discontent, but to show you my condition in this respect. I may say that, under all my frailties and distempers, I find great peace and sweetness in reflecting upon the occasion thereof. It is a part of my glory and joy to bear such infirmities, contracted through my poor and small labour in my Master's vineyard."

No wonder that, when the sentence of death came, it raised no perturbation in Renwick's soul. Life had no attraction for him, death had no terror; the only comforts that had sustained his soul for five long years were beams of heavenly light sent down into the darkness out of that world into which death would immediately introduce him. His patient continuance in his overwhelming labours sufficiently declared his willingness to abide in the flesh if such were the Master's will, but we can well believe that he was *willing rather* to depart and to be with Christ. "I go," he wrote to the same correspondent, on the eve of his execution, "I GO TO YOUR GOD AND MY GOD. DEATH TO ME IS AS A BED TO THE WEARY."

CCCCXCV. When does a Tree Grow? Hos. xiv. 5. "*I will be as the dew unto Israel: he shall grow as the lily.*"

A SHORT time ago a gentleman was preaching in the open air; his subject was "Growth in Grace." At the close of the meeting a man approached him and said: "Our minister has been preaching some excellent sermons on that subject, and I have been trying to grow in grace this long time, but I find I never can succeed." The preacher, pointing to a tree, said, "Do you see that tree?" "Yes," was the wondering reply. "Well, it had to be planted before it could grow. In like manner you must be rooted and grounded in Christ before you can begin to grow." The man understood his meaning, and went away to find Christ; and soon he was rooted in Christ, and brought forth fruit to His praise.

CCCCXCVI. Growth. Hos. xiv. 6. *"His branches shall spread, and his beauty shall be as the olive tree, and his smell as Lebanon."*

HAVE you ever noticed that the trees nearest the light at the edge of the wood have larger branches than those in the interior of the forest, and the same tree will throw out a long branch toward the light, and a short one toward the obscurity of the forest. Just so a man grows towards the light to which he turns. According to the direction in which he turns with supreme affection, he grows.

CCCCXCVII. Critical Times in Life. JOEL iii. 14, *"Multitudes, multitudes in the valley of decision."*

IT has been well said that in every life there is a turning-point, as in a fever, a turning-point that brings either life or death. Napoleon said: "In every battle there are ten minutes on which hangs the fate of nations." Hundreds of soul's battles are fought and won in a few minutes. Unspeakably solemn are the silence and quickness with which these spiritual battles are fought.

CCCCXCVIII. Two Rivers. AMOS iii. 3. *"Can two walk together, except they be agreed?"*

THE Rhone, as it issues from the lake of Geneva and rushes on its arrowy flight, is the most beautiful of rivers—green as an emerald, yet as clear as clearest glass; so that the pebbles on the bottom, where it is twelve feet deep, are as distinctly seen as if they were lying at one's feet.

The Arve—a river of about the same size, and flowing for some distance nearly parallel with the Rhine and but a little way from it—is a dirty stream, carrying with it the wash of the mountains and the mud of the valley.

About two miles below Geneva these two rivers unite, and flow together toward the sea. But, though joined in one channel, they are still for several miles almost as distinct as when they occupied their separate beds. The beautiful Rhone keeps its green clearness on its own side of the channel, while the Arve flows as turbid as ever, from the middle to the farther shore.

So two discordant characters, thrown together by circumstances, often maintain each its own peculiarities; and neither is the wicked sanctified by the just, nor the righteous contaminated by the unfortunate association. In many a family the godless husband goes his own worldly way, while the pious wife lives only nearer the Cross because she cannot enter into her husband's heart.

But, some miles below the junction, the river rushes into a chasm beneath a mountain. When it issues on the farther side it is *one* river—called the Rhone, but in character the Arve. The emerald lost, the purity gone, it is just a common river after the common pattern—opaque and muddy from shore to shore.

So, often—so, *generally*—" evil communications corrupt good manners."

A few days ago, I went with friends to the junction, to see the famous uniting without commingling of waters. The rivers were both unusually low within their banks, and to our surprise the Arve was very nearly or quite as clear as the Rhone. They met and were not to be distinguished in their common channel. My friends, who had been there very often, assured me that they had never seen it so before, that to them it was a phenomenon as strange as the ordinary appearance would have been to me.

Ah! It was not the first time that a muddy character has appeared temporarily as clear and fair as the purest. Even Satan sometimes appears as an angel of light. It will not always do to judge by present appearances. Wait until the rains come. "When affliction or persecution ariseth, immediately they are offended." It must be a sad character, indeed, which is not amiable when its possessor has his own way. And it must be a very bad man who cannot conduct himself respectably for a little while,—especially if he have his own purpose to serve in so doing. Let those who may be tempted to decide hastily in regard to a life-long companionship remember that even the Arve is not always muddy.

CCCCXCIX. Minds like Sieves. JOEL iii. 12, 13.

"*Let the heathen be wakened. Put ye in the sickle, for the harvest is ripe.*"

A SIMPLE Hindoo woman went to receive her weekly

Bible lesson, when the lady missionary found that she had remembered but little of what she had taught her the week before. Being discouraged, she said, "It seems no use teaching you anything; you forget all I tell you. Your mind is just like a sieve: as fast as I pour water in, it runs out again."

The woman looked up at the lady missionary and said, "Yes, it is very true; my mind is just like a sieve. I am very sorry I forget so much; but then, you know, when you pour clean water into a sieve, though it all runs out again, yet it makes the sieve clean. I am sorry I have forgotten so much of what you told me last week; but what you did tell me made my mind clean, and I have come again to-day."

The missionaries at home and abroad go on pouring water into these sieves; and though it runs away and seems to be unprofitably spilled upon the ground, yet the private, the domestic, the public, and the national life of the people is the cleaner for it.

D. Honouring the Sabbath. AMOS viii. 5. *"When will the new moon be gone, that we may sell corn? and the Sabbath, that we may set forth wheat?"*

IN 1633 the town of Taunton had a good Puritan pastor in Mr. George Newton. He was the great light of its Puritanism, and was Vicar of St. Mary Magdalene. Though naturally timid, "strength was made perfect in weakness," and he was not timid in the assertion of his principles, and soon became a noted "gospeller." When the "Book of Sports" came out by order of Council, and was commanded to be read in all the churches, Mr. Newton read it, but said immediately to his congregation, "These are the commandments of men." He then read the twentieth chapter of the book of Exodus, saying, "These are the commandments of God; but whereas in this case the laws of God and the laws of men are at variance, choose ye which ye will obey." Thus he took the side of the Sabbath against the profane decrees of the king.

DI. The Cry from the Depths. JONAH ii. 2. *"I cried by reason of mine affliction unto the Lord, and He heard me; out of the belly of hell cried I, and Thou heardest my voice."*

"YOU want nothing more than this cry. If you cry to God out of the depths, you will cry yourself out of them. Here is a man at the foot of a cliff that rises beetling like a black wall behind him, the sea in front, the clear upright rock at his back, not a foothold for a mouse between the tide at the foot and the grass at the top there. There is only one thing he can do. Shout! Perchance somebody will hear him, and a rope may come dangling down in front, and, if he has nerve, he may shut his eyes and make a jump and catch it. There is no way for you up out of the depths but to cry; and that will bring the rope down."

DII. The Celestial Fauna. MICAH v. 2. *"Though thou be little among the thousands of Judah."*

MR. SPURGEON says: "You can buy complete sets of all the flowers of the Alpine district at the hotel near the foot of the Rosenlaui glacier, very neatly pressed and enclosed in cases. Some of the flowers are very common, but they *must* be included, or the fauna would not be completely represented. The botanist is as careful to see that the common ones are there, as he is to note that the rarer specimens are not excluded. Our blessed Lord will be sure to make a perfect collection of all the flowers of His field, and even the ordinary believer, the every-day worker, the common convert, will not be forgotten. To Jesus' eye there is beauty in all His plants, and each one is needed to perfect the fauna of Paradise. May I be found among His flowers, if only as one out of myriad daisies, who with sweet simplicity shall look up and wonder at His love for ever."

DIII. Practical Christian Teaching. MICAH vi. 8. *"He hath showed thee, O man, what is good; and what doth the Lord require of thee, but to do justly, and to love mercy, and to walk humbly with thy God?"*

"DON'T you think our minister soars very high, sir?" was

once asked of the great Robert Hall by an admiring hearer concerning a minister then residing near Bristol. "Soars high, sir!" exclaimed Hall, with his usual vehemence. "Not at all, sir! What you call high, sir, is simply a foggy atmosphere in which he invariably envelops himself."

DIV. A Law Text. MICAH vi. 8. *"What doth the Lord require of thee, but to do justly, and to love mercy, and to walk humbly with thy God?"*

THE following anecdote is told of the Rev. John Brown, D.D., of Haddington, as illustrating the freedom of his pulpit style from any such doctrinal aberrations as had been by some apprehended. A venerable old man in a congregation not far from his native place had heard the whole Brown family preach through their successive generations. He went a long day's journey to hear another of the race. Being a great enemy of legal doctrine, he was somewhat startled when the text was announced. This was Micah vi. 8, being, in truth, the subject of one of Mr. Brown's Presbytery exercises, "What doth the Lord require of thee, but to do justly, and to love mercy, and to walk humbly with thy God?" He sat deeply interested both in the speaker and in the development of the doctrine; and when all was ended, burst into tears, which he continued shedding for a good while. At length he spoke, "If there was a law text in all the Bible, it was that; but he has preached the sound gospel, for law doctrine was never in his blood."

DV. Where is your God? MICAH vii. 8, 9. *"Rejoice not against me, O mine enemy: when I fall, I shall arise; when I sit in darkness, the Lord shall be a light unto me. I will bear the indignation of the Lord, because I have sinned against Him, until He plead my cause, and execute judgment for me."*

A NONCONFORMIST minister, Mr. Norman, had been condemned to lie in Ilchester gaol for preaching. On his way thither the officers stopped to rest at the sheriff's house. Lady Warre, the sheriff's wife, came to look at the prisoner, and to insult him with cruel words, saying, "Where is your God now, Mr. Norman?" "Madam," he replied, "have you a Bible in the house?" "Yes; we are not so heathenish as to be without a Bible." On getting it into his hands, he turned to Micah and read the words, "Rejoice not against me, O mine enemy: when I fall, I shall arise; when I sit in darkness, the Lord shall be a light unto me. I will bear the indignation of the Lord, because I have sinned against Him, until He plead my cause, and execute judgment for me: He will bring me forth to the light, and I shall behold His righteousness. *Then she that is mine enemy shall see it, and shame shall cover her* which said *unto me*, Where is the Lord thy God? mine eyes shall behold her: now shall she be trodden down as the mire of the streets." The lady retired silenced, and the dealings of God with her family soon made this warning to be noted and remembered.

DVI. A Funeral Sermon. NAHUM i. 3. "*The Lord is slow to anger, and great in power, and will not at all acquit the wicked: the Lord hath His way in the whirlwind and in the storm, and the clouds are the dust of His feet.*"

MASSILLON, one of the famous divines of France, was called to preach the funeral sermon of the departed king. The vast cathedral was crowded. The reigning king, the royal family, the flower of the French nobility, and the members of the chamber were there. The solemn service was intoned. The organ reverberated its awful and impressive sound. The incense pervaded the atmosphere. The priests retired to their seats. The preacher ascended the pulpit. Massillon arose and stood amid that vast assemblage rigid and pale as a statue. A deathlike silence reigned as he stood there saying naught. His gleaming eye alone indicated self-possession. Solemnly he surveyed them all. Now his eye rested on the emblazoned banners and drooping ensigns—now on the glittering coronets of the nobles—now on the royal family, then on the king, until at length he fixed his gaze upon the coffin. Minutes passed. Some thought he was struck dumb before that august assemblage. At last he slowly raised his hand and turned his glance upon the king, saying, with infinite solemnity, "THERE IS NOTHING GREAT BUT GOD."

DVII. Peace on Earth. NAHUM i. 15. *"Behold upon the mountains the feet of him that bringeth good tidings, that publisheth peace!"*

"AT the close of the last war with Great Britain," says an American writer, "the prospects of our nation were shrouded in gloom. Our harbours were blockaded. Communication coastwise between our ports was cut off. Our immense annual products were mouldering in our warehouses. Our currency was reduced to irredeemable paper. Differences of political opinion were embittering the peace of many households. No one could predict when the contest would terminate, or discover the means by which it could much longer be protracted. It happened that one afternoon in February a ship was discovered in the offing, which was supposed to be a cartel, bringing home our commissioners at Ghent from their unsuccessful mission. The sun had set gloomily before any intelligence from the vessel had reached the city. Expectation became painfully intense as the hours of darkness drew on. At length a boat reached the wharf, announcing the fact that a treaty of peace had been signed, and was waiting for nothing but the action of our Government to become a law. The men on whose ears these words first fell rushed in breathless haste into the city to repeat them to their friends, shouting as they ran through the streets, 'Peace! Peace! Peace!' Every one who heard the sound repeated it. From house to house, from street to street, the news spread with electric rapidity. The whole city was in commotion. Men bearing lighted torches were flying to and fro, shouting, 'Peace! Peace! Peace!' When the rapture had partially subsided, one idea occupied every mind. But few men slept that night. In groups they were gathered in the streets, and by the fireside, beguiling the hours of midnight by reminding each other that the agony of war was over, and that a worn-out and distracted country was about to enter again upon its wonted career of prosperity. Thus, *every one becoming a herald*, the news soon reached every man, woman, and child in the city, and filled their hearts with joy."

DVIII. Vigilance. HAB. ii. 1. "*I will stand upon my watch, and set me upon the tower, and will watch to see what He will say unto me.*"

NEARLY two centuries ago about a thousand of the Vaudois, who had taken refuge in Switzerland—all that remained from the many thousands who, by the cruel decree of Louis XIV. of France, had been exterminated—came to a secret, sworn, and invincible determination to make their way through all difficulties, and repossess themselves of their homes in the Cottian Alps. Their valour, their heroism, their contempt of danger, and the constancy and skill with which they met and surmounted all difficulties have never been surpassed in the history of any people. Opposed by armies of more than ten times their number, threading their way over mighty mountains on which lay deep snows, along paths in which alone the chamois or the Alpine mountaineer could keep a footing, travelling through rain and storm, taking no prisoners, but putting to death all who fell into their hands, wresting the very weapons with which they fought from the hands of their enemies, purchasing or conquering their subsistence as they went, seizing bridges in the face of foes who greatly outnumbered them, changing their route a dozen times, to avoid dangers too great to be met without utter annihilation by their little beleaguered and travel-worn band, their eyes were at last delighted with the sight of the familiar mountain peaks that told them they were once more near home. God rewarded such constancy and devotion, and brought them to their dearly loved homes among the mountains, nevermore, let us believe, to be thence driven. "Eternal vigilance is the price of liberty," and the success that crowned their almost superhuman efforts was the reward of a *watchfulness* that waited during years of silent preparation, and that, once they had started, for six long days and nights, gave neither sleep nor slumber to the eyes of their leader. *Watch!* The grim determination that had possessed them as a passion made watching as natural as to breathe. Relax their vigilance? Not for one moment. Miss one golden opportunity for success? Never. Be caught in any snare, though in the very midst of powerful, malicious, and outnumbering foes? Impossible. "*I have a work to* strength, even though they had the will, to tear off the limb in order to save the life. When physical disease and moral depravity clasp and close in upon each other, the soul is overlaid and quenched between. Although the prisoner were willing to part with the right arm, he cannot get it severed. It holds him till the tide rise, and he dies.

"With an earnestness equal to that displayed by the neighbours at Wigton, and with a skill superior, we might save our brother. We could, if we would. By the power of love in all the earlier stages, and by the power of LAW, if the madness proceed to extremities, the community should arise in its might, and rescue the man from himself."

DXI. God's Praise. HAB. iii. 3. *"His glory covered the heavens, and the earth was full of His praise."*

IT is said that once when Sir Michael Costa was having a rehearsal with a vast array of performers and hundreds of voices, as the mighty chorus rang out with thunder of the organ and roll of drums and ringing horns and cymbals clashing, some one man far away up in some corner, who played the piccolo, said within himself, "In all this din it matters not what I do," and so he ceased to play. Suddenly the great conductor stopped, flung up his hands, and all was still—and then he cried aloud, "*Where is the piccolo?*" The quick ear missed it, and all was spoilt because it failed to take its part. O my soul, do thy part with all thy might! Little thou mayest be, insignificant and hidden, and yet God seeks thy praise. He listens for it, and all the music of His great universe is made richer and sweeter because I give Him thanks.

DXII. Seeking Peace for Ten Years. ZEPH. ii. 3. *"Seek ye the Lord, all ye meek of the earth."*

A YOUNG woman in Burmah felt a great wish to learn to read, that she might study the sacred books of her country. After some trouble she was able to read them, and for ten long years she tried to find in their pages the peace for which she longed; but she could not obtain it. One day a friend brought her a Christian tract, which pointed out the only way of rest for a sinner. After some time she heard where the missionary who wrote the tract lived. She soon went in search of him, and when she found him, she was further taught in the truth of God's Word. For some years she lived as a Christian, and then died in the faith. In her last hours she was happy in the thought that she should soon meet her pious teachers who had gone before her to heaven. "But first of all," she said, "I shall hasten to where my Saviour sits, and fall down and adore Him for His great love in sending me those who could lead me in the path to glory."

DXIII. A Melancholy Man. ZEPH. iii. 16. "*In that day it shall be said to Jerusalem, Fear thou not: and to Zion, Let not thine hands be slack. The Lord thy God in the midst of thee is mighty; He will save, He will rejoice over thee with joy.*"

LUTHER, at Wittenberg, seeing a very melancholy man, said to him: "Ah! human creature, what dost thou? Hast thou nothing else in hand but to think of thy sins, on death, and damnation? Turn thine eyes quickly away, and look hither to this man Christ, of whom it is written: 'He was conceived by the Holy Ghost, born of the Virgin Mary, suffered, died, buried, descended into hell, the third day arose again from the dead, and ascended up into heaven,' etc. Dost think all this was done to no end? Comfort thyself against death and sin; be not afraid, nor faint, for thou hast no cause; Christ suffered death for thee, and prevailed for thy comfort and defence, and for that cause He sits at the right hand of God, His heavenly Father, to deliver thee."

DXIV. An Arrow Shot at a Venture. ZECH. ii. 4. "*And said unto him, Run, speak to this young man.*"

ONE Saturday night an earnest minister of Christ studied his sermon, as usual, with prayer, but felt oppressed. In the morning he said, "I cannot preach this; I do not feel the Lord present with me." His wife said, "Pray, 'Get thee behind me, Satan.'" He did, but entered the pulpit with a heavy heart. Service commenced. The time came for the text. He said, "My friends, I cannot tell what oppresses me, but I cannot preach the sermon I have health she was in all respects dutiful and exemplary. But she had not been "born again." She had never *seen* that in the sight of God her own goodness was a worthless thing. She had never "submitted herself to the righteousness of God."

The seeds of consumption were in her constitution. Whilst still young she was laid upon a bed of sickness. She became intensely anxious about her eternal state. Her minister was sent for. He tried to open up to her God's way of saving sinners, for the sake of Jesus. But still her mind continued dark, and her heart unhappy. He saw her often, and on each occasion commended *Jesus* to her as a Saviour, and His perfect obedience and death in the room of sinners as being all that her case could need.

One day when he called, he found her sitting up in bed, supported by pillows, with a look of eager, excited interest upon her face. After a few words of salutation, she said, "Is this what you mean, sir, as the way of salvation, which you have been explaining to me: that Christ's obedience is to gain acceptance *for me*, as if it had been my own obedience: and that all that I have done is to be washed away through the sufferings which He endured for sinners on the cross?" "Yes," said the minister; "that is just it: accept JESUS, and rely on Him *alone* for salvation, and in that moment His sufferings will answer to God for ALL that you have done—for it is ALL sinful; and His perfect obedience will be counted yours. Then God will deal with you as if you had never sinned, but had rendered that obedience yourself." "Do you mean," eagerly asked the dying girl, "that *I* may be saved just in the same way and on the same terms as the most wicked person in the town?" "Yes," answered the minister; "I just mean that." A look of disappointment and dissatisfaction settled upon her countenance. She sat in silence for a little, and then said, very firmly and decidedly, "Well, then, I'll not submit to it." Her anxiety vanished from that hour. From that day forward she refused to converse on the subject of religion. Shortly afterwards she died, in settled, resolute indifference.

DXIX. The Difficult Duty of Prayer. Zech. viii. 21. *"And the inhabitants of one city shall go to another, saying, Let us go speedily to pray before the Lord, and to seek the Lord of hosts: I will go also."*

A Christian brother who had fallen into darkness and discouragement was staying at the same house with Dr. Finney one night. He was lamenting his condition, and Dr. Finney, after listening to his narrative, turned to him with his peculiar, earnest look, and, with a voice that sent a thrill through his soul, said, "You don't pray! that is what's the matter with you. Pray—pray four times as much as ever you did in your life, and you will come out."

He immediately went down to the parlour, and taking a Bible he made a serious business of it, stirring up his soul to God as did Daniel, and thus he spent the night. It was not in vain. As the morning dawned he felt the light of the Sun of righteousness shine upon his soul. His captivity was broken, and ever since he has felt that the greatest difficulty in the way of men's being emancipated from their bondage is that they "don't pray." "Pray without ceasing." "Men ought always to pray, and not to faint."

DXX. Good Counsel. Zech. x. 12. *"And I will strengthen them in the Lord; and they shall walk up and down in His name, saith the Lord."*

The late Duchess of Gordon wrote a letter, a few days before her death, to a young girl whom she had befriended, giving her good counsel, and she concluded thus: "In our weakness His strength is found; and so long as we think ourselves strong in wisdom, purpose, or power, we shall be sure, sooner or later, to find our wisdom folly, our purpose a cobweb, and our power utter helplessness. Therefore my best wish for you is that you may cast all your care on Him who careth for His people, and as my favourite hymn says,—

> 'Lay down in His strong hand,
> So shall the work be done,
> For who can work so wondrously
> As the Almighty One?'"

DXXI. A Shepherd Pastor. ZECH. xi. 4. *"Thus saith the Lord my God, Feed the flock."*

WHEN the Act of Uniformity was passed, in 1662, about two thousand ministers took their stations in the ranks of Nonconformity; many, with their families, had to exchange a life of competency for a life of toil, some adopting the callings of farm-labourers. The lady of a county squire was dangerously ill; the clergyman was sent for, but returned a message that "he was going out hunting, and would come after the hunt was over." "Sir," said one of the servants to the afflicted husband, "our shepherd can pray very well; we have often heard him pray in the fields." The shepherd was immediately summoned to the bedside of the sufferer, and prayed with such fervour that when he rose from his knees the squire said, "You must tell me who and what you are." Upon which the shepherd told him his story, that he was one of the ministers ejected from the Church, and that having nothing left he was now content to submit to the honest and painful employment of keeping sheep. This man was Peter Luce, of Blagmore College, Oxford, and had been noted as a Hebraist in better days.

DXXII. Flowers of Memory. ZECH. xii. 10. *"As one mourneth for his only son."*

AN investigator of pedigrees was searching in a midland county of England for any traces that might still be found of an old family of the district. He went to the records of the church, but their name was not there, it had perished. He repaired to the supposed site of their ancient hall. Not a stone remained to tell its place. Disappointed in these attempts, he accosted an aged peasant: "Do you know anything of the Findernes?"

"Findernes?" was the reply. "We have no Findernes here, but we have Findernes' flowers."

Here was a clue. The old man led the way to a field where there were traces of an ancient terrace.

"There," said he, pointing to a bank of garden-flowers grown wild, "there are Findernes' flowers, brought by Sir Geoffrey from the Holy Land, and, do what we will, they will never die."

There are those that can go back, ten, twenty, forty years, and recall the time when a child was taken from them. It has left no record in the annals of the world: no more mark than the shining pebble that is thrown into the river, when the waters close over it for ever. Is there, then, no trace to be found beneath the heavens of that loved one? Go, ask the mother bereaved so long ago. There, in the old garden of a heart overgrown with many experiences, and shaded with many a sombre spray of ivy and many a weeping branch of cyprus, flourish still the old memories of that cherished child. His winsome ways, his pleasant prattle, his sunny smile, his look of love, are all remembered still. These flowers of memory bloom as fresh as on the day after the little one was gathered home. The snows of winter may have fallen thick upon that mother's head, but touch the old chord, and it will vibrate true and tender as ever. Encourage her to speak upon this theme, and she will pour forth her recollections of her lost one, and will narrate to you the incidents of his sickness and his death with a minuteness and detail that will astonish any one who has not had or lost a child. We lately met a mother whose boy was taken from her more than thirty years ago, who told us, as the tear rose to her eye, that when she is looking after the affairs of her household, she sometimes comes upon his toys, and never without a flood of tenderest memories filling her heart.

DXXIII. The Uses of Affliction. MAL. iii. 3. *"And He shall sit as a refiner and purifier of silver: and He shall purify the sons of Levi, and purge them as gold and silver, that they may offer unto the Lord an offering in righteousness."*

WHEN Mr. Cecil went to college, he had much to bear, both from severe conflicts in his own mind, and also from insulting treatment at the hands of his profligate and ungodly companions. Not yet accustomed to the yoke, these things troubled him more than they would have done afterwards, and he went to walk one day, under their influence, very heavy and sad in heart. The Physic Gardens was the scene which he chose for meditation and relief; and here he observed a very fine pomegranate tree, cut almost through the stem, near the root. Struck with this singular sight, he asked the gardener for an explanation. "Sir," said the man, "this tree used to shoot so strong, that it bore nothing but leaves. I was therefore obliged to cut it in this manner; *and when it was almost cut through, then it began to bear plenty of fruit.*" The answer produced a deep impression upon Mr. Cecil's mind, and he went back to his rooms comforted and instructed. It was then he received his first lesson in the usefulness of trial.

DXXIV. True Courage. MAL. iii. 5. "*And I will come near to you to judgment; and I will be a swift witness against the sorcerers, and against the adulterers.*"

THE boldness of Latimer in rebuking even the king's majesty himself, for conscience' sake, is shown in a well-known anecdote. At the time of Henry's neglect of Queen Anne Boleyn, and his undisguised preference for Jane Seymour, the bishops brought, according to custom, their New Year's gifts to court. "Some," says the old chronicler, "did gratify the king with gold, some with silver, some with a purse full of money; some one thing, some another. But Master Latimer, being Bishop of Worcester, then among the rest presented a New Testament for his gift, with a napkin having this motto upon it, '*Fornicatores et Adulteres judicabit Dominus*'—'Whoremongers and adulterers God will judge.'"

DXXV. "I must Give before I can Pray." MAL. iii. 10. "*Bring ye all the tithes into the storehouse, that there may be meat in Mine house, and prove Me now herewith, saith the Lord of hosts, if I will not open you the windows of heaven, and pour you out a blessing, that there shall not be room enough to receive it.*"

THE venerable Dr. Sewall, of Maine, once entered a meeting in behalf of foreign missions just as the collectors of the contributions were resuming their seats. The chairman of the meeting requested him to lead in prayer. The old gentleman stood hesitatingly, as if he had not heard the request. It was repeated in a louder voice, but there was no response. It was observed, however, that Dr. Sewall was fumbling in his pockets, and presently he produced a piece of money, which he deposited in the contribution box. The chairman, thinking he had not been understood, said loudly, "I didn't ask you to give, Dr. Sewall, I asked you to pray." "Oh yes," he replied, "I heard you, but *I can't pray till I have given something.*"

DXXVI. The Luxury of Doing Good. MAL. iii. 10. *"Bring ye all the tithes into the storehouse, that there may be meat in Mine house, and prove Me now herewith, saith the Lord of hosts, if I will not open you the windows of heaven, and pour you out a blessing, that there shall not be room enough to receive it."*

THE language of Malachi iii. 10 is often used in prayer by those who are not aware that it is rather a challenge than a promise—"Prove me now herewith, saith the Lord of hosts." We naturally ask whether God *does* "open the windows of heaven and pour down blessing" upon the faithful givers of tithes. Instances are not wanting among ourselves to supply the answer. No workers in our day have enjoyed larger blessing than George Müller and Charles Spurgeon, both of whom have, from the beginning of their work, put the sacred rule into practice with believing and humble hearts. Years ago Mr. Spurgeon said: "I knew a lad in Christ once who adopted the principle of giving a tenth to God. When he won a money prize for an essay on a religious subject, he felt that he could not give less than one-fifth of it. He has never since been able to deny himself the pleasure of having a fifth to give. God has wonderfully blessed that lad, and increased his means and his enjoyment of that luxury of luxuries—the luxury of doing good."

DXXVII. Days of Proscription and Persecution. MAL. iii. 16. *"Then they that feared the Lord spake often one to another: and the Lord hearkened, and heard it."*

IN the memoirs of Hannah More, there is mention made of her grandfather, who married into a family zealous for Nonconformity. They boarded a minister in their house, and at midnight pious worshippers went with stealthy steps to hear the words of inspiration from the minister's lips, while Mr. More, with a drawn sword, guarded the entrance from violent or profane intrusion. Mrs. More was also a pious woman, and used to tell her younger relatives, when they complained of the long distance to church, that they would have known how to value Gospel privileges had they lived, like her, in the days of proscription and persecution.

DXXVIII. A Poor Highland Woman. MAL. iv. 2.
"But unto you that fear My name shall the Sun of righteousness arise with healing in His wings."

A POOR Highland woman, unable to read or write, was yet a close observer of nature, and noted how the frail petals of the flax or lint-bell unfolded in the sunshine and closed when his rays were withdrawn. She was very ignorant, her one power being to accept and love the blessings of God, from the "inestimable gift" of His Son to that of the least flower that bloomed in her path. On application to her minister to be admitted to the Lord's Supper, she showed such utter ignorance of the doctrines of the Church, that she was deemed totally unfit to become a communicant. He conveyed this to her as kindly as he could, and she replied, "Aweel, sir, aweel; but I ken ae thing: as the lint-bell opens to the sun, so does my heart to the Lord Jesus!" Here was seed of the Lord's own planting. The Second Adam had been busy in this garden dressing it and keeping it.

DXXIX. Our Evidences. MAL. iv. 2. *"The Sun of righteousness."*

THE Rev. J. H. Evans, of St. John's Chapel, London, on his deathbed sent a message to his people, that he felt his sins and deservings more than ever, but that he stood accepted in the Beloved, notwithstanding all. "In Jesus I stand; Jesus is a panacea." He used to say, "When we look for our evidences, they hide their heads like lilies of the valley, and we are distressed because we cannot find them; but if we look at Christ, the sun arises and they spring up afresh."

INDEX OF SUBJECTS.

Aaron's Rod, 32.
Able to Deliver, 289.
Acorn Shells, 177.
Affection, A Son's, 16.
Affliction, The Day of, 223.
Affliction, The Furnace of, 246.
Affliction, The Mellowing Power of, 148.
Affliction, The Uses of, 317.
Animals, Cruelty to, 105.
Animals, Kindness to, 181.
Answer, A Soft, 183.
Arrow Shot at a Venture, An, 311.
Atmosphere, A Malarial, 224.
Atonement, Belief in the, 255.
Attempting Great Things for God, 255.
Awakening, An, 295.

"Baksheesh," 313.
Balaam's Ass, 202.
Bargains, Three Bad, 12.
Barren Tree, A, 269.
Bed, An Hour or two sooner to, 132.
Beggar, A Pulpit, 165.
Begin at the Beginning, 237.
Benevolence, No Deaths from, 179.
Besieged Town, A, 143.
Beware of the Ivy Green, 225.
Bible, A Soldier's, 222.
Bible in Iceland, The, 70.
Bible in the Heart, Hiding the, 146.
Bible, Penalty of Reading the, 75.
Bible, Ruskin's, 42.
Bible, The Power of a Living, 287.

Bible, The Robber's, 196.
Bishop, An Irish, 163.
Bishop's Veneration for Whitefield, A, 187.
Bitter Cup, A, 256.
Black, Cold, Hard, 278.
Blessing, Times of, 244.
Blocking up the Broad Way, 253.
Body, An Emaciated, 21.
Books, A Chain of Precious, 252.
Books, The Most Unfashionable of all, 46.
Born So, I was, 279.
Boyhood, A Christian, 13.
Boys' Temptations, 172.
Bruised Reed, A, 241.
Building up in their most holy Faith, 32.
Burdens, 106.
Burning with Pure Oil, 23.

Called of God, 46.
Calvin's Motto, 200.
Captive Set Free, The, 78.
Captives, 264.
Card-playing, 72.
Castle of St. Andrew, The, 308.
Cathedral, The Plan of Strasburg, 22.
Cattle on a Thousand Hills, The, 115.
Caught by Guile, 117.
Chariot of Fire, The, 60.
Charity, The Duty of, 30.
Child, A Drunkard's, 199.
Child, Knowing the Scriptures from a, 195.
Child, Story of a Jerusalem, 239.
Children in Prison, 257.

INDEX.

Greedy of Gain, 186.
Groaning but not Grumbling, 282.
Growth, 300.

Hand, The Helping, 200.
Hands, In God's, 162.
Happiness of doing Good, 91.
Hasty Temper, A, 211.
Haus-Segen, The, 39.
Hearing, not Reading, 258.
Heart of Unbelief, The Evil, 279.
Heathen Convert and his Bible, A, 149.
Heathen Honesty, 61.
Heathen, The Conversion of the, 61.
Heathen's Reply to the Jesuit, A, 19.
Heaven, A Message from, 95.
Heaven be? What must, 267.
Heaven, The Arithmetic of, 38.
Heavenwards, 134.
Hell peoples Heaven, The Fear of, 236.
Henry, Philip, 156.
Hidden and Safe, 133.
Highway, The Forest-Guarded, 280.
Home, Nearly, 223.
Home, Sweet Home, 151.
Homesick Mount, The, 16.
Honesty of the Huguenots, 28.
Honour, Worldly, 210.
Hopefulness, Duty of, 111.
Horse, The Pale, 144.
Hour, Our Last, 233.
Huguenots, The Persecution of the, 17.
Human Thought and Heavenly Light, 288.
Humility, 66.
Huntsman, The Wild, 172.
Hymn, A, 109.
Hymn, Charlotte Elliot's, 283.
Hymn, Dr. Ryland and his, 78.
Hymn, The Power of a, 217.

I'll not Submit to It, 313.
Impatience, 183.
Infidel and a Little Girl who was Sorry for Him, An, 85.

Infidel and the Missionary, The, 248.
Innovation, An, 290.
Intellect and the Heart, The, 49.
Intercessor, The Weeping, 268.
Israel, Restoration of, 273.

Japanese Convert, A, 150.
Jesus, Like, 125.
Jesus Opposers, 281.
Jesus? What shall we Give to, 249.
Journey is too Great for Thee, The, 57.

Kind Tone of Voice, A, 190.
Kindness to Animals, 181.
Knowledge, Jargon without, 235.
Knowledge of the Bible, Daniel Webster's, 84.

Labour and Sorrow, 209.
Lambs in His Arms, The, 239.
Lament, A Father's, 53.
Language, One, 8.
Last Hour, The, 229.
Last Hours of Darnley, The, 118.
Legend of St. Marguerite, The, 225.
Leprosy, 26.
Lessons for Children, Three, 166.
Liberality, Duty of, 40.
Liberty to the Captives of Sin, 250.
Life, A Successful, 176.
Life, Critical Times in, 300.
Life, Some to Everlasting, 294.
Life, The Close of, 259.
Light, 228.
Light, Gone into the World of, 264.
Light in the World, 262.
Lips, Watching the, 162.
Living in the Lives of Others, 229.
Loan to the Lord, A, 193.
Lord's Prayer of the Old Testament, The, 123.
Loving God, 38.
Loyalty, 238.

INDEX.

Magnanimity, 9.
Martyr, A Boy, 31.
Martyr, An Old, 290.
Martyr at the Stake, A, 58.
Martyr for Christ, A, 140.
Martyr of the Netherlands, A, 96.
Martyr's Legacy to his Children, A, 89.
Martyrs, The Wigtown, 93.
Meditation, 107.
Melancholy Man, A, 311.
Melancholy, Resistance to, 219.
Memory, Lapse of, 95.
Merchant Prince, A, 87.
Mercies, Daily Insensibility to, 276.
Migrate, About to, 147.
Minds like Sieves, 301.
Minister, A French, 60.
Missionary, A Moravian, 43.
Missionary of the Seventh Century, A, 120.
Money, Accumulation of, 105.
More Light, Lord, 68.
Morning Song of the Christian Church, The, 122.
Moses' Argument, 25.
Mother, Value of a Christian, 206.
Motto, A, 12
Motto, A Bishop's, 228.
Music, The Soothing Power of, 50.
My Ministry, 2.

Name, The Sweetest, 54.
Neptune's Cup, 136.
Nero, 270.
Newton and Jay, 253.
Ninety-and-Nine, The, 275.
No Fear, No Hope, 52.
Noah's Prayer, 7.
Noise, A Mighty, 282.

Ochre Spring, The, 174.
Offering, A Small, 179.
Old Age, 141.

Parable, An Old Hebrew, 117.
Parents, A Question for, 39.
Parents, Ingratitude to, 206.

Parents, One who Delighted to Honour his, 200.
Passover, The, 19.
Pastor, A Shepherd, 316.
Patriot, A, 143.
Peace on Earth, 306.
Peacemaker, A, 151.
People, God's Care of His, 295.
Persecution, 148.
Persecution, Days of Proscription and, 319.
Perseverance, 213.
Pilgrim Fathers, The, 138.
Pilot is on Board, The Great, 17
Pious Son, A, 176.
Playing Cards, 57.
Pliny's Myrtle and Christ's Cross, 273.
Pockets, Look to Your, 20.
Praising God, 103.
Pray, Never be too Tired to, 131.
Prayer, A Man of, 49.
Prayer, God's Readiness to Hear and Answer, 103.
Prayer, Importunate, 75.
Prayer, The Difficult Duty of, 315.
Prayer, The Habit of, 51.
Prayer, The Patience of Unanswered, 65.
Prayer, Touching God in, 293.
Prayer Used of God, Early, 312.
Prayer, Washington at, 68.
Prayers set Aside with Physic Bottles, 297.
Praying and Working, 62.
Praying First, 15.
Praying for What we Do not Expect, 81.
Praying Light-Keeper, The, 241
Preacher, An Eloquent, 209.
Preaching and Praying, 186.
Preaching, Christmas Evans on, 277.
Prophecy Fulfilled, A, 135.
Protection from Evil, 11.
Providence, Interposition of, 153.
Psalm, A Patriotic, 160.
Psalm, A Pauline, 116.
Psalm Beloved by Luther, A, 157.
Psalm, Durie's, 152.

Word of God, Growing Love for the, 67.
Work of God, Helping on the, 13.
Work of God, The Noblest, 21.
Worth and Beauty of a Soul, The, 112.

Wrath, Slow to, 182.

Young Man Void of Understanding, A, 175.
Young, Moral Training of the, 41.

INDEX OF TEXTS.

GENESIS.

	PAGE
i. 1	1
iv. 7	1, 2
iv. 10	2
v. 24	2, 3, 4
vi. 3	5
,, 5	6
vii. 16	6
viii. 9	7
,, 20	8
ix. 13	8
xi. 1	8
,, 9	8
xii. 5	9
xiii. 9	9
xvi. 13	10
xviii. 25	10
xix. 26	11
xxii. 14	12
xxv. 34	12
xxviii. 17	12
,, 22	12, 13
xxxix. 2	13
xli. 9	15
,, 52	15
xlv. 3	16
xlvii. 9	16
,, 29	17
xlviii. 21	17

EXODUS.

	PAGE
ii. 23	17
viii. 26	18
xii. 13	19
xiv. 15	19
xx. 2	19
,, 4	19
,, 7	20, 21

	PAGE
xx. 8	21
,, 12	21
,, 13	21
xxi. 17	22
xxiii. 8	22
xxv. 9	22
xxvii. 20	23
xxix. 44	23
xxxi. 13	24
xxxii. 12	25
xxxii. 24	25
xxxiii. 14	26

LEVITICUS.

	PAGE
xiv. 1, 2	26
xvi. 21	27
xviii. 4, 5	27
xix. 36	28
xxv. 35	30
xxvi. 2	31

NUMBERS.

	PAGE
vi. 25, 26	31
x. 29	32
xii. 3	32
xvii. 8	32
xxi. 4	34
xxiii. 10	35
,, 23	36
xxxii. 23	36

DEUTERONOMY.

	PAGE
v. 17	37
vi. 4	38
,, 5	38
,, 7	39
,, 9	39

	PAGE
xi. 18	39
xv. 7	40
,, 11	41
xxiv. 24	37
xxxii. 46	41
xxxiii. 27	41
xxxiv. 8	42

JOSHUA.

	PAGE
i. 8	42
ii. 1	43
xiii. 33	43
xxiv. 24	44

JUDGES.

	PAGE
v. 16	45

RUTH.

	PAGE
ii. 12	45

1 SAMUEL.

	PAGE
iii. 4	46, 47
iii. 18	48
xv. 11	49
,, 22	49
xvi. 7	49
,, 23	50
xxii. 4	51
xxiv. 19	51

2 SAMUEL.

	PAGE
iii. 33	52
xii. 19	52
,, 23	53
xviii. 33	53
xxii. 3	54
,, 31	54

1 Kings.

	PAGE
xiii. 8, 9	54
xiv. 17	55
xvii. 6	56
„ 18	56
xviii. 21	57
xix. 7	57
xix. 14	58
xxi. 25	59

2 Kings.

ii. 3	59
„ 11	60
iv. 34	60
vi. 15	61
vii. 19	61
xii. 15	61
xx. 5	62
„ 11	63

1 Chronicles.

vi. 49	63
xvii. 16	64

2 Chronicles.

i. 10	64
vi. 40	65
xv. 15	65
xx. 21	66
xxxiv. 27	66

Ezra.

vi. 22	67
vii. 6	67
ix. 8	68

Nehemiah.

i. 6	68
iv. 9	69
viii. 8	70
ix. 17	71
xii. 31	71

Esther.

v. 13	72

Job.

i. 1	72

	PAGE
i. 6	73
„ 21	73, 74
v. 9	74
vi. 8	75
xiii. 15	75
xiv. 14	76
xvi. 22	76
xxviii. 28	77
xxxiv. 18	77
xxxv. 10	78
xxxix. 27	78

Psalms.

i. 4	79
iv. 6	80
v. 3	81
„ 12	82
vii. 11	83
viii. 1	84
„ 2	85
x.	86
xiv. 1	87
xv. 4	87
xvi. 5	88
xviii. 30	88
xix. 1	89
„ 10	89, 90
„ 11	91
„ 13	92
xxiii. 5	92
xxiv. 7	93
xxv. 7	93
xxvi. 8	94
xxvii. 1–14	94
xxvii. 6	95
xxx. 5	95
xxx. 5	96
xxxi. 5	97
xxxi. 23	98
xxxii. 1–11	99
xxxiv. 9	100
„ 10	102
„ 13	103
„ 15	103
xxxv. 28	103
xxxvi. 1	104
„ 6	104
xxxvii. 16	105
„ 26	105

	PAGE
xxxvii. 31	106
xxxviii. 4	106
„ 13	106
xxxix. 3	107
„ 13	107
xl. 3	109
„ 8	109
„ 10	110
xli. 3	111
xliii. 5	111
xlv. 5	112
xlix. 8	113
„ 17	114
l. 10	115
li. 1–19	116
„ 13	117
„ 17	117
lv. 4	118
lvi. 8	119
lvii. 4	120
lx. 1–12	120
lxiii. 1–11	122
lxvii. 1–7	123
lxviii. 1–35	123
lxix. 1	124
lxxi. 1–24	124
lxxii. 4	125
lxxiii. 1	126
„ 22	126
lxxiv. 10	127
„ 16	127
„ 20	128
lxxxiii. 3	128
lxxxiv. 4–12	129
lxxxvi. 7	130
„ 13	130
lxxxviii. 9	131
lxxxix. 26	132
xc. 12	132
xci. 1	133
„ 2	134
„ 15	134
xciv. 2	135
„ 17	136
xcv. 5	136
„ 7, 8	137
c. 1	138
cii. 20	140
ciii. 1	140, 141
„ 5	141

INDEX OF TEXTS.

	PAGE
civ. 34	142
cv. 26	143
cvii. 1	143
,, 18	144
,, 23	145
,, 43	145
cxix. ...	146
,, 9	146
,, 11	146
,, 46	147
,, 54	147
,, 59	147
,, 83	148
,, 86	148
,, 97	148, 149
,, 122	149
,, 130	150
cxx. 7	151
cxxii. 2	151
cxxiv. 1–8	152
,, 2	153
,, 4	154
cxxv. 1–5	156
cxxvi. 5	156
cxxviii. ...	156
,, 2	156
cxxx. ...	157
cxxxiii. ...	159
cxxxvi. ...	160
cxxxvii. ...	160
,, 3, 4	161
,, 4	161
cxxxix. 12	162
cxli. ...	162
,, 3	162
cxliii. ...	163
cxliv. ...	163
cxlv. ...	164
,, 13	164
cxlvi. ...	164
cxlviii. 8	165
,, 17	165

PROVERBS.

i. 8	166
,, 27	166
ii. 8	167
,, 20	168
iii. 9	169

	PAGE
iv. 14	169
,, 15	171
,, 18	171
,, 27	172
v. 22	172
vi. 15	173
,, 27, 28	174
vii. 1	174
,, 7	175
viii. 17	176
x. 7	176
,, 4	177
xi. 18	177
,, 19	178
,, 24	179, 180
,, 30	180
xii. 30	181
xiii. 1	182
xiv. 29	182, 183
xv. i. ...	183
,, 3	183
,, 23	185, 186
,, 27	186
,, 29	186
,, 33	187
xvi. 7	187, 188
,, 24	190
,, 25	190
,, 32	190
xix. 4	191
,, 15	192
,, 17	193, 194
xx. 11	194
,, 22	194
xxii. 6	195, 196, 197, 198
,, 11	199
xxiii. 21	199
,, 24, 25	200
,, 26	200
xxiv. 10	200
,, 11	200
xxv. 11	201
xxvi. 5	202
xxvii. 9	202
xxviii. 25	203
xxx. 8, 9	205
,, 17	206
xxxi. 1	206
,, 11; 12	208

ECCLESIASTES.

	PAGE
i. 2	209, 210
,, 14	210
vii. 9	211
viii. 12	212
ix. 4	213
,, 10	213, 214
,, 18	215
xi. 1	216, 217
,, 6	218
,, 7	219
,, 9	219, 220, 222
xii. 3	223
,, 5	223
,, 14	224

SONG OF SOLOMON.

ii. 15	225
iii. 2	225
iv. 16	225
v. 9	227
vi. 10	228

ISAIAH.

i. 25	228
ii. 11	229
vi. 8	229
viii. 20	230
xi. 6	231
xxv. 1	232
,, 8	232
xxvi. 3	233
,, 8	234
xxviii. 7	234
,, 10	235
xxix. 13	235
,, 23	236
xxx. 33	236
xxxii. 2	236
xxxiii. 17	237
,, 22	237, 238
xl. 11	239
,, 26	240
xlii. 3	241
,, 10	241
xliii. 2	242, 243
,, 8	243
xliv. 3	244
,, 22	244

INDEX OF TEXTS.

	PAGE
xlv. 21, 22	245
xlviii. 10	245, 246
,, 18	247
,, 22	248
xlix. 16	249
,, 24	250
l. 4	252
lii. 7	253
,, 10	253
liii. 1	254
,, 6	255
liv. 2, 3	255
,, 5	256
,, 11	256
,, 13	257
lv. 3	258
,, 12	259
lvii. 15	259, 260
lviii. 13	260, 261
lix. 1	261
lx. 1	262
,, 2	262
,, 19	264
,, 20	264
lxi. 1	264
,, 10	265
lxiii. 13	265
lxv. 17	267

JEREMIAH.

vi. 14	267
x. 1	267
x. 12	268
xii. 5	268
xiii. 17	268
xv. 15	269
,, 16, 17	270
xvii. 9	270
xxiii. 4	270
xxvi. 3	272
xxix. 13	273
xxx. 17	273
xxxii. 37	273
xlviii. 11	274
xlix. 23	274
l. 6	275

LAMENTATIONS.

	PAGE
iii. 33	275
,, 22	276
v. 18	276

EZEKIEL.

i. 3	276
iii. 17	277
xi. 19	278, 279
xviii. 4	280
xxii. 29	281
xxiv. 17	281
xxvi. 13	282
xxx. 24	282
xxxiii. 22	283
,, 32	283
xxxiv. 12	284
,, 29	286
xxxvi. 27	287

DANIEL.

ii. 22	288
iii. 17	289
,, 25	289
,, 21	290
,, 22	290
iv. 35	292
vi. 10	293
,, 20	293
xii. 2	294, 295

HOSEA.

ii. 18	295
v. 15	296
vi. 3	296
,, 4	297
xiii. 2	298
xiii. 14	298
xiv. 5	299
,, 6	300

JOEL.

iii. 12, 13	301
,, 14	300

AMOS.

	PAGE
iii. 3	300
viii. 5	302

JONAH.

ii. 2	303

MICAH.

v. 2	303
vi. 8	303, 304
vii. 8–10	304

NAHUM.

i. 3	305
,, 15	306

HABAKKUK.

ii. 1	307
,, 4	308
,, 15	308
iii. 3	309

ZEPHANIAH.

ii. 3	309
iii. 16	311

ZECHARIAH.

ii. 4	311
iii. 1	312
,, 2	312
iv. 7	313
vii. 11, 12	313
viii. 21	315
x. 12	315
xi. 4	316
xii. 10	316

MALACHI.

iii. 3	317
,, 5	318
,, 10	318, 319
,, 16	319
iv. 2	320